SATIRIC INHERITANCE
RABELAIS TO STERNE

D0146923

R0006024006

Wallace Library

DUE DATE (stamped in blue)
RETURN DATE (stamped in black)

SATIRIC INHERITANCE
RABELAIS TO STERNE

Michael Seidel

PRINCETON UNIVERSITY PRESS
PRINCETON, NEW JERSEY

Copyright © 1979 by Princeton University Press

Published by Princeton University Press, Princeton, New Jersey

In the United Kingdom: Princeton University Press,
Guildford, Surrey

All Rights Reserved

Library of Congress Cataloging in Publication Data will be
found on the last printed page of this book

This book has been composed in VIP Baskerville

Clothbound editions of Princeton University Press books
are printed on acid-free paper, and binding materials are
chosen for strength and durability

Printed in the United States of America by Princeton
University Press, Princeton, New Jersey

PN
6149
S2
S44

FOR
ANN SEIDEL

"*Amor matris*: subjective and
objective genitive."
—James Joyce

"The lamentable change is from the best;
The worst returns to laughter."
                    —*King Lear*, IV, i

CONTENTS

PREFACE   xi

ACKNOWLEDGMENTS   xiii

Chapter One: The Satiric Dispensation   3

Chapter Two: Inheritance and Narrative Mode   26

Chapter Three: The Revisionary Inheritance:
Rabelais and Cervantes   60

Chapter Four: The Internecine Romance:
Butler's *Hudibras*   95

Chapter Five: A House Divided: Marvell's *Last
Instructions* and Dryden's *Absalom and Achitophel*   135

Chapter Six: Fathers and Sons: Swift's *A Tale of A Tub*   169

Chapter Seven: Strange Dispositions: Swift's
Gulliver's Travels   201

Chapter Eight: Things Unborn: Pope's *The Rape
of the Lock* and *The Dunciad*   226

Chapter Nine: Gravity's Inheritable Line: Sterne's
Tristram Shandy   250

CODICIL   263

BIBLIOGRAPHY   267

INDEX   275

PREFACE

"Each man," writes Montaigne, "bears the entire form of man's estate."[1] Inheritance is a powerful metaphor for the preservation of form in whatever context it arises. Partaking of the *hereditas* is to bear in one's own form the potential and the right to continue on. Inheritance both encodes a bodily scheme of transmission and insures a legal transference of substance. In narrative, all movement is a kind of inheritance, a record of individual and cultural transmission, a metaphoric "carrying across" from one time to another, one place to another, one state or estate to another, one plot to another.

The laws of narrative inheritance assume sound donations and healthy conveyances, but laws of any kind will find their violators; systems of any kind, their subvertors. I originally intended to title this book *Mutants Will Be Born* from a phrase in a recent satiric narrative, Thomas Pynchon's *Gravity's Rainbow*, a phrase that describes a process central to satiric creation: "So, when laws of heredity are laid down, mutants will be born."[2] Pynchon establishes a law of inheritance that holds not only for his book but for the mode in which it is offered. His almost consoling "So" invites a more settling conclusion than the narrative delivers. Laws are presumably laid down (if laid down at all) for healthy births. Yet in satire mutants will indeed be born.

This is a book about the satiric violation of narrative lines. Satiric action is a kind of bad seed. Pope describes the satiric action in *The Dunciad* when he depicts the backward birth of an entire culture to its noncreative origin "where things destroy'd are swept to things unborn" (*Dunciad in Four Books*, I, 242). Those coming into their satiric estate

[1] *The Complete Essays of Montaigne*, trans. Donald M. Frame (Stanford, 1958), "Of repentance," III, 2, 611.
[2] Thomas Pynchon, *Gravity's Rainbow* (New York, 1973), p. 275.

generally have no real bearing, although they are represented as if they were entirely self-possessed. By deploying its modal resources against false possession, the fully satiric action converts the promise of inheritance into the conspiracy of degeneration.

All of the major narrative satires I will treat in the following chapters challenge the notion of narrative generation and question the nature of satiric issue: *Gargantua and Pantagruel*, *Don Quixote*, *Hudibras*, *Last Instructions to A Painter*, *Absalom and Achitophel*, *A Tale of A Tub*, *Gulliver's Travels*, *The Rape of the Lock*, *The Dunciad*, and *Tristram Shandy*. These narratives are different in literary intent and execution, and in some cases their strategies are not even exclusively satiric. But each focuses on the properties of inheritance or succession, and each treats the complexities of individual and institutional sufficiency, possession, and perpetuation. My aim in writing about these texts is to come to a critical and theoretical understanding of the nature of the satiric action in an extensive narrative order.

Although most of the works I discuss reflect the strategies and structures of satire during a period of its great narrative ascendancy in England, I hope that in preliminary chapters I can place the satirist and the satiric action in a wider modal and representational context. When conceived as a mode rather than as a generically fixed form, satire has the capacity and power to alter potential in other systems of literary representation. My larger argument for the book will therefore draw on a range of material touching on many aspects of narrative origin, dispensation, and transmission. Throughout I have profited greatly from the work of the extraordinary eighteenth-century encyclopedist of inheritable forms, Giambattista Vico, and from recent work of a modern theorist of origins and violations, René Girard. In subsequent chapters and in a selected bibliography, I will have occasion to acknowledge these debts and many others to scholars, theorists, and critics on whose work I have relied.

ACKNOWLEDGMENTS

I wish I could thank all those whose conversation, heard and overheard, aided me in working out the arguments and general contours of this book. But there is a good chance that many from whom I have pillaged would not choose to have me make public what I have done to their once sound ideas. Therefore, I will acknowledge only those who have read or had the courage to listen to me read portions of the manuscript. My mentors and friends, Earl Miner and Max Novak, have been a source of support to me for many years, and their specific help on aspects of English satire has been invaluable. I have benefited from attention paid to my work by colleagues and good friends, Paul Fry, Alfred Mac Adam, Edward Mendelson, James Nohrnberg, Brigitte Peucker, Jonathan Arac, David Bromwich, Carol Kay, Alvin Kernan, David Quint, and Harris Friedberg. My wife, Maria DiBattista, has taken a great deal of time and care to help me at every stage. Mere thanks seems a paltry gesture, but I thank her anyway.

A year-long grant in 1975 from the National Endowment for the Humanities enabled me to begin work in earnest, and a subsequent shorter term grant from the Andrew Mellon Foundation provided me with crucial time at the William Andrews Clark Memorial Library in Los Angeles. I thank the responsible grantors at both of these programs.

Very little of the material in this book has appeared anywhere else in print, although I have read papers at the MLA, at Yale University, and at Princeton University based on various sections of the manuscript. A much earlier version of the *Hudibras* chapter appeared in the Winter 1971 issue of *Eighteenth-Century Studies*, and some material on satire appeared in an essay, "The Satiric Plots of *Gravity's Rainbow*," in *Pynchon: A Collection of Critical Essays*, ed. Edward Mendelson (Englewood Cliffs, 1978). I have had a great deal of assistance in the preparation of this book from Marjorie Sherwood and Catherine Dammeyer of Princeton University Press. I am very grateful to them for their efforts.

M.S.

NEW YORK CITY   1978

SATIRIC INHERITANCE
RABELAIS TO STERNE

Chapter One

THE SATIRIC DISPENSATION

Questions about the nature of the satiric action generally assume all too easy answers about the nature of the satiric actor. It is one of the more plaguing paradoxes about the satiric mode that the satirist, having taken on a kind of monstrosity as his subject, makes something of a monster of himself. The rhetorical, forensic, and moral justification for satire and for the positioning of the satirist against his subjects tends to ignore the complicity of the satirist in the degenerate record he formally records.

Over thirty years ago, Wyndham Lewis startled readers of satire by arguing that the mode was not even moral.[1] To those who justified the nature of the satiric art by the abiding righteous moral fervor of the satirist, Lewis responded that the curative, meliorative, or restorative role of the satirist is part of a preserving fiction, a mere saving of appearances. The satirist as moral scourge is the imposition of an ethical fabrication upon a literary structure, perhaps an indication of how things may be forced into proper form but hardly a guarantee of how things necessarily shape up. For Lewis satire was a grinning tragedy, the relentless pursuit by the satirist of negative incidentals, a ritualized articulation of damaging facts, nervous impulses in the face of civilized breakdowns.

The satiric representation or fiction refuses to entertain notions of the accommodating, idealizing lie; that is, it refuses to break into normative form. Hence in satiric invec-

[1] Wyndham Lewis, "The Greatest Satire is Nonmoral," in *Modern Essays in Criticism: Satire*, ed. Ronald Paulson (Englewood Cliffs, 1971), pp. 66-79. The original argument appeared in the early chapters of Lewis's *Men Without Art* (London, 1934).

tive the urge to *re*form is literally overwhelmed by the urge to annihilate. The satirist rhymes rats to death, beats to bits with little sticks, strips, whips, mortifies, vexes. But in so doing he is implicated in the debasing form of his action—he is beside himself and beneath himself, something of a beast. According to Plato, the utterer of satiric invective is himself counternormative, that is, against nature. Plato writes in the *Laws*: "the man who utters such words is gratifying a thing most ungracious and sating his passion with foul foods, and by thus brutalizing afresh that part of his soul which was once humanized by education, he makes a wild beast of himself through his rancorous life, and wins only gall for gratitude for his passion" (Loeb trans., 935a).

The satirist is deeply implicated in satire's degenerative fictions precisely because he thrives as the chronicler of degenerative norms. The first represented satirist in Western literature, Thersites of the *Iliad*, is also the most deformed warrior in the Greek camp. In an age of heroic demeanor, Thersites is an ugly being with a hunched back and a tuft of hair growing from a misshapen skull. Such deformity is an insult to heroic proportion. Perhaps Thersites has become a satirist because he is ugly, or, in a more intriguing variant, perhaps being a satirist has made him ugly. He rails against the martial code that determines the propriety of heroic action. Although in the *Iliad* this is not an altogether unreasonable thing to do, it disturbs the heroic sequence. Thus normative form throws a line of defense against Thersites. Odysseus threatens to shame the satirist in a shame culture; he threatens to whip him naked.[2] As satirist, Thersites' words impede narrative action; and as a character in an epic, he is expelled as abnormal.

---

[2] In Lucian's *True History*, Thersites, the offended satirist, brings a charge of libel against Homer for the treatment he receives in the *Iliad*. Odysseus is Homer's lawyer and once again he wins the day (*True History*, 2, 20). Giambattista Vico argues that Thersites, precisely because he was ugly, must have been a plebeian who served the heroes in the Trojan War:

THE SATIRIC DISPENSATION

The plight of Thersites raises some perplexing questions about subverting patterns in satire. Writing on a false but revealing satiric etymology, the satirist as *satyr*, Andrew Marvell points out that the false derivation cuts two ways: "for whereas those that treat of innocent and benign argument are represented by the Muses, they that make it their business to set out others ill-favoredly do pass for Satyres, and themselves are sure to be personated with prick-ears, wrinkled horns, and cloven feet."[3] Marvell knows that he is not working with the Latin derivation of satire (*satura*), but his remarks bring us back to a point of origin of sorts, a point of authority rendered suspect by its very being. The satyr figure is emblematic of the larger structures of satire: to be what it is or to do what it does is to subvert nature. A satyr is half-god, half-beast, and it has access to profound information and knowledge—terrible knowledge that Nietzsche will later reveal in the figure of the satyr Silenus. The satyr appears at the beginning of things as a god-monster and penetrates to the depths of things in echoing life's deep, long cultural moan.

The notion that the satyr figure encompasses in fable the monstrous truths he reveals appears in an early defense of satire, that curious but extremely popular concoction of late sixteenth-century France, *Satyr Menippée*. The English

---

"He was beaten by Ulysses with the scepter of Agamemnon, just as the ancient Roman plebeians were beaten by the nobles with rods over their bare shoulders." See *The New Science of Giambattista Vico*, trans. Thomas Goddard Bergin and Max Harold Fisch (Ithaca, 1970), p. 96. Perhaps the modern satirist beats because he was continually beaten. Bishop Hall, who liked to call himself the first English satirist, entitles one of his works *Virgidemiarum* (from *virgidemiae* or harvest of rods), the implication being that the satirist wields the switch rather than having it wielded against him. His act is a kind of historical revenge. The most thorough discussion of the satirist's status in society is that of Robert Elliott in *The Power of Satire: Magic, Ritual, Art* (Princeton, 1960), a work that has been generative for me in every sense of the word.

[3] Andrew Marvell, *The Rehearsal Transpros'd*, in *The Complete Works*, 4 vols., ed. Alexander Grosart (London, 1873), 3:253.

translation (London, 1594) records that the French authors were also aware that the derivation of the word satire was from the Latin *satura*, but it continues with the inaccurate (and irrepressible) speculation: "But I suppose that the word cometh from the Graecians, who at their publicke and solemn feastes, did bring in upon their states or scaffolds, certaine persons disguised, like unto Satyres, whom the people supposed to be halfe Gods" (p. 202). The satirist is suffered because he has in him something that is sacred and prophetic; he is scorned because he is beastly and profane. Such is the nature of the material he presents. In the later seventeenth century, the illustrator of Grimmelshausen's *Simplicissimus Teutsch* (1669) provided a plate known as the Phoenix Copper, which represented a satyr figure as a Phoenix with one webbed and one shod foot, one visible wing, a horned head, and a bizarrely distorted set of facial features. The Phoenix is a sacred and prophetic image; it keeps giving birth to itself in cycles of destruction and regeneration. Grimmelshausen's profane, deformed Phoenix was meant to embody the action of his narrative: monstrosity perpetuates itself.

From the earlier to the later seventeenth century, the history of critical reaction to satire is the history of an attempt to make satiric forms less noticeably profane and more prophetically accessible. At the beginning of the century satire was resigned to its own vulgarity. In his *Scourge of Villanie* (1599), John Marston announces that his aim is to rail in like fashion against polluting beastliness, and he steadfastly refuses the aid of more refined muses. He invokes "no Dealian deitie, / No sacred offspring of Mnemosyne." Marston rejects the notion of inspiration because an ill wind is blowing out of him—it is not in the nature of satire to require or take in the muse's breath. No "Castalian muse" nor even "sprightly wit" need raise his "flagging wings" nor teach him to "tune these harsh discordant strings." Marston prefers "grim Reproofe" and "stearne hate" for his "Satyres poesie." Something in the satiric act grounds it. In narrative satire, Rabelais had earlier sought the drunken satyr and excused the ascendant Pegasus. He writes in the prologue to the third book of the deeds and sayings of Pantagruel: "Wait a little, till I've swallowed a draught from this bottle. It is my true and only Helicon, my one Pegasus spring, my sole enthusiasm. As I drink I here deliberate, discourse, resolve, and conclude."[4]

As the seventeenth century progressed, the rise of satire was quite literally accompanied by a refined set of notions about its origins and a renewed sense of its public scope. In his *Discourse Concerning the Original and Progress of Satire* (prefixed to his translations of Persius and Juvenal in 1692), John Dryden was intent on disseminating the findings of the classical scholar, Isaac Casaubon. Casaubon had severed the word satire from its supposed etymological forebear, satyr. He derived it from *satura lanx*, a well-filled platter.[5] Metaphorically, one could conceive of the action

[4] François Rabelais, *Gargantua and Pantagruel*, trans. J. M. Cohen (Harmondsworth, 1955), p. 284. Returning to Rabelais by way of Samuel Butler, Henry Fielding invokes the grounded Dionysian muse for one of the introductory chapters of *Tom Jones*: "A modern may with much more Elegance invoke a Ballad, as some have thought *Homer* did, or a Mug of Ale with the Author of *Hudibras*; which latter may perhaps have inspired much more Poetry as well as Prose, than all the Liquors of *Hippocrene* or *Helicon*" (bk. 8, ch. 1). The insecurity of treating subjects of something less than heroic proportion seems reflexively transferred to the act of poetic representation in general, almost as if one must be out of his senses to be a poet and dead drunk to be a satirist.

[5] Following Isaac Casaubon, who in his *De Satyrica Graecorum Poesi et Romanorum Satira* (Paris, 1605) discussed the precise etymology of *satura*, Dryden writes:

But considering Satire as a Species of Poetry; here the War begins amongst the Criticks. *Scaliger* the Father will have it descend from *Greece* to *Rome*; and derives the word Satyre, from *Satyrus*, that mixt kind of Animal, or, as the Ancients thought him, Rural God, made up betwixt a Man and a Goat; with a Humane Head, Hook's Nose, Powting Lips, a Bunch, or Struma under the Chin, prick'd Ears, and upright Horns; the Body shagg'd with hair, especially from the waste, and ending in a Goat, with the legs and feet of that Creature. But *Casaubon*, and his Followers, with Reason, condemn this derivation;

represented in satire as a controlled medley or farrago in the form of an abundant feast. The satirist is feast-giver, or he displaces that role within the work, like Petronius's Trimalchio in the *Satyricon*, or the author of Swift's *A Tale of A Tub* "jumbling fifty Things together in a Dish," or the narrator of *Tom Jones* keeping a "public Ordinary" for all his readers wishing to partake of the stew of human nature.

Something of great power is lost for satire, however, by separating its nature from its more disturbing, though erroneous, etymological origins. Giambattista Vico reverts to older forms when he claims a kind of primacy and universality for satire that he senses was diminished by Roman urbanity and formalization. In trying to make the satirist more polite (that is, in attempting to polish his surfaces or clean up his act, which is what polite means), the Romans civilized an uncivil or disturbed being. For Vico

> satire preserved this eternal property with which it was born: that of expressing invective and insult; for the peasants, thus roughly masked and riding in the carts in which they carried the grapes, had the license—as the vintagers still have in our happy Campania (once called the dwelling of Bacchus)—of hurling abuse at their betters. Hence we may understand with how little truth the learned later inserted into the fable of Pan (since *pan* signifies "all") the philosophical mythology

and prove that from *Satyrus*, the word *Satira*, as it signifies a Poem, cannot possibly descend. For *Satira* is not properly a Substantive, but an Adjective; to which, the word *Lanx*, in *English* a Charger, or large Platter, is understood: So that the *Greek* Poem made according to the Manners of a Satyr, and expressing his Qualities, must properly be call'd Satyrical, and not Satire: And thus far 'tis allow'd, that the *Grecians* had such Poems; but that they were wholly different in Specie, from that to which the *Romans* gave the Name of Satire.

Discourse Concerning the Original and Progress of Satire, in *The Works of John Dryden*, ed. A. B. Chambers, William Frost, and Vinton Dearing (Berkeley and Los Angeles, 1974), 4:28-29.

to the effect that he signifies the universe, and that the hairy nether parts mean the earth, the red breast and face the element of fire, and the horns the sun and the moon. The Romans, however, preserved for us the historical mythology concerning him in the word *satyra*, which, according to Festus, was a dish made of various kinds of foods. Hence the later expression *lex per satyram* for an omnibus law. So, in dramatic satire, which we are discussing here, according to Horace (for no examples of this form have come down to us either from the Greeks or from the Latins), various types of characters made their appearance, such as gods, heroes, kings, artisans, and slaves. But the satire that survived among the Romans does not treat of varied matters, since each poem is devoted to a separate argument.[6]

Vico questions the idealizing balance of satire, discredits its forensically bound structure, and claims, citing Horace, that in its lost dramatic forms satire was universally subversive. For Vico, satire's well-filled dish is the dish that runneth over, whether he speaks of lost dramatic satire or extant Menippean satires. Satire retains the suspicious and disproportionate status of its origins. It is that mode which bursts beyond generic contours. Its untoward, unrestrained, and encroaching characteristics are much like those of farce, which also gains its name from the etymological connection with things either stuffed-in or burst-out. Like farce, satire is conditioned to be out of shape. Its strategies conform to its nature, and the process is still very much with us when a modern narrative satirist such as Vladimir Nabokov ponders what happens when the destructive urge is modally upon him. Whether he tries to hold to form in writing or in the designing of chess problems, Nabokov explains that:

[6] Vico, *New Science*, p. 278.

Deceit, to the point of diabolism, and originality, verging upon the grotesque, were my notions of strategy; and although in matters of construction I tried to conform, whenever possible, to classical rules, such as economy of form, unity, weeding out loose ends, I was always ready to sacrifice purity of form to exigencies of fantastic content, causing form to bulge and burst like a sponge-bed containing a small, furious devil.[7]

✧

One of the difficulties in assessing the nature of larger forms of satire or in reacting critically to the investment of so much literary energy in what is essentially a subversive, deforming mode, touches upon a confusion implicit in the satiric act, a confusion between inspiration and execution. Juvenal said that satire was difficult *not* to write; Dryden claimed that it was very difficult to read. They were perhaps looking at different ends of the same process and ranging between the ease of satiric impulse and the complications of satiric design. Satire is "easy" because its subjects are so tantalizingly manifest, but it is difficult because its strategies are so deceivingly imitative of what it purports to attack. To put it another way, satire is easy because the satirist's impulse is to fight dirty, but it is difficult because the satirist's design is to play it smart.

Freud recognized the connection between the open hostility of satire and its more calculated, enfabled indirection when he plotted the satirist's simultaneous line of attack and retreat. He compares the satiric process to dream-censorship, where the immediacy of a hostile anxiety is recessed into the deeper structure of a "plot" produced to express it. Freud speaks of the dangerous status of those who have "disagreeable truths to tell to those in authority":

[7] Vladimir Nabokov, *Speak, Memory* (New York, 1947; rev. 1966), pp. 289-290.

THE SATIRIC DISPENSATION

If he presents them undisguised, the authorities will suppress his words—after they have been spoken, if his pronouncement was an oral one, but beforehand, if he had intended to make it in print. A writer must beware of the censorship, and on its account he must soften and distort the expression of his opinion. According to the strength and sensitiveness of the censorship he finds himself compelled either merely to refrain from certain forms of attack, or to speak in allusions in place of direct references, or he must conceal his objectionable pronouncement beneath some apparently innocent disguise: for instance, he may describe a dispute between two Mandarins in the Middle Kingdom, when the people he really has in mind are officials in his own country. The stricter the censorship, the more far-reaching will be the disguise and the more ingenious too may be the means employed for putting the reader on the scent of the true meaning.[8]

Attack is a kind of second nature, but defense calls for elaborate systems of retreat. Freud's real interest here is with the dreamer and not the satirist, and of course the difference between the two is that for the dreamer the censorship is affected unconsciously from inside the dream. But it may be that Freud's analogy is stronger than he meant it to be. Satirists generate their own insecurities and then elaborate a fable in which they attempt to displace themselves from what they have generated. Of course the real satiric subject is the degenerative spirit in human nature that can never be restrictively localized anywhere because it is so universally formed. By creating the impression that monstrosities are in front of and "away" from him, the satirist tries to sustain the impression that the monstrous is

[8] Sigmund Freud, *The Interpretation of Dreams*, trans. James Strachey (London, 1953), 4:142.

different from him—that the tub is sufficient to stay the Leviathan. But rarely is that the case.

However, it has always been a persistent part of the satiric fiction for the satirist to try to protect himself from his material. He hopes, almost prays, that whatever out there threatens him does not by a stretch of his own imagination absorb him. Attack is the undisplaced satiric impulse, but escape is the better part of satiric valor. In Pope's *Epistle to Arbuthnot*, for example, the satiric reflex is double. Pope must escape from what he creates. He is more worried about the mass of undifferentiated humanity claiming to like him and to be "like" him than he is about scourging his enemies. It is the "Slaver" that kills "and not the Bite" (l. 106). Pope turns to attack when he thinks he has retreated from contact to the safety of his own home and to the comfort of his doctor's friendship. Only then does he beg his satiric case: "Yet let me flap this Bug with gilded wings, / This painted Child of Dirt that stinks and stings" (ll. 309-310). It ought to occur to Pope, and no doubt does, that his description of Sporus (Lord Hervey) is not altogether different from his own activities as satirist (both inside and outside of his poem).

In a recent speculative essay on the satiric process, Alvin Kernan compares aspects of satiric response to the defense posturings of frightened animals.[9] Kernan is a very measured critic and he refuses to argue more than an analogy, but his speculations are important even if discomfiting. The instinctual distortion of shapes, the emission of odors and poisons, the change of hues, the puffings, coilings, and hissings are defensive gestures of an offensive nature. They are a patterned system of behavior, a reaction to real and imagined threats—usually threats of encroachment or

---

[9] Alvin B. Kernan, "Agression and Satire: Art Considered as a Form of Biological Adaptation," in *Literary Theory and Structure: Essays in Honor of William K. Wimsatt*, ed. Frank Brady, John Palmer, Martin Price (New Haven, 1973), pp. 115-129.

violation. Kernan recognizes that the biological analogy becomes more remote in relation to highly articulated patterns of linguistic energy in satire, but perhaps we can see a kind of middle-order substantiation of Kernan's primary model in an extraordinary scene from Rabelais. At one point in the narrative, Pantagruel's tutor and friend, Panurge, encounters a learned Englishman named Thaumaste. In an elaborately presented satiric agon, Panurge and Thaumaste prepare to posture each other into submission. They engage in combat by signs. Signs may be a form of first speech, "a fantastic speech," according to Vico, "making use of physical substances endowed with life and most of them imagined to be divine."[10] For Rabelais signs are both potent and dangerous, sacred and profane. To those, so to speak, "in the know," the evil eye or the bony finger can render one's victims impotent.[11] Gestures themselves can neutralize.

> Suddenly Panurge lifted his right hand in the air, and placed his thumb inside his right nostril, holding his four fingers stretched out and arranged in their natural order, parallel to the tip of his nose, shutting his left eye entirely and winking with the right, at the same time deeply depressing his eyebrows and lids.[12]

Panurge puts his thumb in his eye, gnashes his teeth, shakes his codpiece, sucks in air, blows up his cheeks, until finally, by dint of grotesque posturing, he wins the day. Thaumaste begins sweating torrents, defecates in profound fear, and submits. At one satiric level Rabelais parodies the obfuscating disputes of the learned perverters of spiritual signs; at a deeper level Panurge becomes an as-

[10] Vico, *New Science*, p. 86.
[11] The first two chapters of Robert Elliott's *The Power of Satire*, "Satire and Magic: History," and "Satire and Magic: Theory," provide a full exposition of satire's debt to ritual postures and powers.
[12] Rabelais, *Gargantua and Pantagruel*, p. 234.

sault artist for a protected Rabelais. In making a spectacle of himself, Panurge absorbs all that is preposterous in the satiric effort. Rabelais merely attends and records.

If confrontation and apprehension are closely related in the ur-satiric scene, the same is generally true for the structured forms of satire. As a subverting and subversive mode, satire possesses purloined territory and the satirist approaches degenerate ground. The satiric act is a kind of trespass. And if the satirist assumes the morally insulating stance, more often than not he suffers the contamination of his own subject. In a recent novel, the German ironist and satirist, Heinrich Böll, comments on the art of garbage collecting as an occupation that instinctively seeks "the appropriate polarization." Böll writes: "Garbage collecting . . . serves the purposes of cleanliness but is regarded as dirty."[13] The dilemma is not a new one. It appears in almost all forms of satire, and it appears most ingeniously in narrative or fabled forms where the satirist works to distance himself from the debasing, deforming, encroaching, and contaminating nature of his subjects by placing surrogate figures into his fictions. He literally invents expendable versions of himself (with whom he is only partially identified) to do his dirty work. The monks in Rabelais "draw on themselves the opprobrium, insults, and curses of the world" because "they eat the world's excrement, that is to say, sins; and as eaters of excrement they are cast into their privies—their convents and abbeys that is—which are cut off from all civil intercourse, as are the privies of a house."[14] Rabelais, of course, is himself as much a monk as an author, but for the purposes of deflecting strategy he allows his surrogates the lesser honor.

The master of satiric deflection, however, is Jonathan Swift. In his short *Meditation Upon a Broomstick*, Swift slips a

[13] Heinrich Böll, *Group Portrait with Lady*, trans. Lelia Vennewitz (New York, 1973), p. 390.
[14] Rabelais, *Gargantua and Pantagruel*, pp. 125-126.

surrogate figure between his zealous self and his anxious self to record the profanation of the satiric act. The moral intent of the cleanser is confounded by the contamination of the satiric action. Beginning life innocently and naturally enough as a tree, the broom works towards its seemingly proper purpose only when it inverts its natural position: "a Tree turned upside down, the Branches on the earth, and the roots in the Air." Swift's broom—a symbol of "mortal Man"—is both purging agent and filthied object, and is compelled to suffer

> a capricious Kind of Fate, destined to make other Things clean, and be nasty it self. . . . He sets up to be a universal Reformer and Corrector of Abuses; a Remover of Grievances; rakes into every Slut's corner of Nature, bringing hidden Corruptions to the Light, and raiseth a mighty Dust where there was none before; sharing deeply all the while in the very same Pollutions he pretends to sweep away.[15]

The complicity of the satirically surrogate mission is still a matter of wary concern in modern literature. In *Malone Dies*, Samuel Beckett tells the story, through Malone, of a certain McMann. McMann, of course, is, like Swift's broom, a satirically conceived human agent—his name means son of man. Conveniently, McMann gets a job as street cleaner in Beckett's dump of a universe. Malone meditates on McMann as broomstick.

> [McMann] himself was compelled to admit that the place swept by him looked dirtier at his departure than on his arrival, as if a demon had driven him to collect, with the broom, shovel and barrow placed gratis at his disposal by the corporation, all the dirt and filth which chance had withdrawn from the sight of the tax-payer

[15] Jonathan Swift, *A Meditation Upon a Broomstick*, in *Works*, ed. Herbert Davis (Oxford, 1965), 1:239-240.

and add them thus recovered to those already visible.
. . . With the result that at the end of the day,
throughout the sector consigned to him, one could see
the peels of oranges and bananas, cigarette-butts, unspeakable scraps of paper, dogs' and horses' excrement and other muck, carefully concentrated all along
the sidewalk or distributed on the crown of the street,
as though in order to inspire the greatest possible disgust in the passers-by or provoke the greatest possible
number of accidents, some fatal, by means of the
slip.[16]

In many ways, the satirist is obsessed by his impulses and
trapped by his designs. If the satirist cannot convince his
readers that they stand like "fair Cloacina," as Pope puts it,
"And minister to Jove with purest hands, " he may at least
be forgiven for breaching the obligations of formal de-
corum because of the risks involved in his chosen profes-
sion. The anthropologist Mary Douglas has written a fascinating short book called *Purity and Danger: An Analysis of
the Concepts of Pollution and Taboo* where she explains the extent to which dirty things constitute a threat to social and
mental order. Dirt is taboo, although different societies
have different notions about what is dirty. Douglas goes on
to suggest that if dirt is matter out of place, perhaps there
is a world of antimatter that belongs to those willing to lay
claim to control over it. Such souls may be social pariahs,
outcasts, very pictures of frustration; or they may be sha-
man and wizards. Or again, they may be satirists ready to
risk exposure to dirt and disorder for the power such a risk
transfers to them.

Granted that disorder spoils pattern; it also provides
the materials of pattern. Order implies restriction;

[16] Samuel Beckett, *Malone Dies*, in *Three Novels by Samuel Beckett: Molloy,
Malone Dies, The Unnamable* (New York: Grove Press, 1965), p. 244.

from all possible materials, a limited selection has been made and from all possible relations a limited set has been used. So disorder by implication is unlimited, no pattern has been realized in it, but its potential for patterning is indefinite. This is why, though we seek to create order, we do not simply condemn disorder. We recognize that it is destructive to existing patterns: also that it has potentiality. It symbolizes both danger and power.[17]

When Wyndham Lewis argues that the satiric action reveals those negative incidentals that constitute the literary articulation of human orders, he formulates for satire a notion of patterned contamination. To place the satirist somewhere near the source of his own vision and to allow him to shape powerfully disordering instincts is to make him into a security risk. The satirist penetrates to origins that are potentially compromising to his subjects, to himself, and to society at large. In effect, satiric activity compromises society's renewing and "cleansing" dispensations—orders that allow for (indeed, insist upon) gestures of polite civilizing that cover over dirty notions. Satiric activity is paradoxical by its very nature. In bringing violations to the surface, the satirist creates that primal scene Lewis calls an orgy of externals. He violates to offer violations.

In pursuing such a possibility, I have been intrigued by a more general argument on the nature of original, mythic, and secular violation recently advanced by René Girard in his two books, *La Violence et le sacré* (Paris, 1972) and *Des Choses cachées depuis la fondation du monde* (Paris, 1978). Girard hypothesizes that legal and ritual systems for human continuity are codifications of originally violent acts or impulses. To penetrate even the most seemingly innocent

[17] Mary Douglas, *Purity and Danger: An Analysis of the Concepts of Pollution and Taboo* (London, 1966), p. 94.

patterns of behavior reveals a kind of regressive complicity. For Girard, violence and its necessary disguising dispensations begin with the biblical account of Cain and Abel, a moment of profound disorder (blood violation) that becomes foundational. According to Girard, historical origin is murderous.

The possibility of "carrying on" demands the postponement of revenge and the displacement of violent cravings into schemes for continuity. Thus the dispensations of history are the beginnings of necessary cover-ups or sanctifications of violence through disguise. For René Girard, the historical and human record of temporal continuity is the accommodation of uneasy memories in the codifying of regressive tendencies so that communal rituals of sacrifice and scapegoatism displace the barbarism of founding acts. Vico notes a custom of the Scythians "to fix a knife in the ground, adore it as a god, and then kill the man with it. This kind of execution the Latins called *mactare*, which remained a sacred term used in sacrifices."[18] Similarly, in his *Genealogy of Morals*, Nietzsche accounts for the atavistic delight in violence by reimagining its presence and perpetuation in systems of Western morality.

---

[18] Vico, *New Science*, p. 305. Later in *The New Science*, Vico explains how in his system all law (and punishment) is disguised in poetic representations: "By its [law's] fictions what had happened was taken as not having happened, and what had not happened as having happened." Vico goes on about jurisprudential fiction:

It rested its entire reputation on inventing such fables as might preserve the gravity of the laws and do justice to the facts. Thus all the fictions of ancient jurisprudence were truths under masks, and the formulae in which the laws were expressed, because of their strict measures of such and so many words—admitting neither addition, substraction, nor alteration—were called *carmina*, or songs, as above we found Livy terming the formula dictating the punishment of Horatius. This is confirmed by a golden passage in Plautus's *Comedy of Asses* where Diabolus says that the parasite is a great poet, for he knows better than anybody how to invent verbal safeguards or formulae, which we have just seen were called *carmina*. (Pp. 342-343)

[Modern man] resists a really vivid comprehension of the degree to which *cruelty* constituted the great festival pleasure of more primitive men and was indeed an ingredient of almost every one of their pleasures; and how naïvely, how innocently their thirst for cruelty manifested itself, how, as a matter of principle, they posited "disinterested malice" (or, in Spinoza's words, *sympathia malevolens*) as a *normal* quality of man—and thus as something to which the conscience cordially says *Yes!* A more profound eye might perceive enough of this oldest and most fundamental festival pleasure of man even in our time; in *Beyond Good and Evil* (and earlier in *The Dawn*) I pointed to the ever-increasing spiritualization and "deification" of cruelty which permeates the entire history of higher culture (and in a significant sense actually constitutes it).[19]

For Nietzsche it is the temerity of penetration into the cruel, Dionysian disorder of human life that constitutes the supreme moments of dramatic tragedy. However, in satire penetration is less the achievement of the subject than the cruel will of the satirist. The satiric scene of violation is a kind of satiric will to power. Pope establishes a satiric sequence in *The Dunciad*: "When Dulness, smiling—'Thus revive the wits!/But murder first, and mince them all to bits" (*Dunciad in Four Books*, IV, 119-120). In the penetrations of satire all actions are never too far from the original violations they harbor: ambition is parricide; schism is fratricide; the denial of posterity is infanticide; inheritance is usurpation. Satire loosens the Scythians' sacrificial knife. Or, to put it another way, satire blows history's cover.

Girard discusses the effect of penetration when he writes of the curse, one of the primary impulses of the satiric spirit. In an essay, "*Les Malédictions contre les Pharisiens et la*

---

[19] Friedrich Nietzsche, *The Genealogy of Morals*, II, 6, in *Basic Writings of Nietzsche*, trans. Walter Kaufmann (New York, 1968), p. 502.

révélation évangélique,"[20] he points to that puzzling passage in the gospels where Christ curses the Pharisees for what is history's first sanctioned cover-up, a form of burial as hypocritical action: "Woe unto you! for ye build the sepulchres of the prophets, and your fathers killed them" (Luke 11:47).[21] Christ exacts payment for the blood of the prophets shed "from the foundation of the world" (Luke 11:50), marks the foundation of the world "from the blood of Abel" (Luke 11:51), and continues with yet another allusion to covering or burying: "For there is nothing covered, that shall not be revealed; neither hid, that shall not be known" (Luke 12:2).

To bury is to put the corpse underground or to put the victim out of sight. In another sense, burial is to hide in hell (hell meaning to cover over). If the buried body is entombed, its place becomes a monumental cover-up, its existence in time, as in history, a fabrication. Sinners of course are buried in their lies, as in Dante's Hell where fraud covers over violence. Christ, because he is a divine scapegoat, is both inside and outside that which is historically covered, and he curses the Pharisees because sacred time will be discovered and uncovered in him—he will in the latter day make historical violators suffer their hypocrisies. In the sequences that Girard describes, history is a community effort in legal attenuation, and only the sacred promise at the end of time will reveal the double-dealing of Cain's secular indemnification.

The satirist, like a prophetic Christ railing at the Pharisees, also denounces the time and the times, also reveals and uncovers the doubleness of action; but unlike Christ, the satirist possesses no certain promise, his fulmi-

[20] René Girard, "Les Malédictions contre les Pharisiens et la révélation évangélique," *Bulletin du centre protestant d'études* 27 (1975): 3-29. The substance of this essay is included in Girard's *Des Choses cachées depuis la fondation du monde* (Paris, 1978).

[21] I cite Luke because Girard cites him. The curse also appears in the gospel according to Matthew.

THE SATIRIC DISPENSATION

nations are very much "in" time. So there is in the satiric act a kind of perverse neutralization of historical progression, a stop without the guarantee of a new start. If for a critic such as Girard history is the encoding of violence, satire is the decoding of violence. If history requires the careful selection of victims, satire turns history into a pattern of universal victimization. If history covers over so that events proceed legally, satire creates a frenzy around points of terminus, penetrates to elaborate moments of regression where origins are ends and where, as in Pope's *Dunciad*, all efforts to continue come to nothing or, as in Swift's *Modest Proposal*, all compensation is overcompensation and primal violations such as cannibalism are all too easily projected as sustaining the *lex per satyram*, the legal serving-up of bodies for the preservation of the system.[22]

In satire the necessary displacements of history—the cover-up rituals—are represented by more overt forms of the violations they are supposed to replace. Girard holds that what was once unthinkable becomes, after a fashion, legal. The satirist maintains that what is represented as legal is really unthinkable. Little is truly conserved in the satiric rendering of human behavior. In revealing anything

[22] Swift's satiric "final solution" to the Irish problem is not without some interesting and overcompensated historical analogues that reflect on Girard's theories. There are two entries in the *Encyclopedia of Religion and Ethics*, ed. James Hastings (New York, 1922), vol. 11, that touch upon Irish violation, sacrifice, and tribute. The first is as follows: "[Irish] Fathers, according to Caesar, had the power of life and death over their wives and children, and the practice of sons not appearing in their father's presence until they had reached manhood may have originated in a judicious concealment by the mothers of the boys from the sight of their fathers, lest the head of the household should decide to reduce the number of his children" (p. 9). The second reads: "To the Fomorians—a group of gods who may have been evil divinities of the Celts, or perhaps the gods of the aborigines regarded by the incoming Celts as hostile to themselves—the Nemedians are said to have given in tribute two-thirds of their children born throughout the year and two-thirds of the year's supply of milk and corn. The Fomorians are here regarded as an actual race; but there is no doubt that they were supernatural beings, and that tribute here means sacrifice, exaggerated though it may be" (p. 11).

about the disguised codes of human action, the satirist reveals too much; in perceiving the nature of original acts, he impedes continuity. In *A Tale of A Tub*, Swift's parodied modern author makes a case against the spirit of penetration on the basis of its unpleasantness.[23] The author's temperament is inimical to the strain of interior processes. Notably, his resistance to penetration is greatest in the *Tale*'s "Digression on Madness," and, as with all arguments in Swift's paradoxical narrative, the author's preference for the surfaces of things goes deeper than he imagines. Perhaps the real threat and danger in satire is that in portraying one sort of action the satirist penetrates to another. In representing surface abuses, he violates continuities. The satirist is himself a mad digression against all ritual and historical cover-ups.

At the very heart of the satiric process is a necessary transformation of compensating actions to forms of hypocritical actions. Satire refuses to recognize the necessity of disguise. False sustenance becomes false utterance, and the revelation of hypocrisy is the satiric dissociation of action and intent. In a narrative satire such as Samuel Butler's *Hudibras*, whose primary subject is hypocrisy, the attack on systems of compensating behavior is so thorough that hypocrisy is the exclusive means by which Butler's creations are allowed to "be." In satire, hypocrisy is, at best, a kind of fraudulent and temporarily secured possession. The satirist either sees all overcompensated behavior as a form of hypocrisy (in which case he portrays the satiric scene as a conspiracy of accommodation), or he goes even further and suspects the very nature of language in fostering hypocrisy. In the first instance, a satirist may write of the satiric sequence as complicitous exchange, a sub rosa

---

[23] Herman Melville's very suspicious confidence man is put in a comparable narrative situation: he complains that he detests "satire and his bosom friend irony," but he exists in a book (*The Confidence Man*) that practices both with a particular vengeance.

acknowledgment of guilt-in-action and guilt *in action*. The conspirators of Dryden's *Absalom and Achitophel* find sustenance in universal hypocrisy: "When Crouds can wink; and no offence be known, / Since in another's guilt they find their own" (ll. 184-185). In the second instance, the satiric charge of hypocrisy is precisely the charge that Christ places at the feet of the Pharisees when in a frenzy of denunciation he accuses them of deficient ritual and defective speech. To guard against hypocrisy (that mode of speech which says one thing and means another) is to distrust the very metaphoric properties of language that carry across codes of meaning.

If satire is the mode of representation that sees one set of actions and knows another, part of the satirist's strategy is to debase metaphors of false conveyance. Satiric subjects such as Swift's author in the *Tale* are forced into positions where their metaphoric conceptions collapse around them. In the introduction to the *Tale* the author pursues meaning to its metaphoric depths—wisdom is "a *Fox*, who after long hunting, will at last cost you the Pains to dig out, . . . a *Cheese*, . . . a *Sack-Posset*, . . . a *Hen*, . . . a *Nut*," all of which contain an inside of substance. By the end of the *Tale*, the author has abjured all substance and the metaphoric language that conveys it—he writes upon the only metaphor left him, that is, "*upon Nothing*."

Satiric action is always double action, a regress in the form of a progress, a presentation in the form of a violation. Pope asks that he be given just enough light to reveal what ought to have remained hidden: "Of Darkness visible so much be lent, / As half to shew, half veil the deep Intent" (*Dunciad in Four Books*, IV, 3-4). Satiric knowledge is somewhat akin to taboo or illegal knowledge.[24] In one of

[24] This is a problem that has concerned such critics as Mikhail Bakhtin and Robert Elliott. Bakhtin, *Rabelais and His World* (Cambridge, Mass., 1968), pp. 6-8 and pp. 196-198, discusses the saturnalian aspect of satire, the notion that an attack on norms (even normative abuses) requires the

the more extraordinary scenes from *Tristram Shandy*, Laurence Sterne captures the penetrable dilemma of satiric knowledge by revealing the discomfort it causes among his comic characters. Tristram's mother, curious about Uncle Toby's amours with the Widow Wadman, is instructed by "the fermentation of that little subacid humour" in Walter Shandy to call her curiosity "by its right name . . . and look through the key-hole." Tristram's father is mortified by his own suggestion, and the narrator comments:

> The mistake of my father, was in attacking my mother's motive, instead of the act itself: for certainly key-holes were made for other purposes; and considering the act, as an act which interfered with a true proposition, and denied a key-hole to be what it was——it became a violation of nature; and was so far, you see, criminal.
>
> It is for this reason, an' please your Reverences, That key-holes are the occasions of more sin and wickedness, than all other holes in this world put together. (Vol. IX, ch. 1)

It is a metaphoric profanation to make a keyhole the thing it is not. Keyholes are for keys, and keys, not eyes, ought to penetrate them. But the keyhole is so conveniently there and so suggestively shaped: it is not enough that it merely serve the purpose of its design, but at the

---

almost ritualistic suspension of those same norms. Bakhtin expands his ideas in *Problems of Dostoevsky's Poetics* (Ann Arbor, 1973), pp. 100ff. Elliott treats the matter of satiric illegality in his chapter, "The Satirist Satirized: Studies of the Great Misanthropes" (*The Power of Satire*, pp. 130-222). In his *Grammar of Motives* (New York, 1945), Kenneth Burke sees something of the same problem of legality in the nature of the satirist's primary literary weapon, irony. Burke writes that "irony is based upon a sense of fundamental kinship with the enemy, as one *needs* him, is *indebted* to him, is not merely outside him as an observor but contains him *within*, being consubstantial with him" (p. 514). For Burke, the true ironist recognizes that "he too was criminal, but that the other man was going to prison for him" (p. 515).

same time it is "too much" if it serves anything more. To look through is at once criminal and irresistible. And of course there is the further suggestion—and this is what makes Sterne so brilliant—that to hint that motives are double and that "things" can admit of more than one function is never to recover from what is discovered. The very shape of the keyhole makes it an image of the act to which it gives access. Seeing is transforming and, in this case, rendering is taboo. Consequently, there is always the temptation for satirists to deny what they are doing at the same time that they are doing it, and this presents the satirist as something of a hypocrite himself. No matter what Walter Shandy's conscience tells him, he encourages Mrs. Shandy to approach the keyhole, and Sterne, willy nilly, is there with them. Of course he reserves the right, as does Baudelaire, to look over his shoulder and implicate someone else, *son hypocrite lecteur*.

Chapter Two

INHERITANCE
AND NARRATIVE MODE

Myths of origin or dispensation trace both the genesis of a race destined to be and the inheritable line a people seem destined to follow. Such narrative recountings extend far back into mythological reserves. Creation myths, *seminarium mundi*, aetiological fables, mark the emergence of enlivened forms from the elemental and undifferentiated "stuff" of nature.[1] The birth of the hero out of the dust of the earth is just such a principle of dispensation where heroism itself is something of a first birth, an act of natural design.[2]

Insofar as it repeats itself in time, birth is a kind of mimesis, and the original of all mimetic action is the inheritance of form from the land. Giambattista Vico writes of "the basic reason why the lands and all goods (for all spring from the land), when they have no owner, revert to the public treasury." For Vico, "inheritances, particularly on the part of legitimate heirs, are said to return (*redire*) to the heirs, though in truth they come to them but once."[3] All returns are original inheritances. As James Joyce writes in *Finnegans Wake*: "on the bunk of our breadwinning lies the cropse of our seedfather, a phrase which the estab-

---

[1] Northrop Frye's theories of myths and modes in his *Anatomy of Criticism: Four Essays* (Princeton, 1957) assume the importance of originating, natural fables. My debt to Frye in this chapter is a great one.

[2] See Otto Rank, *The Myth of the Birth of the Hero and Other Writings*, ed. Philip Freund (New York, 1964). Rank discusses the hero's birth as a kind of double parentage, the ego emerging from nature or a natural state to resist, heroically, the mature but somehow invalid human parent (pp. 84-85).

[3] Giambattista Vico, *The New Science of Giambattista Vico*, trans. Thomas Goddard Bergin and Max Harold Fisch (Ithaca, 1970), p. 180.

lisher of the world by law might pretinately write across the chestfront of all manorwombanborn" (p. 55). Our seed-father Adam's return to earth (or to red dust as his name, Adam, means) is both a secular origin and an abundant, though tainted, promise; hence Joyce's combination of "corpse" and "crops" in "cropse."

In most systems of Western myth, original men are necessarily earth men. Vico writes that "the aborigines were giants, and the term 'giants' properly signifies sons of Earth. Thus, as the fables faithfully tell us, Earth was the mother of gods and giants."[4] Vico sees the sizing or shaping down of these autochthonic monsters as the course of human history, for at first only "the Hebrews retained the normal human stature, to which the descendants of the giants gradually returned."[5] For Vico, "heroic education began to bring forth in a certain way the form of the human soul which had been completely submerged in the huge bodies of the giants, and began likewise to bring forth from the form of the human body itself in its just dimensions from the disproportionate giant bodies."[6]

Heroic narrative action records the struggle to dispense form in the proportioned bodies and careers of kings, warriors, and fathers. In the *Odyssey*, a son (Telemachus) is virtually reborn into status. He travels to collect gifts and substantiate his own worth, acting heroically when his father's old friends recognize in the son's maturing shape the remembered appearance of the younger Odysseus. Dispensation is familial, tribal, and national. Vico writes of epitomes of poetic history—fables of origin, such as Cadmus's founding of Thebes, which literally take nations back into their history through the allegorical routes of fabled genealogy. Vico's emblematic example is the great scepter of Agamemnon in the *Iliad*. The scepter follows the house of Argos: "it came down through the lines of inheritance of

---

[4] Vico, *New Science*, p. 143. [5] Vico, *New Science*, p. 73.
[6] Vico, *New Science*, p. 135.

the royal house of Argos."[7] The first poets, who were also the first men, must "have conceived the second of the Muses, Clio, the narrator of heroic history," writes Vico, and the "first history of this sort must have begun with the genealogies of the heroes, just as sacred history begins with the descendants of the patriarchs."[8]

Transmission or inheritance in narrative is something to be formally achieved in time, something to be moved toward. And the process combines both organic and institutional destiny. Most of the words of inheritance reflect a kind of double structure: beings are of *substance*, and their substance is also their legal *property*. Property is what Vico calls self-possession or self-authority, and the word for *name* in Latin is etymologically linked to the word for rights, *nomen*. In Greek, too, Vico argues, to have character is to have property and to have property is to have rights (the Greek *nomos* or law is close to *nomisma* or money).[9] Character comes from ownership:

> The need for certainty of ownership was a large part of the necessity for the invention of characters and names in the native sense of houses branching into many families, which, with perfect propriety, were called gentes. Thus Thrice-great Mercury, a poetic character of the first founders of the Egyptians, was their inventor of laws and letters. From this *Mercury*, who was likewise held to be the god of com*merce*, the

[7] Vico, *New Science*, p. 209.   [8] Vico, *New Science*, p. 144.
[9] Vico writes that the word "authority" is to be taken "in its original meaning of property. The word is always used in this sense in the Law of the Twelve Tables, and the term *auctores* was accordingly applied to those from whom we derive title to property. *Auctor* certainly comes from *autos* (=*proprius* or *suus ipsius*; and many scholars write *autor* and *autoritas*, leaving out the aspirate" (*New Science*, p. 80). On names, rights, and money, Vico writes: "In Roman law *nomen* signifies right. Similarly, in Greek *nomos* signifies law, and from *nomos* comes *nomisma*, money, as Aristotle notes" (p. 99). In his study of narrative origins, Edward Said discusses the Viconian concept of authority. See *Beginnings: Intention and Method* (New York, 1975), p. 91.

Italians—by a wonderful parallel in thought and expression lasting to our own time—took the verb *mercare*, to mark, in the sense of branding with letters or insignia the cattle or other *merch*andise they have for sale, to distinguish and identify the owners.[10]

Vico's etymologies betray the basis upon which he sees all poetic fable as an expression of foundational laws for preservation and possession. Narrative is the expression of heroic continuity, and to be a hero is to have things to give. He derives the word *hero* from the name of the Goddess Hera. Hera, of course, presided over solemn nuptials, nuptials that in effect legitimized high birth. Vico writes:

> *Heri* had this same meaning in Latin, whence *hereditas* for inheritance, for which the native Latin word had been *familia*. With such an origin, *hereditas* must have meant a despotic sovereignty, and by the Law of the Twelve Tables there was reserved to the family fathers a sovereign power of testamentary disposition.... The disposing was generally called *legare*, which is a prerogative of sovereigns; thus the heir becomes a "legate" who in inheriting represents the defunct paterfamilias, and the children no less than the slaves came under the terms "estate" and "property."[11]

For Vico all beginnings are possessions of a sort: "Possession was originally exercised by continuous physical tenure of the thing possessed.... From this tenure, called *thesis* by the Greeks, Theseus must have taken his name, and not from his handsome posture as the Greek etymologists say, for the men of Attica founded Athens by remaining fixed there a long time."[12] One suspects that Vico's etymologies are no less fanciful than those of the Greek etymologists,

[10] Vico, *New Science*, p. 118. Significantly, Vico goes on to speak of family coats of arms and argues that signs are a kind of possession.

[11] Vico, *New Science*, p. 132.   [12] Vico, *New Science*, p. 339.

but they tell a persistent story, a story of inheritable properties in narrative where man's very being conveys more
than himself or where the self is defined by its very ability
to be more than it seems. His speculation on the etymology
of the word *person* is a pointed example of how men of substance not only dominate but constitute action. Vico rejects
the derivation of *persona* from *persŏnare* or "resound," the
effect produced in the voice from wearing the tragic and
comic masks of Greek drama.

> It must rather have come from *persônari*, a verb which
> we conjecture meant to wear the skins of wild beasts,
> which was permitted only to heroes. . . . Hence the first
> rich spoils must have been these skins of slain beasts
> brought back by the heroes from their first wars,
> which were waged against the beasts in defense of
> themselves and their families. The poets clothe their
> heroes in these pelts, and above all Hercules, who
> wears that of the lion. To such an origin of the verb
> *persōnari*, in the primary meaning which we have re-
> stored to it, is to be traced, we conjecture, the Italian
> application of the term *personaggi*, personages, to men
> of high station and great representations.[13]

Inheritance is the reward for coming into one's own—
one's own self and that which one owns. Similarly, the legal
entity or the legal conception incorporates (that is, the corporation *embodies* or combines) its properties in one body.
Inheritance is thus the most secure promise that time
makes to creation's progeny and the most secure victory, if
such victory can be secured, that civilization celebrates over
regressive potential.

❖

In traditional narrative forms (saga, legend, tale, epic,
testament, heroic romance, chronicle, memoir) what is

[13] Vico, *New Science*, p. 342.

often at issue is the accumulation of potential *through* issue—potential in the sense of energy available for realization. Natural and institutional lines are dispensed, made authoritative and legitimate, given life in time. In the *Aeneid*, Anchises, who embodies the past, points out to his son, Aeneas, who will father the future, how in the shadowy world of Hades the purged souls will reembody in time and take on the precoded shape of imperial Roman citizens. The poem is actually stocked with the race to be, the *gens Romana*. All future is simply latent in the past. Narrative events recount and predict the realization of matter dispensed from loins into law, a realization cleverly parodied in the opening of a satiric narrative like Dryden's *Absalom and Achitophel*, where paternal lust has immediate complications. Of course, it is precisely the basis and line of generation that is questioned in satiric action, a phase of narrative where potential is rendered illegitimate at the source.

Even in narratives that are only "potentially" satiric, the inheritable "action" is not free from subversion. Breaches in lines of continuity generally provide much of the material for narrative conflict. Problems arise from the beginning of time in the violation of original dispensations. The threat to authoritative first actions is a threat to the very nature of being. And problems are multiplied in violations of secondary dispensations, the mimicked, repeated, or perverted promises initially decreed by an authority whose force is unquestionable but sustained by those whose understanding is limited or whose intent is subversive. Superior dispensation narratives have something inferior within them that is literally dying to get out. Violation is a kind of murder at the source, be it the Edenic invasion by sin, the castration of Uranos, the patricide in Freud's primal family, the burying of Osiris's penis. These are "revolting" narrative actions, revolting against those symbols of power and generation that dispense. Mircea Eliade sees all mimicked or secondary dispensations as moving beyond sacred time into a time that by its nature profanes—into a time where imperfections are recorded as history. Linear time is something of life's long disease, and only rituals of cure can re-create the unviolable state: "We get the impression that for archaic societies life cannot be *repaired*, it can only be *re-created* by a return to sources. And the 'source of sources' is the prodigious outpouring of energy, life, and fecundity that occurred at the Creation of the World."[14]

Narrative actions that are reconstituting try, in effect, to redeem violated time, usually with the promise of a new or renewed dispensation. This is the pattern of the Old and New Testaments and, in the literary scheme of things, the pattern for an epic like Milton's *Paradise Lost*. Milton's promise of time allows for the eventual recovery from Sin and Satan by allowing for the possible re-covering of the pair of them in hell. But if we read the plot of the poem without that promise, the nature of its recorded violations reveals much about the frustration of narrative lines of inheritance. Promise is rivalled at the source, mimicked, and rendered imperfect by Satan at the ear of Eve. Satan is a revolutionary who justifies revolt by questioning ultimogeniture as God determines it for his Son. Of course Satan sees himself as the disinherited eldest son, a not unfamiliar pattern from mythic and testamentary sources; and his attempt to regain a lost place is an attempt to reaffirm primogeniture.

> To union, and firm Faith, and firm accord,
> More than can be in Heav'n, we now return
> To claim our just inheritance of old,
> Surer to prosper than prosperity
> Could have assur'd us; . . .
>
> (II, 36-40)

[14] Mircea Eliade, *Myth and Reality*, trans. Willard R. Trask (New York, 1968), p. 30. For a more sustained treatment of the same subject, see

Satan's program reappears in pagan dispensations. Milton compares Satanic history to the account of the infernal gods of Ionia, the saga of Saturn, Jove, and the Titans. Satan becomes a Saturn of sorts in conflict with a Jove who has seized his birthright (and "usurping reign'd"). The Titans (or prior gods become rebels) are then exiled to the west or to the depths (Tartarus). For the Titans as for Satan's host, the underworld is a new place for what is left of an old dominion. Milton's irony here is complex because the allusive connection of satanic and classical revolt tells us that Satan's sense of himself is a living lie. As Saturn he becomes the father exiled by the son to an underworld, but Saturn is also the son who castrated the father (Uranos). Satanic history is part victimization and part wish fulfillment. Satan plays double roles because in breaking union he renders himself schizophrenic. Similarly, his succession is necessarily partible and never again whole. Pandemonium, after all, is the place of many demons, the proliferate inheritance.

The original dispensation that Satan violates is pre-Edenic, and in Book V Raphael explains the inheritable law as uttered by God.

> This day I have begot whom I declare
> My only Son, and on this holy Hill
> Him have anointed, whom ye now behold
> At my right hand; your Head I him appoint;
> And by my Self have sworn to him shall bow
> All knees in Heav'n, and shall confess him Lord:
> Under his great Vice-gerent Reign abide
> United as one individual Soul
> For ever happy; him who disobeys
> Mee disobeys, breaks union, and that day
> Cast out from God and blessed vision, falls

Eliade's *The Myth of the Eternal Return or, Cosmos and History*, trans. Willard R. Trask (Princeton, 1954).

Into utter darkness, deep ingulft, his place
Ordain'd without redemption, without end.

(V, 603-615)

Satan's subsequent argument is that he was prior to
Christ and therefore not to be postponed, a legal term
meaning pushed back from an inheritance. In Book IX he
still worries lest the world, because it was created with better second thoughts, be more glorious than the heavenly
domain he has forever forfeited. He conjectures that God
will naturally create more angels to fill the void in heaven
created by his rebellion or vacation. Satan's proliferate and
rivalling imagination is such that he sees the new earth as a
potential breeding ground for claimants to his old space,
and he fears another postponement from what he thinks is
legally his.

. . . or to spite us more,
Determin'd to advance into our room
A Creature form'd of Earth, and him endow,
Exalted from so base original,
With Heav'nly spoils, our spoils. . . .

(IX, 147-151)

Satan's violation is an act of sophistry that earns him only
an estate subject to a kind of lawlessness and disintegration
that he and his minions pass off as hegemony. Earlier, to
legitimate his status in the eyes of his followers, he had dispensed himself to Paradise to reconnoiter a potentially new
territorial accession. Satan competes because he is disobe-
dient and "breaks union." For those who have literally
given over their ear (disobey: dis ob-audire, not to hear),
temptation is but a prelude to a seemingly more substantial
inheritance.

Division is the first breach in transmission, and the Miltonic account of the Genesis story suggests that Paradise is
ruined when an illegitimate claimant forces the division of
the gift or donation. Satan's inheritance becomes an end-

less division—proliferation without value. He and his minions occupy valueless ground (*Pandaemonium*), a place where the din of language renders only unspeakable things, and where all vitality dies.

> A Universe of death, which God by curse
> Created evil, for evil only good,
> Where all life dies, death lives, and Nature breeds,
> Perverse, all monstrous, all prodigious things,
> Abominable, inutterable, and worse
> Than Fables yet have feign'd, or fear conceiv'd.
>
> (II, 622-627)

Hell is modally more satiric than epic, and the condition of its inhabitants is very close to the permanent condition of satiric being (as Pope will later reveal in *The Dunciad*). Satan's fallen angels have made their own fiery bed, and as victims they are forced to sleep in it. Their condition is potentially satiric because their actions are ritually absurd. They ponder their lot and speak in counsel when we are told that hell has no secrets; they debate the finer points of pure theological issues when they themselves are impure theological issues; they reconnoiter territory when their very settlement is to be unsettled. Of course the larger narrative promise of *Paradise Lost* contains the saving myth of Christ's promised mission for a more just inheritance. Thus when Milton writes that in justifying God to men he "may assert Eternal Providence" (I, 25), he says, in effect, that he will put into sequence or narrate (assert=*adserere*=connect) events seen before (*pro-videre*) and known outside of time (*e-ternal*). That is, Milton intends his full narration to "surround" Satan's temporal and spatial domain. Modally, he buries hell. The depths are a permanent inheritance only for the permanently "descended."

✧

Reaccession narratives record efforts to right the line, to reestablish authorized dispensations, to gain the greater inheritance. In his work *The Birth of the Hero*, Otto Rank traces the prevalence of the myth of the postponed but destined son threatening the suspiciously held position of the father or reigning king (*pater familias*). In describing the morphology of this persistent myth, Rank makes the following observation about the hero's birth: "During or before the pregnancy, there is a prophecy, in the form of a dream or oracle, cautioning against his birth, and usually threatening danger to the father (or his representative)."[15] Rank goes on to describe the process of the hero's expulsion and the circumstances of his necessary return in which he "takes revenge on his father, on the one hand, and is acknowledged, on the other."[16]

Even when the problems of paternal inheritance seem resolved, as in the *Odyssey*, there exists variant versions of the story as a rivalling hero myth. It may not be enough that the son in the Homeric narrative comes into his father's form, that father and son, formerly both dispossessed, restock themselves and diminish the rivals or suitors for their estate. In a lost sequel to the narrative, the *Telegony* (summarized by Proclus), a son, fathered by Odysseus on Circe, journeys to Ithaca and accidentally kills his father. The son, Telegonus, marries the widowed Penelope in a bizarre parallel with the Oedipus story. Not to be out-rivalled, Telemachus marries the deserted Circe. There is no sacred or missionary sanction in this version of the renewed dispensation myth, but perhaps at the simplest level it represents the more basic takeover of the vigorous son from the enervated father. Just such a kernal myth appears in Joyce's *Finnegans Wake* where the waning sexual powers of the old man are challenged. HCE, the Everyman father-hero of the testamentary action, is asked in Phoenix Park by a cad (rival and archetypal son) whether he's "up to it." This is the primal question, the

[15] Rank, *The Birth of the Hero*, p. 65.
[16] Rank, *The Birth of the Hero*, p. 65.

questioning of generative power, the power to go on, to succeed. If the answer is no, then rivalry is almost necessary as a form of renewal; if yes, then rivalry is premature, something akin to the biblical scene in Genesis where Noah is caught with his pants down, so to speak, but is re-covered by at least two of his three sons before he wakes.

Invariably the rival or mimic dispenser is a rebel and, in one fashion or another, a false son. Rivalry hints at that first disinheritable act, sexual displacement. In Hesiod's *Theogony*, Cronos (Saturn) relieves his father, Uranos, of his male member, so that he, Cronos, will himself become the dominant male member. Recognizing the principle of usurpation in his own career, it occurs to Cronos to protect himself against his children by eating them. Such security is short-lived, and in this case civil war is intestinal. Freud plays on a variation of the Theogonic castration for his fable of the primal horde, as does Sophocles in the more sophisticated and troubling saga of Oedipus. Oedipus's tragic inheritance is an uncanny elaboration of the rivalry myth confused by the collapse of generational status— generations both in the sense of coming into being, earth-born (Oedipus is born of the mountain), and in the sense of racial generation, tainted fathers spoiling fated sons, like Ezekiel's fathers who "have eaten sour grapes and the children's teeth are set on edge." The opening words of *Oedipus Tyrannos* ("My children") convey the full irony of Oedipus's plight. He speaks as a father, but his real difficulties arise from his inheritance as a son. His very being, his deadly-footed double curse (swollen-footed deformity), verifies the condition of his inheritance. All rational acuity, all knowing, is subverted by a mythic blight enacted before he was conceived. Oedipus is a descendant of the Theban *spartoi*, earth-born men, earth monsters whose struggle to be born make them contentious from the start as incarnations of rivalry. The myth of the rivalled dispensation is so primal that, as Freud recognized, its destiny is the only available choice, its fate is to be perpetually reenacted. Oedipus lives in a world where the deeds (or thoughts) of the past catch up to the future, where plot doubles back on itself as pathology. Doubleness is too much nature— natural form made monstrous.[17] Oedipus possesses both his legal hegemony, the kingship, and his sexual goal, a queen-wife. But his goal is also his source, his estate descends backwards, he sows where he has been sown. Wherever he turns, he is two-in-one, and it is not surprising that his male offspring are themselves twins and rivals in the continuation of the Theban saga. Rivalry is, in effect, a form of civil war.

The internecine romance is contained within the very idea of narrative conflict. It is as the disheartened princess says in Johnson's *Rasselas*: "children become rivals to their parents . . . [parents] betray each other to their children; . . . by degrees, the house is filled with artifices and feuds" (ch. 26). In order to represent the family romance in all its senses, it was necessary that Johnson see the connection between artifice and feud. He notices an essential disjunctive strategy in narrative. Feud results in artifice or actionable hypocrisy. Or worse, it confuses legality and crime. When Lucan begins his *Pharsalia*, he speaks of wars waged over the plains of Emathia, wars worse than civil (*plus quam civilia*) because waged between kinsmen, Pompey and Caesar. Such a feud leaves peace and legality behind (*hic pacem temerataque iura relinquo*) but confers legality on illegal horrors (*iusque datsum sceleri canimus*). The action turns against the source and threatens the land with generative monstrosities: "Monstrosique hominum partus numeroque modoque / Membrorum matremque suus conterruit infans" ("Women give birth to creatures monstrous in the

[17] For a discussion of the double as monster, see René Girard, *La Violence et le sacré* (Paris, 1972), ch. 6 ("Du désir mimétique au double monstrueux"), pp. 201-234. In my discussion of the Oedipus myth, I am indebted to Girard and to Paul Fry for his essay, *"Oedipus the King,"* in *Homer to Brecht: The European Epic and Dramatic Traditions*, ed. Michael Seidel and Edward Mendelson (New Haven, 1977), pp. 171-190.

size and number of their limbs, and mothers were appalled by the babes they bore," Loeb trans., bk. 1, ll. 562-563). Monstrosity rivals succession.

When it is not monstrously or prematurely rivalled, generational succession provides a means of allowing the old to bow out gracefully while continuing the new in a fully sanctioned order. However, in many of the legends discussed by an interpreter such as Otto Rank, the prematurity of rivalry is more an historical pressure than a family violation. In other words, the impasse of rivalry is broken through by the double action of a hero destined to usurp one kingdom to preserve or redeem another. Escaping death by murder at infancy, Rank's heroes fulfill not only their own but their people's (or race's) fate: Zeus, Isaac, Moses, Oedipus, Cyrus, Christ all fit the pattern. James Joyce names the process "herodatory," a term that incorporates both the threat to lineage in Herod's proposed slaughter of the innocents and the greater Christian promise in the sacred mission or *hereditas*.

Rank also writes of variants of the hero myth, where rivalry is a form of supplantation of the collateral line. In such instances, the sense of renewed dispensation is superseded by self-aggrandizement. Joyce would call the variant "Bettlimbraves," or battling brothers in bed, in which the younger sons, dispossessed by primogeniture, question the "legitimacy" of their older rivals. Rank writes:

> The younger children of a family are particularly inclined to deprive their predecessors of their advantage by fables of this kind (exactly as in the intrigues of history). Frequently they do not hesitate in crediting the mother with as many love affairs as there are rivals. An interesting variation of this family romance restores the legitimacy of the plotting hero himself, while the other children are disposed of in this way as illegitimate.[18]

[18] Rank, *The Birth of the Hero*, p. 70.

Narrative tradition is filled with such stories, beginning
with the accounts of brothers as rivals for a confused or
uncertain patrimony: the Cain and Abel or Esau and Isaac
stories in the Bible, the *spartoi* of the Theban saga, the
Romulus and Remus legend of classical Rome.[19] The
struggle of brothers is essentially based on the premise of
spacing and timing. Two inheritors cannot occupy the
same space at the same time, either physical space or, more
pointedly, psychic space. Cain and Abel are significant in
this respect because the Adamic father, by participating in
the fall, has removed himself from the pattern of dispensation; he has, in effect, made no provision for primogeniture or ultimogeniture because he knows none—he has
lost the ear of God. After the Fall, Cain and Abel seem confused about the nature of primacy. Thus in schemes for
favor, they skip back a generation and appeal directly to
God.

The power of inheritance and primacy among children
is discussed by jurists as part of a mystical code. For example, Pollock and Maitland write of inheritance as it might
apply to the Cain and Abel story. What they see as necessary for a kind of spiritual legality is missing from that
narrative of confused beginnings and old violations.

> To us it must seem natural that when a man dies he
> should leave behind him some representative who will
> bear, or some few representatives who will jointly bear,
> his *persona*. Or again, we may be inclined to personify
> the group of rights and duties which are, as it were,
> left alive, though the man in whom they once inhered
> is dead: to personify the *hereditas*.[20]

[19] René Girard would add the twin sons of Oedipus to the list in discussing the myth of the *frères enemis* (*La Violence et le sacré*, p. 221).
[20] Sir Frederick Pollock and Frederic William Maitland, *The History of
English Law Before the Time of Edward I* (Cambridge, reissued 1968), vol. 2,
p. 256.

In the Cain and Abel story, the *hereditas* is not supposed to be taken personally. The firstborn Cain's offering to God is, for some reason, not favored. Abel's sacrificial lamb takes precedence. In frustration, Cain makes Abel another kind of sacrificial victim, not to God but rather to his own sense of postponed favor. Since he is not a keeper of the sheepfold and since not being a keeper has gained him little, he protests that neither is he, by any means, his brother's keeper. God, of course, has come with questions and not with explanations, and Cain's irony only covers spilled blood. In fact, the spilling of Abel's blood is almost a prior irony, a parody of his own offering to God. Sacrifice itself is both an offering and a violation, perhaps tied to a ritual of taking away that which was once provided, an expiation or displacement of obligation. In jurisprudence, sacrifice rituals are one of many explanations for primogeniture, a simple and no doubt simplistically argued notion that the firstborn is best equipped through exposure and experience to continue a familial obligation to perform sacrifices when the father is no longer able to do so. Pollock and Maitland explain that among certain primitive peoples "the representation of the ancestor by the heir may appear at an early time, because the son must perform sacrificial duties which have been incumbent on his father."[21] Only one member of the family has the right to continue properly, usually the eldest son.

When a satirist such as Alexander Pope traces the patterns of violation in post-Edenic history, he presents a primal scene where sacrifice, a seeming propitiation, is indeed a form of first murder. History is consecrated in blood guilt, and Pope speaks of that prelapsarian state of nature where man "walk'd with beast, joint tenant of the shade," where "No murder cloath'd him, and no murder fed" (*Essay on Man*, Epistle III, 154). The image of man clothed by

[21] Pollock and Maitland, *The History of English Law*, vol. 2, p. 257.

murder or the skin of animals is rich enough in itself, but Pope develops the process of murder into the ritual of sacrifice. The state of nature precludes what is essentially the double, violent, and hypocritical act of sacred profanation. In his *Essay on Man*, he writes:

> The shrine with gore unstain'd, with gold undrest,
> Unbrib'd, unbloody, stood the blameless priest;
> Heav'n's attribute was Universal Care,
> And Man's prerogative to rule, but spare.
> Ah! how unlike the man of times to come!
> Of half that live the butcher and the tomb;
> Who, foe to Nature, hears the gen'ral groan,
> Murders their species, and betrays his own.
>
> (III, 157-164)

Pope is master of the easy idea, but there is a thread running through this passage that is not without a certain complexity. The fall into time is the commitment first to the necessity of murder and then to its ritualization. Violation requires disguise—the postlapsarian shrine is presumably dressed with gold, and the acts thereon performed pass as blessed murder. Animal sacrifice is but a step away from human sacrifice: "The Fury-passions from that blood began, / And turn'd on Man a fiercer savage, Man" (III, 167-168). The stain of violation is historical and organic. In another section of the *Essay*, Pope mocks the idea that man is victimized by a type of ill not of his own generic doing. His example discovers the seed of inheritance in the blood of the violator.

> We just as wisely might of Heav'n complain,
> That righteous Abel was destroy'd by Cain;
> As that the virtuous son is ill at ease,
> When his lewd father gave the dire disease.
>
> (IV, 117-120)

Murder is always original sin, and venereal disease is something of an inheritable reminder. Before Pope, Dryden had drawn the potential for blood violation back to Eden where Adamic man, *autochthonous* or sprung from earth, realizes his futurity in his origin. He writes of the "new made man" barely shaped, still pliable, "confessing still the softness of his clay," but ready to harden up and pass on the principle of revolting sin: "Then, first rebelling, his own stamp he coins; / The murth'rer Cain was latent in his loins" (*Hind and the Panther*, I, 278-279). Adam's profanation makes him a "carrier," and he fathers a son who is literally a carrier in history's service. Cain is a rover, an antithetical type of the wandering hero. His fate is perpetual displacement, and the line of his inheritance is generically unstable. In the *Beowulf* epic, Grendel and Grendel's mother are lineal descendants of the race of Cain, a race consisting of monsters, ogres, trolls, and giants. It is said in the narrative that Grendel has only a mother and no known father, nor is it clear whether any monsters similar to Grendel and his mother ever existed before, almost as if Cain alone need be the only patriarch of a house in which every generation takes on monstrous shape. In more modern times the violation of Cain still falls back into the faults of fathers. In *Finnegans Wake*, Joyce's fable of gigantic backsliding, the Adamic man is all men, father and son, dispossessed but legally sanctioned, homeless but a wandering founder of new territory, new cities. Joyce writes of the primal or original sinner and monstrous violator who becomes through shifting pronouns the historical son or inheritor: "My fault, his fault, a kingship through a fault! Pariah, cannibal Cain" (p. 193).

One might speculate that in the Cain and Abel story the firstborn farmer kills the secondborn herdsman because he somehow fears that the sacramental transmission of spiritual strength from the source has been inexplicably denied him. Pascal, writing a note to himself in his *Pensées*, gains a stark insight into the process of confused priority and violation: "In the letter on injustice perhaps include: The absurdity of the eldest son having everything, 'My friend, you were born on this side of the mountain, so it is right that your elder brother should have everything.' 'Why are you killing me?' "[22] Pascal leaves his formulation ambiguous. Exactly who is killing whom? Without law the issue *is* ambiguous, and even stipulated division is preferable to murder. Voltaire, writing half in jest as usual, sees in the feudal refinement of laws of primogeniture a solution to the notion of primal rivalry.

> The law giving the entire fief to the eldest son is excellent in an age of anarchy and pillage. Then the eldest is the captain of the castle, which sooner or later is assailed by brigands; the younger sons are his chief officers, and the farmers his soldiers. The only thing to fear is lest the younger son assassinate or poison the Salic lord, his eldest brother, to become master of the hovel in his turn, but these cases are rare, because nature has so combined our instincts and passions that we have greater horror of assassinating our eldest brother than we have a craving to take his place.[23]

Of course, the Cain and Abel story knows less fraternal forbearance (elder or younger brother) and more primal rivalry. Yet the historical killer Cain continues on. His mark both damns and legalizes (indemnifies) him. Because he shall go on to found cities, his violation is paradoxically civilizing—his mark becomes him. The biblical account bears comparison with the fratricidal saga of the founding of Rome that, because it involves the twins, Romulus and Remus, draws even more difficult lines of priority and inheritance.[24] Romulus, too, builds a city on the bones of the dead. Joyce describes the process in *Finnegans Wake* in a

[22] Blaise Pascal, *Pensées*, ed. and trans. A. J. Krailsheimer (Harmondsworth, 1966), p. 34.
[23] Voltaire, *Philosophical Dictionary*, trans. Peter Gay (New York, 1962), entry under "*Des loix*," pp. 364-365.
[24] For a general study of the subject, see J. H. Becker, *The Twin Saga as the Key to the Interpretation of Ancient Tradition* (Leipzig, 1891).

phrase that includes both relations and foundations: "And that was how framm Sin fromm son, acity arose" (p. 94). Joyce's "framm" contains the brotherly ("fra") component. Greece's first city is similarly a city of brotherly unlove. Thebes arose from the remnants of the *spartoi*, men born brothers from dragon teeth. They are born fighting: teeth are first contentious and then civilizing. In myths of agricultural origin, the *spartoi* mark off or cultivate the land as would the teeth of a plow. In fact, Vico derives the term *urbs* from the curved furrows of demarcation in planted fields. One such furrow "Remus jumped over . . . to be killed by Romulus and thus, as Latin historians narrate, to consecrate with his blood the first walls of Rome."[25]

In narrative action, the rivalry of brothers does not necessarily abate even if the inheritance is secure. Law does not preclude the desire to be first and the need to have it all. The Bible provides a more complicated and extended version of the Cain and Abel story in the account of Jacob and Esau, the sons of Isaac. The outlines of the story are revealing. The younger son, Jacob, disguised as the elder, Esau, receives a blessing at the hands of his blind father. He had already bargained Esau out of his birthright for a bowl of potage. Isaac tells the disguised Jacob, "be lord over thy brethren" (Gen. 27:29). His blessing is ambiguous for reasons beyond Jacob's counterfeit status. Ultimogeniture, or youngest son inheritance, becomes law by mistake but is given sanction in Israel's future. Redeeming narratives justify mistakes, but not immediately. When Isaac later speaks to his true elder son, he blesses Esau in a way that seems to sanction civil war. Esau complained he was a two-time loser—Jacob had taken both his birthright and his blessing. What is done cannot be undone, but Isaac tells Esau: "by thy sword thou live, and shalt serve thy brother; and it shall come to pass when thou shalt have the domin-

[25] Vico, *New Science*, p. 149.

ion, that thou shalt break his yoke from off thy neck" (Gen. 27:40).

The seeds of fraternal rivalry are planted, and Esau reveals his intent: "The days of mourning for my father are at hand; then will I slay my brother Jacob" (Gen. 27:41). But such an intent is displaced by the more important, saving missions of history. The narrative itself disperses its participants when Jacob and Esau literally "go away" to avoid confronting one another. Instead of dwelling on old violations, Jacob is given the name *Israel*. He takes the name of a people's larger inheritance or dispensation. Later, he is reconciled to Esau by a clever willingness to call himself, in contradistinction to his fraudulently gained blessing, his brother's servant (Gen. 32:18). Esau gains back in the courtesy of address what he had lost in the subterfuge of design. The dispensation of "Israel" takes precedence over the impulse to fratricide. The pattern of the narrative is an accommodation of the Cain and Abel story, a displacement, as René Girard would see it, of violation into law. The destiny of Israel, after all, is God's law. Despite the artful, tactful, and ritual "servitude" of Jacob to Esau, Esau knows full well that Jacob is no one's servant but God's.

✧

Inheritance in narrative is potentially proffered, threatened, and reconstituted. The inheritable action, however, carries with it not only a progressive promise but a regressive threat. Properties of transmission are both conveyed and "descended." If inheritance is considered as descent, the very word implies a succession or plot that is spatially a falling off as well as temporally a continuing on. Descent is downwards, and the metaphoric configuration of "line"[26]

[26] Vico writes: "the Romans set forth their genealogies by placing the statues of their ancestors in rows along the halls of their houses, and these rows were called *stemmata*. (This term must have been derived from *temen*,

INHERITANCE AND NARRATIVE MODE

in inheritance is not lost on precise legal commentators such as the jurist Bracton, who argues that an inheritance is as a heavy body that falls downwards; it cannot fall upwards.[27] Such a conceit calls to mind the parody of patrimonial lineage in Sterne's *Tristram Shandy*, where to inherit is to fall prey to heavy things or to have heavy things fall prey to a kind of Shandean gravity. Triptolemus, one of the strangely named attendants at Walter Shandy's table, offers the following opinion: " 'Tis a ground and principle in the law, said *Triptolemus*, that things do not ascend, but descend in it; and I make no doubt 'tis for this cause, that however true it is, that the child may be of the blood and seed of its parents——that the parents, nevertheless, are not of the blood and seed of it; inasmuch as the parents are not begot by the child, but the child by the parents . . ." (vol. IX, ch. 29).

Along the line inheritance marks in time, the notion of advance is perilously close to the prospect of descent. In divine or theological schemes, the descent of man *is* a fall into time. Previous or more heroically endowed orders generally were not only before but above. Vico writes: "we may observe generally that the most ancient cities and almost all the capitals of peoples were placed on the crests of mountains, while the villages on the other hand lie scattered on the plains. Such must be the origin of the Latin phrases *summo loco, illustri loco nati*, to signify nobles, and *imo loco, obscuro loco nati*, for plebeians; for the heroes dwelt in the cities, the *famuli* in the plains."[28]

---

thread; whence *subtemen* for the thread that is carried under as weft in weaving cloth.) The jurisconsults later called these genealogical rows *lineae*, or lines, and down to our time *stemmata* has kept the meaning of family arms" (*New Science*, p. 142).

[27] Pollock and Maitland (*The History of English Law*, vol. 2, p. 286), cite Bracton, f. 62b: "Descendit itaque ius, quasi ponderosum quid cadens deorsum, recta linea vel transversali, et nunquam reascendit ea via qua descendit post mortem antecessorum."

[28] Vico, *New Science*, p. 139.

INHERITANCE AND NARRATIVE MODE

To descend from on high is a fall in stature. Near the end of the first book of the *Iliad*, during a council on Olympus concerning the course of the Trojan War, Hephaestus pleads with Hera not to contravene an action initiated by the highest born, Zeus. Hephaestus, a god made for trouble, remembers all too well the time long before when Zeus cast him headlong from the heights of Olympus. His descending flight terminated, uncomfortably, hours later on the isle of Lemnos, a fall Milton remembers as well in *Paradise Lost* when he insists that his own Mulciber's plunge from the heavens ("from Morn / To Noon he fell, from Noon to dewy Eve," I, 742-743) predates and relocates the Hephaestean accident.

The literal descent from a heroic place is also the descent from a heroic condition. In falling, Hephaestus suffers an injury or deformity. He is a hero *de*formed, and his descent renders him generically deficient, nonheroic. When he reappears in the *Odyssey*, he is involved in the burlesque double cross of Mars and Aphrodite narrated by the Phaeacian bard. That sequence, too, turns on a tumble, a descent into indignity. In his concept of the Olympian pantheon as part of an enfabled allegory for class conflict, Vico sees Mars and Hephaestus as diminished types, gods brought beneath heroes, brought down to the level of "plebeians who served the heroes in war."[29]

In a sense all movement in narrative time is descendent movement. Life quickens by the touch of gods from high places.[30] And it is only divine, semidivine, or specially dispensed heroes such as Hercules, Theseus, Odysseus, Aeneas, Christ, and the pilgrim Dante, who prove their special or higher powers by surviving descents into hell— the literal end of the inheritable line. To return to the above is to defy time and gravity; to remain in hell is to be-

[29] Vico, *New Science*, p. 165.
[30] For a general study of the theme of epic descent, see Thomas Greene, *The Descent from Heaven: A Study in Epic Continuity* (New Haven, 1963).

come part of the unregenerative world. Vico writes of the underworld as that place where human seeds are impotent, where there is no more succession, where the temporal line becomes a depleted estate. The satanic characters in *Paradise Lost* are exiled to such a place as are the characters who perpetually occupy exhausted ground in a satiric narrative like Pope's *Dunciad*. For Vico, as for Pope, the underworld need not even be underground so long as all who inhabit it are beyond giving anything but confusion and darkness to their posterity.

Finally the underworld was taken to be the plains and valleys, as opposed to the lofty heaven set on the mountaintops. In this underworld the scattered vagrants remained in their infamous promiscuity. The god of this underworld is Erebus, called the son of Chaos; that is, of the confusion of human seeds. He is the father of civil night (in which names are obscured), even as the heaven is illuminated by the civil light with which the heroes are resplendent. Through this underworld runs the river Lethe, the stream of oblivion, for these men left no name of themselves to their posterity, whereas the glory of heaven eternalizes the names of the illustrious heroes. From this underworld Mercury with his rod bearing the agrarian law summons the souls from Orcus, the all-devouring monster. This is the civil history preserved for us by Vergil in the phrase: *hac ille animas evocat Orco*. That is, he redeems the lives of bestial and lawless men from the feral state which swallows up all mankind in that they leave nothing of themselves to their posterity.[31]

The narrative tradition that records descent plots the general lineage of the displacement of higher forms by lower, so that forms like mock-heroic or counterepic are,

[31] Vico, *New Science*, pp. 221-222.

after a fashion, all descent.[32] Their inheritance is but a notch above burlesque. In the best of the mock-heroic narrative forms there is almost an elegiac strain that sings of lost tradition, all "Classic learning lost on Classic ground," as Pope puts it. The peculiar relation that descendent or, in some cases, deficient, lower generic forms have to higher is, of course, a complicated and protean subject. The threat to the line of descent in narrative tradition is a threat to the modal integrity of forms conceived as "higher" and derived from legitimate literary sources. In Swift's *Battle of the Books*, the goddess of Criticism, Momus, descends to her son Wotton, parodying the descent of Thetis to Achilles in the *Iliad*. Momus reveals herself to her son by throwing monsters into his mouth. In other words, she reveals the monstrosity of her being, and she displays to her son the nature of his own origin. Swift continues to play on the line of descent and diminution when he places the modern poet-translator, Dryden, against the ancient poet-translated, Virgil. The scene is a parody of Glaucos and Sarpedon in the *Iliad*. Dryden "soothed up the good *Antient*," with lifted visor revealing a shrunken pea-head within. He "called him *Father*, and by a large deduction of Genealogies, made it plainly appear, that they were nearly related."[33] The ancestral is that which is bigger, and for Swift

[32] In his *Secular Scripture, A Study of the Structure of Romance* (Cambridge, Mass., 1976), Northrop Frye writes of mode and narrative movement: "The radical of satire, as Lucian established long ago, is a descent narrative" (p. 120).

[33] Jonathan Swift, *The Battle of the Books* in *A Tale of A Tub, To Which is added The Battle of the Books and the Mechanical Operation of the Spirit*, ed. A. C. Guthkelch and D. Nichol Smith (Oxford, 1958), p. 247. The entire matter of the ancient-modern controversy was, by its nature, related to questions of cultural inheritance. In the Preface to his collected poems of 1717, Pope made the connection explicit: "they who say our thoughts are not our own because they resemble the Ancients, may as well say our faces are not our own, because they are like our Fathers." Earlier, in *An Essay of Dramatic Poesie*, Dryden had presented the modernist viewpoint in the voice of Neander. Neander's argument employs the metaphor of inheritance in examining the properties passed from one generation to

things have indeed fallen off. Dryden's claim of near relation is less the honoring of anteriority than the catachrestic representation of what Pope was later to call the rhetorical art of sinking in poetry or *peribathous*.

Although the complexities of descent in narrative action are all based in one way or another on the insistent confusion of the directional fall with the progressive line, the varieties of debasement are limitless. Aristophanes provides a version of mythic-satiric descent in the tale he tells for the Platonic *Symposium*. The slightly tipsy and hiccup-ridden satiric poet is asked to speak on love, and he obliges with a descent myth that accounts for the origin of desire. The creature Man begins as a monster, an extraordinary hermaphrodite whose power was such that it constituted a direct threat to the ascendant order, the Olympian gods. Aristophanes describes the ur-man.

> In the first place, there were three kinds of human beings, not merely the two sexes, male and female, as at present: there was a third kind as well, which had equal shares of the other two, and whose name survives though the thing itself has vanished. . . . Secondly, the form of each person was round all over, with back and sides encompassing it every way; each had four arms, and legs to match these, and two faces perfectly alike on a cylindrical neck. There was one head to the two faces, which looked opposite ways; there were four ears, two privy members, and all the other parts, as may be imagined, in proportion. The crea-

---

another. For the Restoration, older geniuses such as Shakespeare, Jonson, and Fletcher are spent: "We acknowledge them our Fathers in wit, but they have ruin'd their Estates themselves before they came to their childrens hands. There is scarce an Humour, a Character, or any kind of Plot, which they have not us'd. All comes sullied or wasted to us: and were they to entertain this Age, they could not now make so plenteous treatments out of such decay'd Fortunes." See *An Essay of Dramatick Poesie and Shorter Works*, in *The Works of John Dryden*, ed. Samuel Holt Monk and A. E. Wallace Maurer (Berkeley and Los Angeles, 1971), 17:73.

ture walked upright as now, in either direction as it pleased; and whenever it started running fast, it went like our acrobats, whirling over and over with legs stuck out straight. (Loeb trans., 190a)

According to Aristophanes, Zeus's scheme is to divide and conquer. Zeus wishes, in effect, to reduce the threat to his line by mitigating the power of the line beneath him.

"Methinks I can continue that men, without ceasing to exist, shall give over their iniquity through a lessening of their strength. I propose now to slice every one of them in two, so that while making them weaker we shall find them more useful by reason of their multiplication." (Loeb trans., 190c)

The descendant line bifurcates and its power diminishes. Zeus counters violence with violence and rearranges monstrous properties. To be weaker is to be less, to have less to pass on. Descent, if accompanied by degeneration, is a kind of negating inheritance. The interior revolt or descent story is as old as the myths of the descendant ages of man and the flight of Astraea from the throne of justice at the time of momentous corruption. Hesiod's account in *Works and Days* significantly sets the process of Iron Age decay in the midst of the larger family romance: "The father will not agree with his children, nor the children with their father, nor guest with his host, nor comrade with comrade; nor will brother be dear to brother as aforetime" (Loeb trans., 180-184). Hesiod writes that the firstborn of degenerate generations will be old men at birth, or at least look old, thus subverting the image if not the sequence of regeneration and inheritance.

In many narrative structures and even in some philosophic ones a descending action is countered by a restoration or reascent. In the *Politicus*, for example, Plato speaks of an inverted condition in which God abandons control of the universe and everything moves in a direction away from unified order: all is disordered, polluted, anatropic.[34] It is only the resumption of a kind of universal control that restores order (*Politicus*, 269c-273d).[35] For Plato, here and elsewhere, there is an implicit connection between good form and continuity. Generation is the "elevation" of the spirit. Diotima of the *Symposium* speaks of love as the desire to seek the ultimate inheritance, immortality, in perpetuating the beautiful: "So when a man's soul is so far divine that it is made pregnant with these from his youth, and on attaining manhood immediately desires to bring forth and beget, he too, I imagine, goes about seeking the beautiful object whereon he may do his begetting, since he will never beget upon the ugly" (Loeb trans., 209b). The perfection of being invites continuation; the prospect of degeneration signals the beginning of the end. To be dispirited, as Plato conceives it, is to be ugly.

With the voice of the satyrlike Socrates at his perpetual disposal, Plato keeps offering up degenerative sequences from which the overall form of his dialogues will ultimately recover. Degeneration is always a form of descent or bad breeding. The interior revolt in the *Republic* comes about because the city or soul begets its own demise—its seeds of destruction are within. The same is true for the narrative structure of the dialogue. In its middle books, the *Republic* suffers a revolt against its utopian form that is reconstituted by the upward bound *Myth of Er* at the end. Plato's fable charts the regressive course of the city in the image of a monstrous, decaying corporation.[36] The ideal body and soul (civic and organic) in a sense "freaks out."

[34] For a discussion of the anatropic order in the works of Plato, see John Wild, *Plato's Theory of Man* (Cambridge, Mass., 1948), p. 36.

[35] Sanford Budick makes great use of the myth of the *Politicus* in discussing the restorative civic conception of Augustan public verse. Budick's chapter on *Absalom and Achitophel* is especially revealing in this light. See *Poetry of Civilization: Mythopoeic Displacement in the Verse of Milton, Dryden, Pope, and Johnson* (New Haven, 1974).

[36] The metaphoric connection between the body politique and the natural body is, of course, one of the oldest tropes in literature. Hobbes still

But since for everything that has come into being destruction is appointed, not even such a fabric as this
will abide for all time, but it shall surely be dissolved,
and this is the manner of dissolution. Not only for
plants that grow from the earth but also for animals
that live upon it there is a cycle of bearing and barren-
ness for soul and body as often as the revolution of
their orbs come full circle, in brief courses for the
short-lived and oppositely for the opposite; but the
laws of prosperous birth or infertility for your race,
the men you have bred to be your rulers will not for all
their wisdom ascertain by reasoning combined with
sensation, but they will escape them, and there will be
a time when they will beget children out of season.
(Loeb trans., 546a-b)

Such "begetting out of season" produces a series of typed
deformations each germinating into a more deficient seed
than the one preceding it. The result is a formal monster-
soul, a generically unstable form, "a single shape of a manifold and many-headed beast that has a ring of heads of
tame and wild beasts and can change them and cause to
spring forth from itself all such growths" (Loeb trans.,
588c). Plato's beast is a parodic and full inversion from the
philosopher-king, a beast undifferentiated from its progeny just like Spenser's Error or Milton's Sin. Such a crea-

---

employs it in *Leviathan*: "Amongst the infirmities therefore of a commonwealth I will reckon in the first place, those that arise from an imperfect
institution, and resemble the diseases of a natural body, which proceed
from a defectuous procreation" ("Of Commonwealth," pt. 2, ch. 29). Sir
William Temple repeats the essentially Platonic paradigm of civic-organic
decay in his essay "Of Popular Discontents": "Could we suppose a body
politic framed perfect in its first conception or institution, yet it must fall
into decays, not only from the force of accidents, but even from the very
rust of time; and, at certain periods, must be furbished up, or reduced to
its first principles, by the appearance and exercise of some great virtues or
some great severities." See *The Works of Sir William Temple* (London, 1814),
3:37.

ture has only a distantly "formed" past and no future to speak of.[37]

Nonsatiric works in the narrative tradition invariably modify violations at the beginning and end of a line—they cover up degenerative potential by implying that a series of time that reasserts the integrity of human and institutional lines exists beyond the bounds of a regressive action. The very title of Dante's *Divine Comedy*, for example, echoes the eschatological program of recovery promised in the sequence of its movements. In its divine sense, comedy is the cosmic circle, the return to a first and "moving" promise. Only hell is descendent and degenerative. In the fourteenth canto of the *Inferno* we meet a Dantesque icon of Hesiod's fallen history, the Old Man of Crete within the mountain of Ida. His head is of fine gold, his breast and arms of silver, his torso brass, his legs iron, his right foot of primordial clay. The tears of the Old Man well up, gather, and form the descendent and underground rivers of hell: Acheron, Styx, Phlegethon, and Cocytus. To move down is to move in the temporally and spatially wrong or *sinister* direction, away from the reinheritable source. In the full *Comedy*, the forward, progressive, and ascendant canticles pass beyond the backward and descendent one. It is in the *Inferno* that the satiric element is literally captured in hell's frozen wastes. The *Inferno* is the satiric descent, the narrative bottoming out where Satan, a goatlike satyr, beats his futile wings.[38] He is, of course, unmoved and unmoving as

[37] Northrop Frye sees satire as displacing the giants and monsters of romance with "the mythical form of society, the hydra or fama full of tongues, Spenser's blatant beast which is still at large" (*Anatomy of Criticism*, p. 229).

[38] In an essay on the *Inferno*, James Nohrnberg argues that the canticle embodies the fallen status of a giant being.

Out of such observations emerges the image of Hell as a gigantic, shadowy creature suffering the interior life of the fallen man. It breathes with the lovers; it is nourished with the gluttons; it is irrigated with the polluted river of tears; it is steeped in the blood of our violence. It ruminates upon the sinners immersed in its fluids and cathe narrative action passes him by in such a manner that Dante's participants may look down upon what has been voided by the world.[39]

Similarly, Satan's projected fate in Milton's *Paradise Lost* is to be captured in hell. He has something of a free reign until his satiric place, his hell, is covered over at the Last Judgment. Before then, Satan's domain is the world of all degenerate being. Milton keeps telling us that, despite Satan's heroic mimicry and his stately forbearance, he essentially displays bad form or "bad eminence" (II, 6). *Bad* is not a casual Miltonic word; it derives from the Old English "baeddel," and it means impure of gender, hermaphroditic. Satan's bad form is narrative action gone bad, made impure, descendent, promiscuous. Bad form needs to be controlled, cast out, or covered by hell. Outside hell, Satan contaminates and devalues all spaces, all dispensations. In effect, he brings his bad form to bear on the newly created world, a kind of action that in its fully satiric articulation is a complete usurpation.

If degeneration and disinheritance predominate, satire takes over the body or "corporation" of an action. Of course, even a satiric action can be recaptured within a greater narrative promise of renewal or cure, a more just corporature as Vico would put it. In a narrative such as Dryden's *Absalom and Achitophel*, the expulsion of the satiric line (the biased line of inheritance or the line of bastards) is

---

nals, and it is half-poisoned on the wastes that clog its visceral foul pouches. Finally, though locked by an icy waste that is all impasse, it is voided by a cathartic vision of evil.

See, "The *Inferno*," in *Homer to Brecht*, p. 98.

[39] In his *Anatomy of Criticism*, Frye comments on this scene from the *Inferno* at the end of his discussion of the satiric mode: "Tragedy and tragic irony take us into a hell of narrowing circles and culminate in some such vision of the source of all evil in a personal form. Tragedy can take us no farther; but if we persevere with the *mythos* of irony and satire, we shall pass a dead center, and finally see the gentlemanly Prince of Darkness bottom side up" (p. 239).

part of the recovering ritual of the action, a ceremony of restoration. But in a more fully sustained satiric action the line of degeneration is permanently marked. For example, Dryden begins his *Mac Flecknoe* with a statement of satiric succession and descent: "All human things are subject to decay / And, when Fate summons, monarchs must obey" (ll. 1-2). At poem's end the summons of fate is reified in the image of life's more base descendent processes. Dryden's elder Flecknoe is the victim of a subterranean wind and a fall through a trap door, something akin to Swift's later elevation of the spirit and debasement of the body.[40] The true satiric descent takes place on the jakes, and the dethroned father's call of nature in *Mac Flecknoe* ("Trust nature, do not labour to be dull," l. 166) suggests the intentional confusion in satiric action between origins and ends, between the substance of birth's labors and the substance of wit's productions. In satire, the act of carrying on is also the act of finishing off.

Giambattista Vico writes that decay is "expressed very sagaciously in the verb *corrumpi*, signifying the breaking down of all the parts composing a body, as opposed to *sanum*, for the sound and healthy condition of all the parts in which life consists."[41] Decay is the final condition of material degeneration, a condition nowhere more prominently sustained than in one of the original documents of the satiric narrative tradition, Petronius's *Satyricon*. The *Satyricon* is a celebration of human waste.[42] Most of its narrative action takes place inside Trimalchio's house or inside

[40] Michael Wilding suggests that Mac Flecknoe's reception of a "double portion of his Father's Art" demands a more alliterative cadence, and he is surely right. See "Allusion and Innuendo in *Mac Flecknoe*," *Essays in Criticism* 19 (1969):355-370.

[41] Vico, *New Science*, p. 215.

[42] Mikhail Bakhtin argues that Menippean forms of satire (of which the *Satyricon* is a prime example) are related to celebrations of profligate energies—saturnalia or "carnival." These are times of inversion, lawlessness, and radicalization. See Bakhtin, *Problems of Dostoevsky's Poetics*, trans. R. W. Rotsel (Ann Arbor, 1973), pp. 100ff.

a brothel. In fact, the *cena* becomes, satirically, a model of ingestion and expulsion. Trimalchio's porter refuses to let the guests out the door through which they entered, arguing that what comes in one way must go out another. Many of the *Satyricon*'s interpreters believe that the narrative is a parody of epic movement, specifically a parody of the Homeric revenge motif where the god Poseidon puts the epic hero in perpetual motion. If so, the *Satyricon* not only substitutes peristalsis for peripateticism but it substitutes Priapus for Poseidon in taking satiric revenge against the exhausted sexual and material line. After the *cena* we encounter such scenes as that between a drunken Encolpius and Circe, where Encolpius curses his recalcitrant member for betraying him in a moment of great need, for reducing him in his prime to a state of weakness and impotence. He begs his member to perform, but in a gesture of embarrassment it recedes further into hiding and droops toward the ground like a tired poppy on its stalk.

Toward the end of the narrative, the *Satyricon* takes a utopian turn, but its action still represents a "state" of satiric exhaustion. Voyagers approach the city of Croton, the true *urbs satirae*, after a shipwreck. They occupy a disinherited and degenerate place.

> In this city the pursuit of learning is not esteemed, eloquence has no place, economy and a pure life do not win their reward in honour: know that the whole of the men you see in this city are divided into two classes. They are either the prey of legacy-hunting or legacy-hunters themselves. In this city no one brings up children, because anyone who has heirs of his own stock is never admitted to dinner or the theatre; he is deprived of all advantages, and lies in obscurity among the base-born. (Loeb trans., 116)

In a ruse to exploit the Crotonians, Petronius's traveller, Eumolpus, remarks that in some countries the heirs to a man's estate must eat him at his death. This is the *Satyricon*'s final debased inheritance, an image of consumption and cannibalism. The land knows no natural heirs, just appetites. Eumolpus taunts: "Operi modo oculos et finge te non humana viscera sed centies sestertium comesse": "Just shut your eyes and dream you are eating up a solid million instead of human flesh" (Loeb trans., 141). On this cannibalistic note the extant manuscript of the *Satyricon* ends.

Chapter Three

THE REVISIONARY INHERITANCE: RABELAIS AND CERVANTES

Later satirist-admirers of Rabelais and Cervantes paid homage to these great forebears for selective parts of their satiric vision. At the beginning of *The Dunciad*, Pope gives his friend Swift a choice of attitudes: "Whether thou chuse Cervantes' serious air, / Or laugh and shake in Rab'lais' easy Chair" (1728 *Dunciad*, I, 19-20). Sterne, who swears "by the ashes of my dear *Rabelais*, and dearer *Cervantes*," listens in dismay as Walter Shandy advises his brother Toby to abandon these authors in his pursuit of the Widow Wadman because laughter precludes lust. Perhaps Samuel Butler, whose knight and squire have a Panurgian capacity for sheer verbiage and whose muse is "Cervantick" in the extreme, gets closest to the mark without even mentioning Rabelais or Cervantes. He simply describes satire quixotically as "a kinde of Knight Errant"[1] fated to wander and destined to do no good whatever.

Gargantua and Pantagruel and *Don Quixote* are revisionary narratives. They absorb the structures, genres, modes, and properties of precedent forms and reissue them in ways that measure the larger inheritance of the Renaissance and post-Renaissance imagination. Both Rabelais and Cervantes play upon a traditional configuration of narrative movement: errantry. Whereas heroes usually wander through error into purpose, the subjects of Rabelais' and Cervantes' narratives engender mistakes. The satiric plot has strategies devised to keep it on the wrong track, to confuse its status, to undermine its purpose. In the darker

[1] Samuel Butler, *Characters and Passages From Note-Books*, ed. A. R. Waller (Cambridge, 1908), p. 469.

books of Rabelais, wanderings separate action from value; in the second part of *Don Quixote* (before the knight's recovery), the powers of the errant imagination grow sinister and impassive.

Rabelais and Cervantes heap material upon the frame of their narratives' suspect actions, they overjustify plots of origin, they repeat fears of sterile being and mad growth. Both *Gargantua and Pantagruel* and *Don Quixote* manifest a kind of obsession with illegitimate beginnings, forced dispensations, and complex, even redundant, movements. The revisionary urge in Rabelais and Cervantes does not divorce narrative event from an inheritable past; rather it casts satiric action as a bizarre form of that which is all too readily familiar. Rabelais makes a monstrosity of heroic genealogy by returning to those original mighty men or giants, and Cervantes reconditions chivalric romance as the product of sterile dementia.

One of the first indications of generic subversion in satiric literature is the claim of truth as a narrative privilege. Lucian hints that the mere mention of history in the presentation of the seemingly ludicrous forces attention to matters that would be better left unexplored. To fabricate or protest the truth is virtually to ensure that what readers are about to experience is a lie. Furthermore, to insist that what any intelligent reader perceives as a fictional construct is indeed an historical record is to make the very issue of authority or "legitimacy" part of the fictional subject at hand. For his own sometimes oblique and unsettled reasons, the satirist taunts his readers into a double perspective on all "seeming" action. Rabelais feigns horror that anyone should think him a liar: "Heaven forbid that we should in any way resort to myth in this most truthful history."[2] Cervantes implicitly makes the same claim for

---

[2] François Rabelais, *Gargantua and Pantagruel*, trans. J. M. Cohen (Harmondsworth, 1955), p. 425. Subsequent references will be to this edition and will be cited by page number in the body of the text.

Don Quixote by the elaborate energy he generates in tracking down, verifying, even "dead-ending" his sources. Of course to the extent that he, as narrator, admits his reliance on the record of the historian Cide Hamete Benegeli, who is a Moor and therefore a liar, Cervantes further complicates his own case. On the one hand, he concocts a bogus history; on the other, he is in league with his readers as a commentator upon inauthenticity.[3] The ironic perspective on represented action is thus the first step in revising the norms upon which narrative action is sustained.

When Lucian writes what he calls a "True History" he makes something of a mockery of single perspective. True history is itself redundant, and by saying the same thing twice Lucian succeeds in unsaying it. The audacity of the title separates the very notion of history from the lie that is to follow, but it also joins those forms that proclaim to be histories (or true narrations) with the outrageous narrative vehicle Lucian readies himself to present. In other words, it is the intent of his satire to imitate into oblivion precedent lies that have been taken as truths. And if we are likely to miss his point, Lucian explains his procedure and his work as "a more or less comical parody of one or another of the poets, historians and philosophers of old, who have written much that smacks of miracles and fables" (*True History*, 1, 2). He announces himself as the greatest of historians, that is, as an absolute liar, descended from and legitimized by none other than Homer, the first fabulist: "Many others, with the same intent, have written about imaginary travels and journeys of theirs, telling of huge

---

[3] The whole problem is further complicated by the appearance of characters within *Don Quixote* such as the *picaró* in disguise, Ginés de Pasamonte, who claims to have written his own life, partly by depositing a manuscript in prison and partly by simply living it. For an excellent discussion of the Pasamonte sequence as it regards Cervantes' use of multiple narrative authorities, see Claudio Guillén, "Genre and Countergenre," in *Literature as System: Essays Toward the Theory of Literary History* (Princeton, 1971), pp. 147-157.

beasts, cruel men and strange ways of living. Their guide and instructor in this sort of charlantry is Homer's Odysseus" (*True History*, 1, 2). Swift's Gulliver is patterned in the same mold, with the added irony that Gulliver protests the accuracy of his "true history" by repeating Sinon's poignant words from the *Aeneid*: "Nec si miserum Fortuna Sinonem / Finxit, vanum etiam mendacemque improba finget" ("A Voyage to the Houyhnhnms," ch. 12). "Fortune may have made Sinon miserable, but she has not made him a liar"—and this from Sinon who is lying to the Trojans about a gift horse. Swift puts his satiric truth-teller, Gulliver, into the same position, although Gulliver, poor fool, does not know it when he thinks he is telling the truth about horses in the last book of *Gulliver's Travels*.

In satiric narration, irony is a negation of true histories or at least a negation of that phase of narrative that counts on making such things as saga, legend, myth, fable, and determinative allegory *seem* legitimate or authoritative. There is a sense in which irony must come at the end of inheritable literary transmissions, so that irony is a step in the direction of revision. Vico writes of irony as subverting the singleness of vision that first produced "believable" poetic fictions.

> Irony certainly could not have begun until the period of reflection, because it is fashioned of falsehood by dint of a reflection which wears the mask of truth. Here emerges a great principle of human institutions, confirming the origin of poetry disclosed in this work: that since the first men of the gentile world had the simplicity of children, who are truthful by nature, the first fables could not feign anything false; they must therefore have been, as they have been defined above, true narrations.[4]

[4] Giambattista Vico, *The New Science of Giambattista Vico*, trans. Thomas Goddard Bergin and Max Harold Fisch (Ithaca, 1970), p. 90.

To suspend disbelief in narrative is to believe in a naive kind of truth. It is interesting, in this sense, that Horace would exact the principle of *in medias res* for the larger epic action. To begin in the middle of things is a way of avoiding the overt act of legitimization and foundation that at the beginning invariably comes across either as a naive myth or a blatant lie. If Spenser were, for example, to begin the *Faerie Queene* by seeking to establish an original authority other than the general Arthurian image of knighthood,[5] he would lose the easy and simple access to errantry he gains with the *in medias res* opening of "A Gentle Knight ... pricking on the plaine." It is when the fable is rendered suspect at the source that the satiric action assaults conventional narrative patterns and allows itself space for usurpation. Thus Rabelais declassifies ancient narrative secrets on the basis of an authority whose source always remains questionable. He explains in one very suspicious digression how the great in Elysium have learned the exquisite pleasure of goosedown ass-wipes. The burlesque belittles and befouls narrative and historical ancestry: Xerxes hawks mustard, Romulus taxes salt, Numa sells nails, Brutus and Cassius are land surveyors, Cicero is a blacksmith's bellows man, Achilles has ringworm, Agamemnon licks dishes, Nestor is a snatch thief, Darius, a cleaner of cesspools, Marcellus, a beansheller, Scipio Africanus hawks lye, Priam sells old rags, Lancelot of the Lake is a flayer of dead horses, Pope Calixtus is a cunt shaver, Dido sells mushrooms (p. 266). The revision here is an extreme form of satiric burlesque, an ironic dispensation redoing a source or series of sources so that suspicion is not only attendant upon recorded action but is *part* of that action.[6]

✧

[5] Arthur is analogous to "th' Author selfe," and the poem is generated by him as well as about him. See James Nohrnberg, *The Analogy of the Faerie Queene* (Princeton, 1976), p. xiii.

[6] Incorporated in the general structure of Rabelais' narrative burlesque

Rabelais' Gargantuan narrative begins with a suspicious pregnancy that has exceeded its expected term. Whereas Swift will later argue in *A Tale of A Tub* that "*Going too long* is a Cause of Abortion as effectual, tho' not so frequent, as *Going too short*," Rabelais protests not only the organic possibility but the legal integrity of such a birth: "My masters, the Pantagruelists of old, have confirmed what I say, and have declared the birth of a child born of a woman eleven months after her husband's death not only to be possible but also legitimate" (p. 46). Of course, Gargantua's father is not yet dead, so Rabelais adds to an organic oddity a legal contingency not even relevant to his fable. In defending the possibility of the action he is about to describe before it even ensues, Rabelais' protest belies its original intent. Illegitimacy overwhelms the narration. Because the eleven-month term is possible in pregnancy, Rabelais advises his readers (or fine lechers as he calls them) to mount any willing widow within a period of "two months after their husband's decease." By so doing, "if they conceive in the third month, their issue will be the dead man's legal heir" (p. 47). What begins as a defense of organic probability has turned to a scheme for covering up illegitimacy. Bastardy becomes a legitimate legal fiction. The line of argument here mimics the satiric procedure: in protesting the likelihood of the sequence he is about to narrate, Rabelais both bastardizes the literary event and seeks to make that which has been bastardized legitimate.

At the same time as such generic and legal shenanigans are taking place, Rabelais presents the monstrous birth as a parody (in its healthiest sense) of the miraculous birth of

---

is part of a larger plan in which, according to Mikhail Bakhtin, a "downward movement animates all his images, all the leading episodes, all the metaphors and comparisons. Rabelais' world in its entirety, as in every detail, is directed toward the underworld, both earthly and bodily." See *Rabelais and His World* (Cambridge, Mass., 1968), p. 370. For a more balanced and normative reading of the narrative, see Donald M. Frame, *François Rabelais: A Study* (New York, 1977).

THE REVISIONARY INHERITANCE

the hero. The pregnant mother, Gargamelle, eats too much tripe. She is overstuffed, and in this sense embodies both the actual subject of the narrative, Gargantua, and the metaphoric equivalent of parodic material: tripe. She is literally the vehicle for the farce that is to come—farce meaning that which is "stuffed." Augustine remarked that the human subject, born between urine and feces, is victimized from the onset by its origins, and Rabelais proves the case. Too much is going on below for Gargamelle, so she evacuates *all* her bodily holdings. In the descend*ent* and descend*ant* action of satiric narrative too much is always going on below, and it is only natural that a complementary profanation precede the hero's birth. The child, past term in this defecatory confusion, leaps up and bursts through the matrix at the top into the hollow vein and out his mother's ear, a satiric homage to the idea of annunciated birth. In the double action of release and birth not only is the legitimacy of the pregnancy at issue but so is the nature of the issue produced.

Rabelais again protests that this sequence could, after all, happen. He is a true historian and can cite precedents, especially in Pliny. But then again Pliny, like Cide Hamete Benengeli in *Quixote*, is a "barefaced liar" (p. 53), although Rabelais is "not such a barefaced liar as he was" (p. 53). If we are reading in the proper satiric spirit, we are reading the potential for regression into every statement of narrative advance: for Rabelais the very fullness of the human experience depends on the paradox of progress in regress, growth in retardation.[7] It is perhaps an accident of literary gestation that we have *Gargantua and Pantagruel* in the sequence in which we do. Rabelais actually conceived of Pan-

[7] Mikhail Bakhtin (*Rabelais and His World*) sees the grotesque principle of growth as essential to Rabelais' spirit: "The body discloses its essence as a principle of growth which exceeds its own limits only in copulation, pregnancy, childbirth, the throes of death, eating, drinking, or defecation. This is the ever unfinished, ever creating body, the link in the chain of genetic development, or more correctly speaking, two links shown at the point where they enter into each other" (p. 26).

tagruel before Gargantua (already a figure of legendary proportion in folklore), and he wrote the life of the son before the father. The sequential rearrangement of books is a regression of sorts, righting the circumstantial advanced timing of the son coming before the father. That which is compositionally second comes first for the ease of Rabelaisian chroniclers who have fabricated the joint title, *Gargantua and Pantagruel*. In Rabelais, as in Laurence Sterne, no sequence comes easily.

Even in Gargantua's birth there is the suggestion that sequence has been thrown out of order. The giant child receives his eponymous name in a kind of gasped wonder at supersession. Grandgousier, the child's father, is astounded by his son's size: "Gargantua," he marvels or "Que grand tu as" (p. 53), and the child shall be what he is first called. The narrator jokingly assumes that Grandgousier refers to his son's gullet; the reader is meant to assume that Grandgousier can barely imagine the size of his son's generative organ ("What a big one you've got!"). In a sense, the father is immediately displaced or rivalled without the child having passed through conventional stages of growth and maturation. Gargantua's organ at birth dwarfs the organ that produced him, just as Rabelais' satiric conception of heroic manifestation skips back over the inheritable heroic tradition to the original giants born of earth. In the very opening sentence of his Gargantuan chronicle, Rabelais refers us to the "great Pantagrueline Chronicle" for all knowledge of "Gargantua's genealogy and of the antiquity of his descent" (p. 41). When we arrive where we are directed, we hear of a dispensation that is not unfamiliar to the satiric scene and that has been discussed earlier in light of René Girard's views on violent beginnings. Giants are proportioned by the fruit of the earth's loins.

It is fitting that you should note, therefore, that at the beginning of the world—I am speaking of a distant date, more than forty times forty nights ago, to count

by the method of the ancient Druids—a little after
Abel was killed by his brother Cain, the earth, being
soaked in the blood of the righteous, was that day so
very fertile in all those fruits that from her loins she
bears for us, and especially in medlars . . . (P. 171)

This second fruit is both blessed and tainted by blood
violation. Those eating of it perform a kind of sacramental
parody noted by Rabelais—and he wants "to take particular care not to be" mistaken—which seemed a second original sin in that "a variety of accidents befell" the celebrants
(p. 172). All "were afflicted with a most horrible swelling on
the body, but not all in the same place" (p. 172). Monstrous
growths included the swelling of the shoulders; the
lengthening "of that member which is called Nature's
labourer, so that it grew marvellously long, big, stout, fat,
lusty, and proud, after the ancient fashion, so much so that
men made use of it as a belt, twisting it four or five times
round the body" (p. 172); the enlarging of the ballocks; the
growth of the legs, nose, and ears; the extension of the
torso "from whom came the giants, and from them Pantagruel" (p. 173).
What follows in the chronicle is a parodic genealogy of
giants, a true descent. But Rabelais once again doubles
back on himself and doubts his authority in asserting it.
The sequence is most suspicious in its presentation of the
unbreached line from the giant Hurtali who "reigned in
the time of the Flood" (p. 173).

I know very well that in reading this passage, you
will feel in your hearts a very reasonable doubt and ask
how it is possible that this should be so, seeing that at
the time of the Flood the whole world perished except
Noah and seven persons with him in the Ark, amongst
whom the said Hurtali is not included. No doubt the
question is well put and quite justified. (P. 174)

Rabelais' answer is that Hurtali sat astride the ark, thus revising those "Hebraic bagpipers" who compile older testaments. The satirist always has an answer when multiple authorities mock the very idea of true authority. Pantagruel is the product of an unbroken satiric line. And his entrance into the light is but another version of the satiric obliteration of matrix. Gargantua comes with an accompanying substance, thus identifying his genre; Pantagruel arrives in so monstrous a fashion that he destroys his mother's form: "for he was so amazingly large and so heavy that he could not come into the world without suffocating his mother" (p. 174). This prompts Gargantua to ask an essentially Rabelaisian question: Shall he weep at his wife's grotesque death, or shall he laugh at his son's grotesque birth? It is a property of Rabelaisian satire to reconstitute malaise. So Gargantua bellowed like a cow for his dead wife, but "when Pantagruel came into his mind, he suddenly began laughing like a calf" (p. 177).

Rabelais begins his first two generational installments with monster forms bursting in upon narrative spaces. The threat of disproportion is such that giants will make life dangerous for others or will be made to feel out of place themselves. The comic gesture in the continuing books of Rabelais is to make the monstrous seem normal.[8] Such a process is at the heart of the Rabelaisian mythos.[9] For the

---

[8] Thomas Greene, *Rabelais, A Study in Comic Courage* (Englewood Cliffs, 1970), calls the principle of comic encompassment in Rabelais the "embrace of lunacy" (p. 10). His phrase is a good one because it suggests the reflexivity of the comic-satiric process: lunacy both embraces and is embraced.

[9] Bakhtin argues that Rabelais' means for accommodating his satiric system of monstrosity into a reconstituting vision depends upon the folk roots and myths of medieval tradition. He claims that artistic expression from the later Renaissance to the neoclassical period was attached solely to a sense of proportion, to a need to cover up protuberances and blemishes, to a desire to separate an essential self from a world body. Bakhtin writes of "the peculiar drama of the material bodily principle in Renaissance literature—the drama that leads to the breaking away of the body from the single procreating earth, the breaking away of the body from the col-

comic Rabelais, life itself is a giant body manifest in the body politique, in the Church as the body of Christ, in the very expanse of a growing, humanistic Renaissance world. Rabelais' comedy absorbs his satire and protects his heroes, just as Pantagruel protects his armies from the storm by covering them with his tongue. For Rabelais, the tongue is the most versatile and regenerative of comic symbols.

The truly satiric process in Rabelais occurs only when the degenerative sum of the parts adds up to more than the reconstituting condition of the whole. Rarely does this take place. Rabelais' genius can reconstitute most anything, which brings to mind not only the two unseemly pregnancies[10] and births that begin his book but which recalls the image from his opening prologue, where he explains by analogy the double processes of the satiric mode. Rabelais writes of that time when

> Alcibiades, in that dialogue of Plato's entitled *The Symposium*, praises his master Socrates, beyond all doubt the prince of philosophers, he compares him, amongst other things, to a Silenus. Now a Silenus, in ancient days, was a little box, of the kind we see to-day in apothecaries' shops, painted on the outside with such gay, comical figures as harpies, satyrs, bridled geese, horned hares, saddled ducks, flying goats, stags in harness, and other devices of that sort, light-heartedly invented for the purpose of mirth, as was Silenus him-

lective, growing, and continually renewed body of the people with which it had been linked in folk culture" (*Rabelais and His World*, p. 23). To go too far into the politics of these aesthetics is a praiseless folly, except to say that Bakhtin's point (if it is a point and not a Marxist brief) suggests that the satiric mode is most degenerate when the "individual body was presented apart from its relation to the ancestral body of the people" (p. 29).

[10] Bakhtin points to another image to refer to the Rabelaisian process. He writes of the Kerch terra-cotta figurines of senile, pregnant, and laughing hags as emblems of the kind of grotesque comedy or satire in Rabelais. The figurine collection is ambivalent: "It is pregnant death, a death that gives birth" (*Rabelais and His World*, p. 25).

self, the master of good old Bacchus. But inside these boxes were kept rare drugs, such as balm, ambergris, cardamum, musk, civet, mineral essences, and other precious things. (P. 37)

On an obvious level, Rabelais announces the problem of external form versus internal value, a matter of traditional concern in any defense of satire. There is no disputing that the vehicle for conveyance, the *silen*, is ugly. So was Socrates, that mocking satyr: "For to view him from the outside and judge by his external appearance, no one would have given a shred of an onion for him, so ugly was his body and so absurd his appearance, with his pointed nose, his bovine expression, and his idiotic face" (p. 37). Socrates' wisdom was concealed within, but "had you opened that box, you would have found inside a heavenly and priceless drug: a superhuman understanding, miraculous virtue, invincible courage, unrivalled sobriety, unfailing contentment, perfect confidence, and an incredible contempt for all those things men so watch for, pursue, work for, sail after, and struggle for" (p. 37). Thus the satiric act can be said to represent or portray varieties of ugliness by assuming their external shape, but clever readers of satire will be able to uncover the rare quality of imaginative wisdom within.

Rabelais leaves untold that part of the Silenus myth that so captivated Nietzsche in the nineteenth century—the part that tells of wisdom's terror and the advantages of dying young to avoid its revelations. But he does amend his conceit to allow for a less comfortable reading of satiric revelation. Rabelais asks whether his readers have ever seen a dog discover a marrowbone. If so, "you must follow this dog's example, and be wise in smelling out, sampling, and relishing these fine and most juicy books, which are easy to run down but hard to bring to bay. Then, by diligent reading and frequent meditation, you must break the

bone and lick out the substantial marrow" (p. 38). But marrow attracts maggots in a more ambiguous version of penetration: "Interpret all my deeds and words, therefore, in
the most perfect sense, show deep respect for the
cheeselike brain that feeds you on these delicate maggots,
and do your best to keep me always merry. Now be cheer-
ful, my dear boys, and read joyfully on for your bodily
comfort and to the profit of your digestions" (p. 39).
Rabelais begins with an image of his art as pregnant wisdom and ends with the rewards of drunken peristalsis. As
he feigns more and more agitation in the prologue, he
hints that his readers are no doubt singularly unfit to profit
from his narrative at all, but that the last laugh is reflexive:
he, Rabelais, was as drunk writing it as his readers will be
reading it.

That Rabelais wants it both ways, comically and degeneratively, is witnessed by the prologue to Book Five, the
last book (of debated authenticity). Rabelais speaks of a
world before his own time that was "gormless," a Langue-
docian adjective "signifying unsalted, saltless, tasteless, and
flat. Metaphorically it means foolish, simple, devoid of intelligence, and cracked in the upper storey" (p. 601). Presumably the present, humanistic world is less gormless
than the foolish past. How did this come to be? Rabelais
proposes that the world became wise in the Jubilee Year
31, that is, in those years of the present century to 1550.
And it did so by reading his books of Pantagruelism, books
constructed on the principle of nonsensical wisdom. In an
odd sense, then, Rabelais stands at the crossroads of what
he calls the "Gothic" past and the expectant present, the
crossroads of an Erasmian folly and a Rabelaisian recovery.
But as is his custom, Rabelais turns the argument around
later in the prologue. Ironic wisdom cuts deep. Only a "few
relics remain of those snivelling and Gothic times" (p. 603),
and in the face of Gallic overrefinement Rabelais has reserved the right to "hiss and cackle like a goose among the

swans," if his readers merit the abuse. And they do. The program for intellectual recovery becomes what it always is in Rabelais, an evacuation of the body, a renewal wherein like is drawn to like. His readers must not only purchase his books "but gulp them down as an opiate cordial and absorb them into your systems. Then you will discover what good there is in them, ready for all gentle beanshellers to extract" (p. 605).

Rabelais is never certain just what it is he has chosen to present to his readers as narrative. Nor is he certain in what estimation his readers should hold his work, or he his readers. In the prologue to his third book, Rabelais tells the story of Ptolemy presenting to his Egyptian subjects the booty of various conquests, including one freak camel and a slave half white, half black. The Egyptians were appalled, and Ptolemy "discovered that they took more pleasure and delight in the handsome, the elegant, and the perfect than in ridiculous and monstrous objects." Rabelais points out that this "example sets me wavering between hope and fear, uncertain whether I may not meet with an unpleasant reception instead of the appreciation I expect" (p. 285). He worries lest he offend rather than serve, lest he annoy rather than amuse, lest he displease rather than please. And he worries lest his fate as satirist be the same as Euclio's cock, "the creature that discovered the treasure with his scratching and had his throat cut for his pains" (p. 285). Rabelais swears by Hercules, however, that this will not happen to him, and he counts on his renewing comic spirit to protect him from a satirist's end: "they will never take in bad part anything that they know to spring from a good, honest, and loyal heart. I have so often seen them take the will for the payment, and be content with it, when that was all the debtor had" (p. 286).

It is in Book Three, of course, that we encounter Panurge's famous defense of the system of indebtedness, a system that turns on an appeal to the larger satiric body of narrative evacuation, intake, expansion, and continuation.[11] Rabelais' economic-organic metaphor represents the loan of the whole to the part, a natural gesture that Panurge compares to the Saturnian age of golden abundance on earth. The comparison is important because it counters the political and generic decline of the fourth book, where the reign of injustice or the Iron Age is compared to the monstrosity of antinature, or Lent. Life and health for Rabelais are the release or freeing of the body—a liberty to live, eat, drink, pass nature's products, and pass through nature. Such a liberty is later subverted by the allegorical monsters, Clawpuss, Greed, and Lent. The impulse in Rabelais' narrative is to fight off these monsters as one would fight off death. Although it may appear in Rabelaisian satire as if the dead take over from the living and sustain their satiric inheritance ("Is it not set out in the old customs of our most noble, most ancient, most beautiful, most flourishing, and most wealthy kingdom of France, that the dead shall seize the quick—that is shall, before dying, confer his properties upon him?" p. 440), it is possible to react to death in two ways. On the one hand, the

---

[11] If Rabelais treated the creditor-debtor relationship from the perspective of the satiric debtor, three hundred years later Nietzsche treated it from the perspective of the creditor. And what he has to say bears on another aspect of the satiric response:

[The creditor knows] the pleasure of being allowed to vent his power freely upon one who is powerless, the voluptuous pleasure *"de faire le mal pour le plaisir de le faire,"* the enjoyment of violation. This enjoyment will be the greater the lower the creditor stands in the social order, and can easily appear to him as a most delicious morsel, indeed as a foretaste of higher rank. In "punishing" the debtor, the creditor participates in a *right of masters*: at last he, too, may experience for once the exalted sensation of being allowed to despise and mistreat someone as "beneath him"—or at least, if the actual power and administration of punishment has already passed to the "authorities," to *see* him despised and mistreated. The compensation, then, consists in a warrant for and title to cruelty.

The Genealogy of Morals, II, 5, in *Basic Writings of Nietzsche*, trans. Walter Kaufmann (New York, 1968), p. 501.

dying or dead "entail" the living—they will them into their incorporated woes as Swift later wills the satirically dead astrologer Partrige into "an *uniform'd* Carcass" who "walks still about, and is pleased to call it self *Partrige*."[12] On the other hand, the living simply refuse to die, as Rabelais interprets inheritance: "Without health life is a decrepitude; life is only the image of death. So, when you are deprived of health—that is to say dead—seize the quick, seize health, which is life" (p. 440).

The doctrine of indebtedness enunciated by Panurge may be sophistic, but in effect it buys time for the living. What life "needs" life borrows. Its economy is an open system, organic and communal, whose end is continuation. Panurge exults.

> "God's my life, I drown, I perish, I lose my way when I begin to consider the profound abyss of this world of lenders and owers. It is, believe me, a divine thing to lend, a heroic virtue to owe. Yet this is not all. This borrowing, owing, lending world is so good that when this act of feeding is over, it immediately thinks of lending to those who are not yet born, by that loan perpetuating itself, if it can, and multiplying itself by means of its own replicas; that is children. For this purpose each member cuts off and pares away some of the most precious of its nourishment, and sends it below, where Nature has prepared fitting vessels and receptacles for it, through which it descends to the genitories by long and circuitous windings. There it receives proper form and finds fitting places, in man and woman alike, for the conservation and perpetuation of the human race. This is all done by loans and debts, one to another; whence it is called the debt of marriage." (P. 301)

[12] Jonathan Swift, *Bickerstaff Papers*, ed. Herbert Davis (Oxford, 1940), p. 162.

That Panurge's principle of indebtedness should lead to marriage (an uncompleted quest in the Rabelaisian comedy) is fitting indeed. Marriage is the double emblem of comedy—the human bond and the socialization of nature into law, or liberty into legal license. It is a union whose end is reproduction. In one of Rabelais' earlier books, Gargantua explained the principle of divine and human comedy in a letter to his giant son. His subject was marriage.

> Among the gifts, graces, and prerogatives with which the Sovereign Creator, God Almighty, endowed and embellished human nature in the beginning, one seems to me to stand alone, and to excel all others; that is the one by which we can, in this mortal state, acquire a kind of immortality and, in the course of this transitory life, perpetuate our name and seed; which we do by lineage sprung from us in lawful marriage. By this means there is in some sort restored to us what was taken from us by the sin of our first parents, who were told that, because they had not been obedient to the commandment of God the Creator, they would die, and that by death would be brought to nothing that magnificent form in which man has been created.
>
> But by this method of seminal propagation, there remains in the children what has perished in the parents, and in the grandchildren what has perished in the children, and so on in succession till the hour of the Last Judgment, when Jesus Christ shall peacefully have rendered up to God His Kingdom, released from all danger and contamination of sin. Then all generations and corruptions shall cease, and the elements shall be free from their continuous transformations, since peace, so long desired, will then be perfect and complete, and all things will be brought to their end and period. (P. 193)

Gargantua provides what is the full narrative cycle of creation—that which is dispensed, altered through corruption, and restored in perfection. Man remains indebted until his debt is paid for him. Depending upon what phase of the inheritable cycle gains narrative prominence, an action is by emphasis degenerative or restorative. In the later and darker books of Rabelais, that part of the debt of man that perverts or denies seminal propagation falls due. If Rabelais' giganticism and Panurge's indebtedness accommodate the properties of transmission in comedy, an allegorical figure such as Lent in Book Four depletes those same properties satirically. King Lent is the dying body of satire with a "brain of the size, colour, substance, and strength of a male flesh-worm's left ball" (p. 513). His external configuration is all mechanical, and so, too, his internal. In a sense, King Lent has no organic structure he can call his own—he is the body displaced into antimatter: " 'That's a strange and monstrous anatomy of a man, if I should call him a man,' said Pantagruel. 'What you say reminds me of the shape and anatomy of Misharmony and Discord' " (p. 519).

Pantagruel's analogous reminiscence sets Panurge's fable of counterdispensation in motion. What Panurge knows of Misharmony and Discord is applicable to the satiric birth. Panurge sounds like both Diotima and Aristophanes of Plato's *Symposium*.

Physis—Nature, that is—in her first delivery brought forth Beauty and Harmony, without physical copulation. For she is most fertile and prolific in herself. Antiphysis, who has always been Nature's enemy, was immediately jealous of these beautiful and noble offspring and, to be even with her, gave birth to Misharmony and Discord, by copulation with Tellumon. They had spherical heads, as round as footballs, and not delicately flattened on either side as human beings have theirs. Their ears were high on their heads, and stuck up like asses' ears. Their eyes stood out of the heads on the ends of bones like heel-bones, without eyebrows, and were as hard as crabs' eyes. Their feet were round, like tennis balls, and their hands and arms faced backwards, in reverse. They walked on their heads, continually turning cartwheels, arse over tip, with their legs in the air. (Pp. 519-520)

The desire of the satiric mother or matrix (Antiphysis) is to pass off her creation as superior. Such a wish is not unlike that of Pope's Dulness whose preformal world hatches from the pagan seed of chaos. The inheritable satiric universe to which Rabelais gives more and more space as Pantagruel seeks that Renaissance underworld connection, the Northwest Passage, is something akin to an astronomical black hole. It attracts the falling end products of creation as Antiphysis "attracted every fool and madman to her side, and won the admiration of every brainless idiot, of everyone, indeed, who lacked sound judgment and common sense" (p. 520). Erasmus had already praised folly— the satiric world after Rabelais awaited the inheritance of Pope's Dulness.

✧

If Rabelais' narrative divides its time between anatomical comedy and satiric denaturing, Cervantes' *Don Quixote* combines the formulation of an idiosyncratic, comic "character" with the satiric deformation of the chivalric romance. Late in the seventeenth century, Sir William Temple wrote about the revisionary effect of one work on the imperial history of a nation. The conclusions he records are drastically oversimplified, but they are also symptomatic of the fading power of at least one set of inheritable literary norms.

An ingenious Spaniard at Brussels would needs have it, that the history of Don Quixote had ruined the Spanish monarchy; for, before that time, love and valour were all romance among them; every young cavalier that entered the scene, dedicated the services of his life to his honour first, and then to his mistress. They lived and died in this romantic vein. . . . After Don Quixote appeared, and with that inimitable wit and humour turned all this romantic honour and love into ridicule; the Spaniards, he said, began to grow ashamed of both, and to laugh at fighting and loving, or at least otherwise than to pursue their fortune, or satisfy their lust; and the consequences of this, both upon their bodies and their minds, this Spaniard would needs have pass for a great cause of the ruin of Spain, or of its greatness and power.[13]

Temple's "ingenious Spaniard" is probably not a trustworthy historian—he ignores too much, and he conveniently forgets what he ignores. But it is hard to read works written in the seventeenth century (whether in Spain, on the Continent, or in England) after *Don Quixote* without considering the content of Temple's remarks as they touch upon literary pressures—pressures that affect the characteristic kinds of actions or powers of actions, as Northrop Frye would call them, that are manifest in given historical periods.[14] If Temple's Spaniard has not established the full record of history, he has at least established a fable of change that is *itself* perceived by Temple (for one) as part of a process of historical delimitation.[15] Even if what passes

[13] Sir William Temple, *The Works of Sir William Temple* (London, 1814), 3:485.

[14] See Frye's "Historical Criticism: Theory of Modes," in *Anatomy of Criticism: Four Essays* (Princeton, 1957), pp. 33-67. When the change in what seems a radical mode or hierarchy of presentation is turned towards the expectations of a receiving (or reading) audience, the sense of historical sequence is still preserved. Hans Robert Jauss makes this case in an adaptation of Frye's general scheme to phases of reception history. Jauss links the admiring audience to the exemplary hero, the sympathetic audience to the imperfect hero, the cathartic audience to the suffering hero, and the ironic audience to the "missing" hero. See Jauss, "Levels of Identification of Hero and Audience," *New Literary History* 5 (1974): 283-317.

[15] The same fable is reiterated by a modern structuralist critic, Robert

for change is some form of exaggerated, partial, or suspicious recollection, that recollection may contribute to the fashioning of minds that perceive and thus enact change. In this sense, it is rewarding to read Temple's remarks on *Don Quixote* as historically formative no matter what manifold difficulties Spain may have been experiencing in or about 1605. The narrowness of Temple's causal range is finally less important than his insight that Cervantes' novel possesses a revisionary power beyond its own status as a confined literary structure.

Cervantes was in many ways engaged in the controversy over the nature of narrative forms that had occupied so much theoretical time of the continental critics of the Renaissance. By the early seventeenth century the debate turned not only on the structure of the classical epic and the vernacular *romanzi* but towards the accommodation of native "realistic" forms that were to evolve as comic histories and comic narratives. Realism in narrative is necessarily relativistic—it is tied to systems of revision. As Proust writes: "So from age to age is reborn a certain realism which reacts against what the previous age has admired." For the later Renaissance and earlier seventeenth century, realism would have primarily meant a more carefully represented set of local conditions in narrative, a more accurate and discriminating depiction of social class, a narrative ear attuned to local speech, an attempt to record recognizable geographical places, an attention to national and regional custom.

In a wider sense, for those like Rabelais experimenting not so much with realism in the middle and later sixteenth

Scholes: "In examining the history of narrative, we see that specific fictional genres, as they become emptied of contextual value, seek to compensate for this by formal elaboration until they die either of their own weight or through parody, which often means by having forced upon them a system of contextual reference they are too fragile to sustain—as when Cervantes forces the chivalric romance to refer to contemporary Spain." See Scholes, *Structuralism in Literature* (New Haven, 1974), p. 94.

century but with modal combinations from epic to burlesque to utopia, or for those like Cervantes working with
the appropriation of various "fictions" within generic
boundaries, the crucial question was the relation of narrative to antecedent and ancestral models. In some measure,
these models were inevitably heroic—but it is too simple to
say that in the counterstructures of narrative all heroic potential is lost. Change is a complex notion, and its sometimes hidden processes seem to release a conserving instinct in a culture or a literature. Therefore one of the
more convincing measures of change is the extent to which
some will go to resist it. The literary idea of the heroic dispensation, for example, is one not easily abandoned in any
age. Even in the later Renaissance, heroism supposedly still
measured that which is truly "conserved." To accept the
heroic as a viable literary mode has little to do with the degree of accommodation between heroic actions and the actual (or "realistic") world, but it has everything to do with
the accommodation between what is represented and what
is received as the higher truth of representation. Heroic
status is closely related to actions that a culture "imagines"
as normative and determinative, so that the nature of
valued action is the property of heroic power (for the
Greeks, heroes were *andres epiphaneis* or fully manifest men
of action). Thus to attack the heroic for its improbability (as
many from the later sixteenth through the eighteenth centuries did) is to get the priorities of a normative argument
reversed. Some, such as Giambattista Vico (a great defender of the heroic dispensation), try to set the priorities
aright:

> The human mind is naturally impelled to take de-
> light in uniformity. This axiom, as applied to the fa-
> bles, is confirmed by the custom the vulgar have when
> creating fables of men famous for this or that, and
> placed in these or those circumstances, of making the
> fable fit the character and condition. These fables are

ideal truths suited to the merit of those of whom the vulgar tell them; and such falseness to fact as they contain consists simply in failure to give their subjects their due. So that, if we consider the matter well, poetic truth is metaphysical truth, and physical truth which is not in conformity with it should be considered false. Thence springs this important consideration in poetic theory: the true war chief, for example, is the Godfrey that Torquato Tasso imagines; and all the chiefs who do not conform throughout to Godfrey are not true chiefs of war.[16]

It is the poet's war chief who is real because he is what he is imagined to be. In *Don Quixote* there is an innkeeper who believes in the literal truth of the actions recorded in the knightly fables—but he has managed to keep the distinction clear between truth and misappropriation: "I shan't ever be such a fool as to turn knight-errant, for I'm quite aware that it's not the fashion today to do as they did in the olden days when those famous knights are said to have roamed the world" (p. 324).[17] Don Quixote, who is less able to distinguish between the metaphysical and the physical, carries Vico's speculative uniformity into reality. At the heart of *Don Quixote* is not so much the rejection of a heroic nature as the confusion of separable orders, a confusion that results in a divorce from one's senses, a leave-taking. For Quixote, the imagination is too deeply implicated in the heroic configuration or, in a sense, too radically separated from it.

In any age or period revisionary potential is often the test of separating or discriminating powers: To what extent do older norms reflect contemporary range? To what extent are older perceptions disjunctive? In an enigmatic but revealing entry in his *Pensées*, Pascal comments on a

[16] Vico, *New Science*, pp. 31-32.
[17] Miguel de Cervantes, *Don Quixote*, trans. Walter Starkie (New York, 1964). All references in the chapter are to Starkie's translation.

mighty god disturbed by the human conception of a bounded and worldly universe. Pascal is neither blasphemous nor overly sceptical; he merely mocks the inappropriate and inadequate norms of a geocentric being in a decentered space. God embodied by man is god burlesqued.

> If you want him to be able to find the truth, drive away the creature that is paralysing his reason and disturbing the mighty intelligence that rules over cities and kingdoms.
> What an absurd god he is! Most ridiculous hero![18]

At the end of the previous century, Montaigne had written of a more middling order of heroism. Although the hero had once been the imaginative measure of perfect proportion, Montaigne's contemporary adjustment cannot bear heroic shape.

> The value of the soul consists not in flying high, but in an orderly pace. Its greatness is exercised not in greatness, but in mediocrity. As those who judge and touch us inwardly make little account of the brilliance of our public acts, and see that these are only thin streams and jets of water spurting from a bottom otherwise muddy and thick; so likewise those who judge us by this brave outward appearance draw similar conclusions about our inner constitution, and cannot associate common faculties, just like their own, with these other faculties that astonish them and are so far beyond their scope. So we give demons wild shapes. And who does not give Tamerlane raised eyebrows, open nostrils, a dreadful face, and immense size, like the size if the imaginary picture of him we have formed from the renown of his name?[19]

[18] Blaise Pascal, *Pensées*, ed. and trans. A. J. Krailsheimer (Harmondsworth, 1966), p. 43.

[19] *The Complete Essays of Montaigne*, trans. Donald M. Frame (Stanford, 1958), "Of repentance," III, 2, 614-615.

In the middle of the seventeenth century, Thomas Hobbes had defined heroic self-transformation as a species of insanity. Quixotic at best, the imagination is a double dose of decayed sense when compounded by normative models of literary and national heroes: "So when a man compoundeth the image of his own person with the image of the actions of another man, as when a man imagines himself a Hercules or an Alexander, which happeneth often to them that are much taken with the reading of romances, it is a compound imagination and properly but a fiction of the mind."[20] Hobbes centers on an aspect of what for Cervantes had been a fictional program. His Quixote negotiates between imagined heroic paradigms and the contingent realities (or sanities) of seventeenth-century Spain. But Cervantes was not so ready as Hobbes to dismiss the imagining power. Rather, he asks a satirist's question: What do the rituals of romance (chivalric delusion) cover up? We begin at the satiric source, a kind of gestational prison. Obsessed with legitimation and authorial lineage, Cervantes expresses a progenitorial and congenital wish:

> Idle reader, you need no oath of mine to convince you that I wish this book, the child of my brain, were the handsomest, the liveliest, and the wisest that could be conceived. But I could not violate Nature's ordinance whereby like engenders like. And so, what could my sterile and uncouth genius beget but the tale of a dry, shriveled, whimsical offspring, full of odd fancies such as never entered another's brain—just what might be begotten in a prison, where every discomfort is lodged and every dismal noise has its dwelling? Repose, a quiet corner, fragrant fields, cloudless skies, murmuring brooks, spiritual calm—all contribute their share in making the most barren muses teem and bring forth to the world such offspring as will fill it

[20] Hobbes, *Leviathan* (London, 1651), pt. 1, ch. 2.

with wonder and delight. And if a father should happen to sire an ugly and ill-favored child, the love he bears it claps a bandage over his eyes and so blinds him to its faults that he reckons them as talents and graces and cites them to his friends as examples of wits and elegance. (P. 41)

The narrative gets started, in effect, by fathering itself from the rank and sterile confines of Cervantes' prison cell. There is an immediate connection between the generation of odd fancies and the deranged spaces in the mind of Cervantes' chivalric surrogate, Don Quixote. Our first sight of Don Alonso Quijano (Quixote) suggests that the gentleman-farmer is imprisoned by another kind of sterility. With no family to speak of, wizened, gaunt, around fifty, possessor of a diminishing estate, Quijano exchanges property for fancy: "he sold many acres of arable land to purchase books of knight-errantry" (p. 57). The land was fertile; the books "dried his brains." Cervantes employs almost the same language for the condition of his creation as he had for his own condition. Quixote's pursuit of chivalry was "the oddest fancy that ever entered a madman's brain" (p. 59).

Later in the narrative, an ecclesiastic attendant of the Duke and Duchess's court berates Quixote for what has somehow gotten into his head: "And you, numskull, who put it into your head that you are a knight-errant and that you conquer giants and capture miscreants? Go on your way, with good luck to you as my parting words. Go back to your home and rear your children, if you have any, and look after your estate and give up roaming through the world, swallowing wind and making yourself the laughing-stock of those who know you, and those who do not" (pp. 751-752). Of course, this is precisely what Quixote cannot do: "Now tell me, your reverence, for which of the follies that you have noticed in me do you condemn and abuse me, and bid me go home and look after my house and wife and children, without knowing whether I have any?" (p. 753). Quixote's only children, like those of Cervantes, are brain-children. When in Part II the fanciful knight is raised from the vision-breeding Cave of Montesinos, Sancho greets his master with these words: "Welcome back, master, we fancied you were staying down there to found a family" (p. 684). Metaphorically, Sancho's fancy is accurate. From the Cave of Montesinos, Quixote delivered himself up to bear a full bodied narrative vision; from prison, Cervantes bore the vision that became *Don Quixote*.

The notion that both Cervantes and his creation are one of a kind, one against the world, self-generators, has come down as the traditional "romantic" reading of the narrative. But surely more is involved. The conception of a disordered character—a character disordered because he thinks himself necessary—fascinated Cervantes as an historian of promiscuous mental spaces. Human delusion is both an object of satire and a subject of satiric imitation. Quixote, like Cervantes, generates an imagined space and protects it. He creates his own dilemma. Quixote leaves home three times; each time the circle around his home territory widens. As the circles expand so, too, do the problems of inviolable space. First Quixote travels alone, pays the price for his transforming powers, and gives his nag Rozinante free reign in leading him home. In his second journey, Quixote is attended by the materialistic squire, Sancho Panza. Their wanderings are interfused with and confused by a set of rival actions whose multiple resolutions send Quixote home as a prisoner in a cart. The third voyage begins with the second part of the adventures, at which point Quixote's very story has become a shared cultural document. He carries with him the reputation of a madman, and he is publicly used and abused. In his last journey he reaches the shores of Spain at Barcelona, and this compass (even more than the sojourn at the Duke and Duchess's) is too much for him. When Quixote looks at the sea wherein his epic forebears sailed, he is virtually over-whelmed by the Mediterranean, the real place for all imag-ined heroes. Shortly thereafter he is defeated by Sanson Carrasco, the bachelor disguised as the Knight of the White Moon (that is, a feigned lunatic), and he gives up his fantastic conception of chivalric purpose. Quixote snaps into a kind of sanctified sanity and lets his friends mourn the passing of a more antique vision. The expanding circles of the book touch not only on the absurdity of dementia but on the agony of uncontrolled mental spaces. By the end Cervantes seems to have both deepened the problems of his hero and altered the tone of his fiction.

As an author, Cervantes complicates the pattern of his narrative effort in a way not altogether different from that of his knight. In his first prologue, Cervantes creates a character, a friend, who identifies the subject of the book as "one long invective against the books of chivalry" (p. 46). Cervantes does not object to this characterization, but as with the early outings of Quixote it is too simplistic. Cer-vantes' intent changes radically when he discovers, well after the completion of Part I and during the composition of Part II, that another author has issued a bogus continua-tion that threatens the integrity of his satiric enterprise. One Alonso Fernández de Avellaneda, a plagiarist and—what is worse in Cervantes' estimation—a usurper, has en-croached upon private terrain. Usually the satirist thrives on proliferation, which is, after all, his own narrative strat-egy (too much of anything insures the devaluation of the object). Indeed, it is a kind of false and proliferate continu-ation of the chivalric tradition in modern Spain that gener-ated the plot of Cervantes' own narrative in the first place. Cervantes even admits in the prologue to Part II that Avel-laneda's one saving grace is that he has, to some extent, understood the subversion practiced by Cervantes: Avel-laneda sees the principle of the original *Don Quixote* as "more satirical than exemplary" (p. 526).

It seems odd, then, that Cervantes, who had based his claim to narrative space on the revision of previous narrative structures, would feel that, having trampled the ground walked on by others, he had the right to complain that already trespassed ground was being trespassed upon again. After all, to Cervantes' delight his satiric effort courted popular success. Success breeds imitation. One particular imitation debased Cervantes' original, and he felt contaminated. (More likely, he felt his grip loosening on the potential audience for Part II.)

Cervantes thus finds himself in the complicitous position of attacking a subsequent satirist and defending a precedent lunatic (Quixote). He protects his literary property and the "originality" of his sired form, its rights and its domain. As a satirist, he wishes to insure a literary hegemony just as Quixote, a madman, wishes to insure a chivalric hegemony. But in both cases the wish is tainted by the nature of the property protected. The satiric domain is not easily occupied nor comfortably held. Within this territory attack and defense begin to look alike, and the neat distinctions between satiric objects and satiric objectives begin to break down. Cervantes admits that his narrative is a satire on books of chivalry, but its design, in part, takes the shape of a series of chivalric quests. What the Canon, a decidedly unpleasant character, says of chivalric books at the end of Part I can with a stretch of the parodic imagination apply to Cervantes' strategy in satirizing them.

> I have never seen a book of chivalry with a whole body for a plot, with all its members complete, so that the middle corresponds to the beginning and the end to the beginning and the middle. Instead, they are composed of so many limbs that they seem rather to have been intended to form a chimera or monster than a well-proportioned figure. Moreover, they are uncouth in style, their adventures are incredible, their amours licentious, their compliments absurd, their battles bor-

ing, their speeches doltish, their travels ridiculous, and finally, they are devoid of all intelligence and therefore deserve to be expelled from a Christian republic as a useless race. (P. 478)

To some extent Cervantes would agree. But to some extent he would also agree with the Curate, who defends books of chivalry for their imaginative space—"the opportunity that they offered a good intellect to display itself. For they presented a wide and spacious field through which the pen might run without any obstacles" (p. 479).[21] To parody these forms, Cervantes lets Quixote's mind (if not his own pen) run amuck, but his satiric territory extends farther yet. His scope in *Don Quixote* takes in not only chivalry but an entire range of narrative forms: *romanzi*, exemplary tales, pastoral romances, fabliaux, farces, even puppet shows. There are bizarre sequences in *Don Quixote* that presumably do not grow out of the demented chivalric brain of Quixote himself. Lunatics wander through the Sierra Morenas; disguised aristocrats devise bloodcurdling revenge plots; entire populations lament in shepherds' garb; long-lost family members reunite in instances of remarkable coincidence. The nature of the supposedly sane world around Quixote is often as narratively bizarre and suspect as the most attenuated adventures of the Quixotic model, Amadis of Gaul. Quixote's madness can be dismissed as imaginatively pathological, but the attendant plots generated in *Don Quixote* have as their excuse only the satiric imagination of a fictionally parodic spirit (Cervantes himself).

But woe to that scoundrel Avellaneda who usurps the space of that spirit. Cervantes wants revenge, and he will get it. In his second prologue he has become even more

[21] These are two of Cervantes' many contributions to the debate that had been raging on the Continent (even before the publication of *Orlando Furioso*) over the heroic and *romanzi* forms. See Bernard Weinberg, *A History of Literary Criticism in the Italian Renaissance*, 2 vols. (Chicago, 1961).

like his own knight errant. He defends his imaginative estate—the rights of his bastard child's narrative inheritance—and he does so on virtually the same grounds as might Quixote. In fact, when Quixote hears of the spurious continuation of his adventures he is as furious as his creator. First he claims that his patience may not prevent him from taking vengeance on Avellaneda, then, upon hearing that the spurious adventures place him in Saragossa, he protests: " 'For that reason,' said Don Quixote, 'I will not set foot in Saragossa, and so the forgery of this new historian shall be exposed to the eyes of the world, and mankind will be convinced that I am not the Don Quixote of whom he speaks' " (p. 953). In other words, Quixote will literally reclaim himself and his own space. For Cervantes, this is one of the larger themes of the entire second half of his book. He and his knight are rivalled, and the usurping imagination takes on a sinister cast. Figures such as the Duke and Duchess devise rival actions that not only allow Quixote to compromise himself (as he had on his own initiative in Part I) but that force the doleful knight into a pattern of inaction. Quixote is literally depressed by his rivals—he withdraws and sulks. Cervantes' fiction is peculiarly modern in this sense. When Quixote's madness is no longer his alone, he abandons its pursuits. It is one thing for a satiric victim, a madman, to force the world into the confines of his distorted vision; it is quite another for a Spanish Hidalgo, suddenly famous as a quixotic being, to perform to the dictates of a pair of sadists or a rival author.

The darkening and deepening texture of the second part of *Don Quixote* is forecast in the prologue. With the redirection of satiric focus, the position of the satirist is less clear, less firm. Cervantes seems plagued in the second prologue, and his struggle for authority tells us a good deal about satiric encroachment, aggression, violation, and insecurity. He begins thinking about a matter that always engages satirists: To what degree is the very satiric enterprise vulnerable as a violating force? Cervantes assumes that his readers are, in a sense, loyal to him, although that notion itself may be part of a saving fiction. Readers of Part I will expect him to avenge his honor against that rat of a thief, Avellaneda, who has kidnapped his work and his subject's "life." But that very expectation is a version of the "errant-ry" plots that were subject to such abuse in the first part of *Don Quixote*: "God bless me, how eagerly you must be await-ing this prologue, illustrious, or perhaps plebeian, reader, expecting to find in it vengeance, quarrels, and abuse against the author of the second *Don Quixote*" (p. 525). Cer-vantes coaxes: "You would like me to call him an ass, a fool, and a bully, but I have no intention of doing so. Let his sin be his punishment—let him eat it with his bread, and there let it be" (p. 525). The Dantesque solution initiates a more complex strategy of indirection. Cervantes supposes that Avellaneda lacks courage; he "does not dare to appear in the open field and under a clear sky" (p. 526). It is a good thing this is so, even if fictionally so, because the conditions for a duel are remarkably like the conditions for a chivalric joust. Cervantes is ready to defend his honor, but he is not quite ready to defend his imaginative space in exactly the same manner as would Don Quixote.

Open attack is all impulse, and even Quixote conceives of redirection as the better part of valor. Cervantes will take another, and cleverer, satiric tack. He will distance himself from Avellaneda and suggest that anyone else happening to meet the spurious author relay to him two simple stories—stories that turn out to be something more than simple. The first is as follows.

> There was a madman in Seville who had the craziest notion that ever entered a madman's brain. He made a tube out of a cane, sharpened it at the end, and picked up a dog in the street or elsewhere. He would then hold down one of the animal's hind legs with one foot

and lift up the other with his hand. Next, inserting his tube in the right place, he would blow into it, as hard as he could till he had blown the dog up as round as a ball. Then, holding it up in this way, he would give it a couple of slaps on the belly and let it go, saying to the bystanders—and there were always plenty of them: "Your worships perhaps think that it is an easy thing to blow up a dog?" Does your worship think it is an easy thing to write a book? (P. 527)

Cervantes, who writes of the fancy that enters Quixote's mad brain, has already described his own book as the odd fancy of a sterile brain. If in this anecdote Avellaneda is to be taken as the madman of Seville, we are dealing with yet another unbalanced author(ity). Furthermore, the last rhetorical question suggests an uncomfortable relation among seemingly disparate activities: madness, rectal inflation of dogs (which Swift may have remembered for one of the more famous experiments recorded by Gulliver at the Academy of Lagado), and the writing of books. Cervantes, Quixote, and Avellaneda blow all forms out of proportion upon encountering them. The anecdote reflects a kind of lunatic disgust, and the rhetorical question at the end—if it is to be taken at all seriously—is a rather dubious defense of art as the divine afflatus. Cervantes must sense this. Hard on the heels of the first anecdote comes a second that refines the notion of artistic purity and provides more discriminating distinctions between lunatic and author.

> And if my story does not suit him, you can tell him this one, dear reader, which is also about a madman and a dog:
> In Córdoba there was another madman whose habit was to carry in his hand a piece of marble or stone of no light weight, and when he met with an unwary dog, he would go up close to him and let the weight fall plump on top of him. The dog, in a panic, would yelp

and bark up three streets without stopping. It so happened once that among his victims was a hatter's dog of whom his master was very fond. The stone came down, struck his head, and the battered beast uttered a dismal howl. His master saw the deed, flew into a rage, picked up a yard measure and rushed out after the madman, and beat him until he had not a whole bone in his body. At every blow he gave him, he shouted: "Dog thief! My pointer! Didn't you see, cruel brute, that my dog was a pointer?" And repeating many times the word 'pointer,' he sent the madman away beaten to a pulp. The madman learned his lesson and went off, and for over a month he did not appear in public. But at the end of this time he reappeared with an even heavier weight, and he would go up to a dog, and staring at him from head to foot, not caring or daring to let the stone fall, he would say: "This is a pointer! Beware!" In short, all the dogs he met, whether mastiffs or curs, he called pointers; so, he never dropped his stone again. Perhaps the same may happen to this story teller, who will not risk discharging any more the load of his wit in books, for bad books are harder than rocks. (Pp. 527-528)

This picaresque miniature effects a more satisfying transfer between the satiric act and the satiric object. Now the dog is a purebred—a pointer—and not a stray. The madman's relation to it, perforce, must change. Since he, like Avellaneda, has no capacity to discriminate between what is pure and what is mixed, he would do well to leave off his efforts altogether. Or, at least, Cervantes advises as much for Avellaneda in relation to the pedigreed *Don Quixote*. The purebred has the potential to continue its line, to keep its recognizable proportions, its delineations. If Cervantes' first anecdote draws the spurious author nearer than desirable to the world of *Don Quixote*'s satiric distortions, the second establishes the rights of the prior book as a new pure breed, an authorized form of narrative. It is precisely this impulse throughout the seventeenth century to give newer, larger, comic, and satiric forms a status of their own that is paramount here. Later critics such as Sorel and Dryden will argue specifically for the legitimization and integrity of forms like the *roman comique* or the heroic satire, and even in the form he satirizes Cervantes sees the opportunity for the elevation of prose-parody. What the Curate says of the chivalric romance holds for Cervantes' comic-satiric rendering of it: "For the loose structure of those books gives the author the chance of displaying his talent in the epic, the lyric, the tragic, the comic, and all the qualities included in the pleasing sciences of poetry and rhetoric, for the epic may be written in prose as well as in verse" (p. 479). Throughout the seventeenth and surely by the eighteenth century, Cervantes' fiction had earned its pedigree. A writer such as Fielding will spend considerable time in the Preface to *Joseph Andrews* or in the introductory chapters to the books of *Tom Jones* extolling the virtues, range, and scope of what he calls the "comic epic-poem in prose." Rabelais' satiric anatomy may have been an ur-version of such a mode; Cervantes' *Don Quixote* is a more refined "original" whose hero is at least scaled down to proper size even if his experience-starved and memory-saturated mind generates extravagancies on the dry plains of La Mancha.

Chapter Four

THE INTERNECINE ROMANCE: BUTLER'S *HUDIBRAS*

What finally unsettles Don Quixote in the first part of his adventures is not the penetrability of his antique vision but the disjunction of chivalric codes and modern "capacities." As an uncommon hero, his greatest enemy is advanced technology.

> When I consider this, I have a mind to say that I am grieved in my soul at having undertaken this profession of knight-errantry in so detestable an age as this we live in. For although no peril can daunt me, still it troubles me to think that powder and lead may deprive me of the chance of making myself famous and renowned for the strength of my arm and the edge of my sword over all the known earth. But Heaven's will be done! I shall win all the greater fame if I am successful in my quest, for the dangers to which I expose myself are greater than those that did beset the knights of past ages. (P. 392)

Quixote's heroic body is vulnerable because he is an actor in an increasingly relativistic comedy where the power of action rivals the refinement of artillery. The hero gives up his mind to protecting his bodily extensions; he is a kind of *tic nerveux* in the levelling scheme of a mechanistic universe. In the beginning of his *Leviathan*, Thomas Hobbes builds a system on the basis of a recreated or artificial man—a new Adam for the materialist order—and his modern "genesis" is an implicit critique of older dispensations, special heroic destinies, and inherited strengths. After creating his new man, he proceeds to speak about man's natural condition:

THE INTERNECINE ROMANCE

Nature hath made men so equal, in the faculties of
the body, and mind; as that though there be found
one man sometimes manifestly stronger in body, or of
quicker mind than another; yet when all is reckoned
together, the difference between man and man, is not
so considerable, as that one man can thereupon claim
to himself any benefit, to which another may not pretend, as well as he. For as to the strength of body, the
weakest has strength enough to kill the strongest,
either by secret machination, or by confederacy with
others, that are in the same danger with himself.[1]

The notion of levelling had a considerable impact in altering the contours of heroic literature throughout the
seventeenth century.[2] Antiromance engendered its own
tradition as it had in Lucianic times past,[3] and by mid-
seventeenth century even such an essentially nonsatiric
poet as Abraham Cowley was referring to the older heroic
efforts of his literary forebears (and some of his peers) as
the *"Cold-meats* of the *Antients,"* a heap of "antiquated

---

[1] Thomas Hobbes, *Leviathan* (London, 1651), pt. 1, ch. 13.

[2] In his Preface to *Gondibert*, William Davenant argues that the tired tactics of older forms of heroic romance and epic avoid rather than address
necessary new norms of heroic activity. He wishes to recall the ethos of
heroism without entailing all the fussy embellishments of romance. He attacks Spenser for his romance finery and Lucan for his condescending
historical extravagance. If Davenant diagnoses the weak ground of
heroism, he fails to prescribe the cure. Like Hobbes, who answered Davenant with a rigid geographical *schema* for generic sanctity, Davenant is
committed to a generalized moral system. He divorces the heroic mode
from its sense of the marvelous, he denies the particularizing power of the
national epic, and he ends up in the modified Christian land of Lombardy
where aristocrats make love and war. The strongest case made for the
partial success, if not for the validity, of Davenant's program is argued by
Earl Miner in his *The Restoration Mode from Milton to Dryden* (Princeton,
1974).

[3] The most thoroughgoing call for a reassessment of narrative aims
based on principles of counterheroism came from Charles Sorel in his review of the state of French narrative, *Bibliothèque françoise* (1664). See
English Showalter, Jr., *The Evolution of the French Romance, 1641-1782*
(Princeton, 1972).

Dreams of senseless *Fables* and *Metamorphoses*."[4] When Milton turned to his tragic theme in the ninth book of *Paradise Lost* he dismissed the chivalric muse as good only for the relation of "long and tedious havoc fabl'd Knights / In battles feign'd" (ll. 30-31). For Milton, romance and even the martial conventions of the classical epic were the *rejecta membra* of fallen civilizations; in fact, the battles in heaven of *Paradise Lost* and the regrouping of Satan's pandemonic host have been treated by some as structurally close to burlesque.[5] Though it may be that "greatness of Arms" was still the dominant measure of heroism for Dryden at the end of the century as it was for Cervantes at the beginning, for others the case was put somewhat differently. Samuel Butler writes: "It is a heavy case, no doubt, / A man should have his Brains beat out, / Because he's tall, and has large Bones; / As men kill Beavers for their stones" (*Hudibras*, I, ii, 31-34).[6] In his "Character of a Hero," Butler suggests what Hobbes had suggested earlier.

A Hero was nothing but a fellow of great Stature, and Strong limbes, who was able to carry a heavier load of Armes on his Back, and strike harder Blows, than

---

[4] Abraham Cowley, "Preface to Poems (1656)," in *Critical Essays of the Seventeenth Century*, ed. J. E. Spingarn (Bloomington, 1957), 2:88-89.

[5] See, for example, Michael Wilding, "The Last of the Epics: The Rejection of the Heroic in *Paradise Lost* and *Hudibras*," in *Restoration Literature: Critical Approaches*, ed. Harold Love (London, 1972), pp. 91-120. In *Imagination and Power: A Study of Poetry on Public Themes* (New York, 1971), Thomas Edwards makes the point that "future [post-Miltonic] poets would face the task of assessing politics and power without serious appeal to heroic images, but if this was a loss of a useful standard of judgment, it brought a compensatingly closer and more demanding involvement of imagination in the contingent, unformulaic nature of modern politics" (p. 44). As is well known, Milton, Dryden, and Pope all pondered and rejected the notion of a national epic with pronounced romance elements. In Pope's case, he never got beyond a prospectus for an epic on Brutus, that Tudor joy-child who supposedly connected the original Britons with remnants of the Trojan empire.

[6] This and all subsequent references to *Hudibras* refer to John Wilders' edition, *Samuel Butler: Hudibras* (Oxford, 1967).

those of lesser size. And therefore since the invention of Guns came up, there can be no true Hero in great Fights, for all mens Abilitys are so leveld by Gun-shot that a Dwarf may do as heroique feat of Armes that way as a Gyant. And if he be a good marksman, be too hard for the Stout Hector and Achilles too.[7]

With its displaced centers of war and love, Butler's *Hudibras* is the *summa* of counterromance in the seventeenth century. The steel-witted Lady of the poem rejects Hudibras' chivalric court, his materially "high Heroique fustian," as a mere "Poetique Fiction." And Butler on occasion comes forward in proper person to set his poem's record straight. His spirit is less forbearing than even that of Cervantes at his most satiric: *Hudibras* is nowhere without the chivalric romance, and yet it occupies a no man's land because of it:

> Certes our Authors are to blame,
> For to make some well-sounding name
> A pattern fit for modern Knights,
> To copy out in Frays and Fights,
> (Like those that a whole street do raze,
> To build a Palace in the place.)
> They never care how many others
> They kill, without regard of mothers,
> Or wives, or children, so they can
> Make up some fierce, dead-doing man,
> Compos'd of many ingredient Valours,
> Just like the Manhood of nine Taylors.
> (I, ii, 11-22)

"Dead-doing" and "deed-doing" are not orthographical inconsistencies lost on Butler, for whom the strategy of burlesque attack renders all heroic actions vulnerable to a

[7] Samuel Butler, *Characters and Passages From Note-Books*, ed. A. R. Waller (Cambridge, 1908), p. 468.

sense of disproportionate if grotesquely comic agony.
Perhaps the experience of almost continual warfare of one
kind or another (mostly internecine) from the end of the
sixteenth throughout the seventeenth century in Europe
affected all literary rendering of martial action. No doubt
the most bizarre account of the warrior in burlesque appears not in Butler but in Grimmelshausen's picaresque
narrative, *Simplicissimus Teutsch*. We are spared few of the
uncomfortable details of the Thirty Years War in Germany. Grimmelshausen's burlesque of the greater national
dispensations justifying the wars becomes an overt attack
on the principles of heroic determinism. At one particularly discouraging point in the narrative, he presents a
German fanatic who believes he is Zeus and who predicts
the dawning of a German imperial power under the aegis
of a Hero whose actions would be guided by the Olympian
lunatic's will and whose mission would displace the factions
and feudal remnants of the German nations. This seventeenth-century vision of a German *Reich* (or, at its best, a
Virgilian *pax germania*) is interrupted at the penultimate
moment of its pronouncement when the fanatic is beset by
fleas. War and peace take on bodily dimensions. The fanatic lets down his breeches and begins scratching with besotted fury.

A few chapters earlier, Grimmelshausen's soon to be
lionized folk hero, Simplicissimus, had conceived of the
war effort as internecine on a bombastic but reduced plane:

> One time my lieutenant colonel was ordered to ride
> to Westphalia on a special mission. If he had then had
> as many men as I had lice, he would have frightened
> the whole world. But since he hadn't, he had to proceed carefully and hid in a forest between Hamm and
> Soest. At that time my pedicular enemies had reached
> the height of their glory. They were plaguing me so
> much with their undermining tactics that I thought
> they would soon take up quarters between my skin and

flesh. No wonder the Brazilians eat lice—anger and the spirit of revenge drives them to it! One time, when part of the cavalrymen were feeding their horses, while others slept or kept a lookout, I could no longer stand the annoyance and stepped aside under a tree to do battle with my enemy. Though others put on their armor when they fight, for this battle I took mine off and started such a murder and a massacre that my swords (both thumbs) were dripping blood, and corpses (or dead skins) fell everywhere. The ones I didn't kill I chased out into the cold world and let them take a walk under the tree.[8]

In burlesque the heroic body is out of control. Even the heroic gods lose their prerogatives. Zeus's thunder, a fearful crack in the firmament, becomes a burlesque crack of the fundament. Burlesque heroes keep their supposed status but lose their balance, or, to put it another way, they keep their names but lose their bearing. Of course, the machinery of burlesque is available to any period. Thus in *Hudibras* Samuel Butler suggests that the descent of the hero is timeless, and like Lucian he argues that the first practitioner of the inverting or bastardizing art was Homer himself. Referring to a participant in the burlesque bear-baiting scene of his narrative, Butler writes:

> He was of great descent and high,
> For Splendor and Antiquity,
> And from Celestial origine
> Deriv'd himself in a right line.
> Not as the Ancient *Hero's* did,
> Who, that their base births might be hid,
> (Knowing they were of doubtful gender,
> And that they came in at a Windore)
> Made *Jupiter* himself and others

[8] J.J.C. von Grimmelshausen, *Simplicissimus Teutsch*, trans. George Schulz-Behrend (Indianapolis, 1965), p. 118.

THE INTERNECINE ROMANCE

O'th' Gods Gallants to their own mothers,
To get on them a Race of Champions,
(Of which old *Homer* first made *Lampoons.*)
(I, ii, 207-218)

The burlesque artist appropriates not only the fables of the heroes but also the intent of the fabler. Homer is remembered for the narrative digression of the bard in Phaecia who lampoons Hephaestus, Mars, and Aphrodite. In *Hudibras*, of course, Butler's strategy is not so much to lower high-mindedness as to send middling spirits up. Heroic errantry is brought to its knees where it meets—in full hypocritical pose—the praying and babbling apostates of the internecine dispensation.[9]

❖

Samuel Butler's *Hudibras* takes as its titular hero a deformed and impoverished colonel in a land ravished by civil war. The narrative's controlling action centers on the possession of a widow's jointure—a small inheritance that stands for the real subject of the poem, the schismatic, divided, devalued "estate" of the English historical scene. Samuel Johnson praised *Hudibras* as "one of those compo-

[9] It is extraordinary how many chivalric and allegorical schemes served as the basis for a host of English Civil War romances, romances that circumstantiated specific events leading to and through the Wars and Interregnum by portraying the entangled heroic affairs of pastoral aristocracies on the islands of Sicily and Sardinia. Curious and tortuous romances such as *Theophania: or Severall Modern Histories Represented by way of Romance: and Politickly Discours'd upon* (1655)—possibly by Sir William Sales—or Richard Braithwaite's *Panthalia: or the Royal Romance, A Discourse stored with infinite variety in relation to State Government* (1659) try, with too much seriousness and much too little success, to recreate the transition from Tudor to Stuart rule in England or the intrigues of a decade of civil war on remote islands and pastoral places of the sunny Mediterranean. Samuel Butler writes of these efforts: "Some force whole Regions, in despight / O' Geography, to change their site: / Make former times shake hands with latter, / And that which was before, come after" (*Hudibras*, II, i, 23-26). Patience is a necessary virtue for the gentle skimmer of these narratives.

sitions of which a nation may justly boast," and there is at least the suggestion in his remark that the narrative embodies a national theme. Indeed it does. *Hudibras* is the skewed epic of the Wars and Interregnum, a major satiric spectacle of the nation's apostolic mind. In the Restoration and for decades after, *Hudibras* stood as the very record of internecine dispossession. Both Charles II and Andrew Marvell memorized a good deal of the poem. Swift memorized almost all of it. But modern commentators merely poke at it as they would a beached whale and read the narrative intermittently for its bizarre tropes, its encyclopedic outrageousness, its factional invective, its absurd rhymes ("*hickup*" and "*prick up*," "Engins" and "Penguins," "Greek" and "squeek," "Obnoxious" and "Hiccius Doctius," "Magicians" and "piss in"). *Hudibras* deserves better.[10] The narrative is expansive—it is not *just* the freak of Butler's slightly drunken genius—and its larger narrative strategies, its saving (or covering) fictions, and its material and motivational penetrations were unabashedly mined by satirical writers for decades.[11]

[10] *Hudibras* has received extensive local commentary in Roger L'Estrange's "Key" to *Hudibras* in *Butler's Posthumous Works in Prose and Verse . . . with a Key to Hudibras by Sir Roger L'Estrange* (London, 1715), the editions of Zachary Grey, *Hudibras in Three Parts . . . with Large Annotations and a Preface*, 2 vols. (London, 1744), Treadway Russel Nash, *Hudibras*, 2 vols. (London, 1835), and John Wilders, *Samuel Butler: Hudibras*. Treatments of the poem as narrative are sparse, but the following critics discuss various aspects of the poem at varying lengths: Ian Jack, *Augustan Satire, 1660-1750* (Oxford, 1952), Ruth Nevo, *The Dial of Virtue: A Study of Poems on Affairs of State* (Princeton, 1963), Thomas Edwards, *Imagination and Power*, (New York, 1971), Earl Miner, *The Restoration Mode*, (Princeton, 1974), and George Wasserman, *Samuel "Hudibras" Butler* (Boston, 1976).

[11] In his essay, "Of Poetry," Sir William Temple describes the potential for poetic representation in his age, and his conclusions conform almost exactly to the narrative program of *Hudibras*: "Besides, our different opinions in religion, and the factions they have raised or animated for fifty years past, have had an ill effect upon our manners and customs, inducing more avarice, ambition, disguise (with the usual consequences of them) than were before in our constitution. From all this it may happen, that there is no where more true zeal in the many different forms of devotion,

THE INTERNECINE ROMANCE

As participants in a civil war satire, the characters in *Hudibras* pretend to a personal and national integrity that they in fact do not possess. The narrative's action— Hudibras' attempt to separate the Widow from her previous jointure—is, like civil war itself, a schismatic act. All that is predisposed to joining terminates in division. That is why marriage, a potential union, is so central a parodic goal in the poem. Hudibras seeks property through a symbolic "jointure." He ends, however, as he begins: divided and barely self-possessed. Butler keeps the factions in the land apart as he keeps the sexes apart, and the domestic scheme of *Hudibras* is written large in the historical scheming of propertied factions in England. What was at issue, according to one historian, "was the ownership of the soil of England."[12]

Hudibras' marriage fable tests the personality of history and finds the internecine romance wanting in commitment. For Butler the "Good Old Cause" is feminine in gender, and his Presbyterian heroes "espoused" it when she "Had store of Money in her Purse, / When he took her for bett'r or worse" (III, ii, 107-108). If the war effort is a

---

and yet no where more knavery under the shows and pretences." See *The Works of Sir William Temple* (London, 1814), 3:440. As late as 1743 Pope associates the theme of cultural anarchy with the subject of Butler's great civil war satire. We hear of Cibber's loyalties: "Dulness! whose good old cause I yet defend / With whom my Muse began, with whom shall end" (1743 *Dunciad*, I, 165-166). Even Laurence Sterne (in one of his convoluted pieces of literary historiography in *Tristram Shandy*) sees in the Civil War and post-War period an onslaught against wit (which he calls a *"hue* and *cry,"* mimicking parliamentary rhetoric). The "cause" against wit has set the materialist scene of affected gravity ever since, and Sterne goes so far as to implicate Locke who was gulled by his times into attacking wit in his *Essay Concerning Human Understanding.* Sterne calls that attack (again with the results of the Civil War and 1688 Revolution in mind) "the *Magna Charta* of stupidity ever since" (vol. 3, ch. 20).

[12] H. N. Brailsford, *The Levellers and the English Revolution* (Stanford, 1961), p. 11. Brailsford is far from the only historian to make this point, and the issue of sequestered estates was one of the more tangible realities of the Wars before and after the restoration of the Stuart monarchy.

female partner in a material alliance, it follows that Hudibras' pursuit of the Widow is the return of the Presbyterians to something like a monarchical suit. Butler has coded the Royalists into his poem as the "Wicked," in contrast to the Dissenting "Saints." So it is no surprise to hear of the Widow: "She's of the *Wicked*, as I guess, / B'her *looks*, her *language*, and her *dress*" (II, ii, 251-252). When the major Presbyterian forces sought the hand of the Crown in preparing for the Restoration, they also prepared to secure what dominion they could rather than risk a greater factional dissolution that threatened again after the death of Cromwell. Hudibras' marriage proposal makes historical sense in light of a passing remark about Presbyterian motivation made by Butler later in the poem:

> For who e're heard of *Restoration*,
> Until your *thorough Reformation*,
> *That is the Kings, and Churches Lands*
> *Were Sequestered int'other hands?*
> For only then, and not before,
> Your eyes were opened to restore.
> (III, ii, 1227-1232)

Butler maneuvers the marriage plot so that it seems to exist in the allegorical "no-time" of the poem—between the actual Wars and the Restoration settlement. In another sense, the progression from the initial public riots of Part I (bearbaiting), to the Skimmington in Part II, to the long "Rump" canto digression of Part III suggests that the temporal lineaments of the narrative extend from the 1640s to the 1660s.[13] When Butler abandons the forward move-

---

[13] Original commentaries on *Hudibras* (such as L'Estrange's "Key" and the voluminous notes of Zachary Grey, Butler's splenetic Tory editor) were keen on identifying the impersonated historical characters in the poem, but of greater interest is the ironic progress piece that Butler sets up in the poem's alternating sets of alliances. He writes to Oxenden of the allegory's subjects: "Butt I Assure you my cheife designe was onely to give ye world a Just Acct of ye Ridiculous folly & Knavery of ye Presbiterian

ment of the fable and has his characters "speak" history, he announces the undisplaced issues of his poem. The early argument between Ralpho and Hudibras over synods and bears, for example, reflects not only the division of parties during the Wars but the changed circumstances of the post-Cromwellian era. When Ralpho compares bears (a monarchical symbol) to synods (presbyteries), he hints at a kind of interchangeability in historical patterns. Later, he links the Presbyterian forces not only to the monarchy but to the religion of the enemy: "*Presbyterie* does but translate / The Papacy to a *Free State*" (I, iii, 1201-1202).

Ralpho repeats the essential argument of the poem: after the fall of Cromwell the Younger's government the Presbyterians assisted in ushering back the monarchy. Such a conspiratorial theory of alliances, of course, justifies the Independents' grab for power earlier in the 1650s. Ralpho's betrayal of Hudibras in the third part of the poem suggests the principle of political relations after the fighting of the Wars. And the whole of the poem appears to move from the late squabble of the second Civil War, to the machinations of the 1650s (a dark age of skulduggery and prognostication: hence Sidrophel, the poem's astrologer), to the recriminations of the early Restoration in the form of retrospective backbiting and scapegoating. Before the Restoration (or before the marriage of Presbyterian and Royalist factions), the *Presbyter* and *Independent*, having usurped all the King's lands, began proceedings against each other: "Laid out their Apostolick Functions, / On Carnal Orders and *Injunctions*" (III, ii, 47-48). Property is always the "plot" around which the poem centers.

> For when, like Brethren and Friends,
> They came to share the Dividends,
> And ev'ry Partner to Possess,

& Independent Factions then in power" (for the text of the reprinted letter, cf. Wilders, *Samuel Butler: Hudibras*, Appendix A).

> His Church and State Joynt-Purchases,
> In which the Ablest Saint and Best,
> Was Nam'd in Trust by all the Rest,
> To pay their Money, and instead
> Of ev'ry Brother pass the Deed:
> He streight converted all his Gifts,
> To pious Frauds and holy Shifts,
> And setled all the others Shares,
> Upon his *outward Man* and's *Heirs*.
> Held all they claim'd as Forfeit Lands,
> Deliver'd up into his hands,
> And past upon his Conscience,
> By *Pre-intail of Providence*
> Impeach'd the rest for Reprobates,
> That had no Titles to Estates;
> But by their Spiritual Attaints,
> Degraded from the Right of Saints.
>
> (III, ii, 55-74)

Of course the narrative's satiric condition both fosters and impedes conspiratorial grabs. At the end Hudibras is still suing for what he was denied at the beginning. As far as the Widow is concerned, Hudibras' very being is "immaterial" to her although it is desperately material to him. In his "Heroical Epistle" to his Lady, Hudibras makes the case for marriage and possession. His argument is part of the massive social and political subterfuge represented by Butler throughout the poem—an argument for the control of England's usurped estate.

> For Women first were made for Men,
> Not Men for them.———It follows then,
> That Men have right to every one,
> And they no freedom of their own:
> And therefore Men have pow'r to chuse,
> But they no Charter to refuse.
>
> ("To his Lady," 273-278)

As was made clear earlier, Hudibras knows full well that he needs title only as legal sanction for dominion. His suit to the Widow asks for what is in effect the legalization of line. All his chivalric gestures are counterfeit.

> For what can we pretend to inherit,
> Unless the *Marriage-deed* will bear it?
> Could claim no Right to Lands, or Rents,
> But for our Parents settlements:
> Had been buy younger *Sons o'th'Earth*,
> Debar'd it all, but for our Birth,
> What Honours, or Estates of *Peers*
> Could be preserv'd but by their Heirs?
> And what security maintains
> Their Right, and Title, but the *Banes?*
> What Crowns could be Hereditary,
> If greatest *Monarchs did not marry?*
> And with their *Consorts*, consummate
> Their weightyest *Interests of State?*
>
> (III, i, 833-846)

The suit is clearly political: the dispossessed Hudibras senses that "when we once resign our Pow'rs, / W' have nothing left, we can call ours" (III, i, 967-968). The Lady is onto him. Marriage in satire is not what it is in comedy, and union for the sake of greed is an unresolved bond. In a conceit literalizing the idea of marriage as the joining of properties, the Lady compares the marriage act to burying the dead: "Cast *Earth, to Earth,* as in the *Grave,* / To Joyn in Wedlock all they have" ("Ladies Answer," 127-128). Chivalry is that which can be carried home: all "Languishing Transports, are Fond / Of *Statute, Mortgage, Bill, and Bond*" ("Ladies Answer," 87-88). The Widow's idea of re-marriage to a Presbyterian is a satiric diminution.

> (For what's infer'd by *T'have* and *t'hold,*
> But something past away, and sold?)

That as it makes but one, of two,
Reduces all things else, as low.
(III, i, 575-578)

The Widow's or Lady's role in *Hudibras* forces the action
in the poem to sustain a certain divisiveness—it forces
hypocrites to reveal themselves. When at the end the narrative returns to a kind of Edenic battle of the sexes, it re-
plays the original dispensation as satiric schism without the
eschatological promise of *re*union. Such is the ironic nature
of dispensation in *Hudibras*. Its domestic squabble signals
its regressive form and "talks up" its larger failings.
Whereas Butler's early critics had identified the subject of
the poem as simple hypocrisy,[14] in a wider sense hypocrisy
is a breached dispensation, a verbal schism, a perpetual
seeming instead of being. The narrative texture of *Hudibras* mimics the schismatic fabric of history—the living of
the lie, the fraudulent covering over of motivational intent
with the parodic gestures of verbal errantry. Butler's characters are not great fighters, but they *are* fast talkers.

Butler knows that in periods of civil discord the representation of the divisive scene requires the deployment of
faction as a kind of literary con game: "For as two Cheats
that play one Game, / Are both defeated of their Aim: / So
those who play a *Game of State*, / And only *Cavil* in Debate, /
Although there's nothing lost nor won, / The Publick Business is undone" (III, ii, 155-160). The spirit of the factional
cheat is central to every relationship in the poem: Hudibras
versus Ralpho, the Widow versus Hudibras, Hudibras versus Sidrophel, the two politicians in the "Rump" canto. All
relations are unstable, and they follow a predictable pat-

---

[14] John Dennis writes of *Hudibras*: "The violence and virulence of the
contending Parties in *England*, have, I am afraid, been one great cause,
why we have had no just satire in *England*, since the author of *Hudibras*
published his, which seems to me, to be a very just one on Hypocrisy." See
"Letter to Sir John Edgar," in *Critical Works of John Dennis*, ed. Edward
Niles Hooker (Baltimore, 1943), 2:210.

tern: the con game leads to the double-cross leads to the drubbing. Allies convert to enemies, protagonists to antagonists, co-conspirators to double-dealers. The climax of the poem turns on hypocritical exposure. Disguised as a demon inquisitor, Ralpho forces Hudibras into the material truth. Or to put it another way, Hudibras turns witness against his material self. The factionalist is anarchic.[15]

> *What made thee break thy Plighted Vows?*
> That which makes others break a House.
> And hang, and scorn ye all, before
> Indure the Plague of being poor.
> (III, i, 1237-1240)

Ralpho the Inquisitor asks the question that reduces all behavior to a Hobbist state of nature, a perpetual civil war: *"What Laws, and Freedom, Persecution?* / B'ing out of Pow'r and Contribution" (III, i, 1283-1284). "Contribution" *is* power in *Hudibras*; but in a world in which no one contri-

---

[15] Butler has written that civil war is the expression of a primitive ambition and want: "The Ambition of some men and the wants of others are the ordinary causes of all Civil Wars" (*Characters and Passages From Note-Books*, p. 383). The notion is Hobbist and becomes commonplace even in the wider sense of all warfare. Swift writes in the opening of his *Battle of the Books*: "it very seldom happens among Men to fall out, when all have enough: Invasions usually travelling from *North* to *South*, that is to say, from Poverty upon Plenty." See *A Tale of A Tub, To Which is added The Battle of the Books and the Mechanical Operation of the Spirit*, ed. A. C. Guthkelch and D. Nichol Smith (Oxford, 1958), p. 218. During this age, the prejudice of the propertied against the unpropertied was the axis upon which political theory turned. Sir William Temple writes of a pattern that Butler's Hudibras might well understand: "There is one universal division in all states, which is between the innocent and criminals; and another between such as are, in some measure, contented with what they possess by inheritance, or what they expect from their own abilities, industry, or parsimony; and others, who, dissatisfied with what they have, and not trusting to those innocent ways of acquiring more, must fall to others, and pass from just to unjust, from peaceable to violent . . . yet the last, when they have gained enough by factions and disorders, by rapine and violence, come then to change their principles with their fortunes, and grown friends to established orders and fixed laws." See *Works* (1814), 3:37-38.

butes, no one holds power. The internecine condition is debilitating. That a domestic parable of marriage stands at the parodic core of the poem is doubly ironic in this sense, because in civil conflict factional extremism attacks the nature of the state as model family—it is as Thucydides writes of the internecine romance: "Family relations were a weaker tie than party membership, since party members were more ready to go to any extreme for any reason whatever."[16] To hunger for power is to divide the national inheritance, to generate rivalries. According to Thucydides on the subject of the Greek civil wars:

> So revolutions broke out in city after city, and in places where the revolutions occurred late the knowledge of what had happened previously in other places caused still new extravagances of revolutionary zeal, expressed by an elaboration in the methods of seizing power and by unheard-of atrocities in revenge. To fit in with the change of events, words, too, had to change their usual meanings. What used to be described as a thoughtless act of aggression was now regarded as the courage one would expect to find in a party member; to think of the future and wait was merely another way of saying one was a coward; any idea of moderation was just an attempt to disguise one's unmanly character; ability to understand a question from all sides meant that one was totally unfitted for action. Fanatical enthusiasm was the mark of a real man, and to plot against an enemy behind his back was perfectly legitimate self-defense. Anyone who held violent opinions could always be trusted, and anyone who objected to them became a suspect. To plot successfully was a sign of intelligence, but it was still cleverer to see that a plot was hatching.[17]

[16] Thucydides, *The Peloponnesian Wars*, trans. Rex Warner (Harmondsworth, 1954), p. 243.
[17] Thucydides, *The Peloponnesian Wars*, pp. 242-243.

THE INTERNECINE ROMANCE

Thucydides' observation that schismatically distorted events invite the perversion of language is a crucial one for a satirist such as Butler. Hypocrisy represented in narrative action is a kind of logomachy, and civil war is a deterioration of mind and language. *Hudibras* seems a static poem because talk overwhelms the depiction of narrative events, but in another sense talk is action for Butler—his poem conforms to James Joyce's later alteration of the typical romance formula, "thou art in perilous ways," to an even more dangerous errantry, "thou art in parlous ways." Language in the poem is itself schismatic; for every "why" Hudibras, has a "wherefore." The Civil Wars are a "tongue fight," as Butler calls them. Oaths have the same integrity as obligations—none at all. At one point Ralpho tries to convince Hudibras that he need not keep his verbal oath to the Widow. Oaths, of course, are the very basis of chivalric obligation, but Ralpho transforms heroic romance into internecine politics—much the same transformation that Butler adapts for the structural basis of his narrative.

> For, breaking of an *Oath* and *Lying*,
> Is but a kind of *Self-denying*,
> A *Saint-like virtue*, and from hence,
> Some have broke *Oaths*, by *Providence*:
> Some, to the *Glory of the Lord*,
> *Perjur'd* themselves, and broke their word:
> And this the constant *Rule* and *practice*,
> Of all our late *Apostles Acts* is.
> Was not the *Cause* at first begun
> With *Perjury*, and carry'd on?
>
> (II, ii, 133-142)

The language of obligation is not only chivalric but legal. And one of Butler's sustained efforts is to make the language of law adjustable to the politics of civil fraud: "Who though their *bus'ness at the Bar* / Be but a kind of *civil War*, / In which th' ingage with *fiercer Dudgeons* / Then e're the

Grecians did, and Trojans" (III, iii, 441-444). Legal battles, battles of words, paper wars are all part of the internecine "wrangle / About the slightest fingle fangle" (III, iii, 453-454). Thomas Hobbes, who translated Thucydides, realized from a theoretical perspective what Butler was to conceive from a narrative perspective: civil war is an epistemological crisis—it affects ways of knowing. To wit is to outwit, to con.

> Furthermore, since the combate of Wits is the fiercest, the greatest discords which are, must necessarily arise from this Contention; for in this case it is not only odius to contend against, but also not to consent; for not to approve of what a man saith is no lesse than tacitely to accuse him of an Errour in that thing which he speaketh; as in very many things to dissent, is as much as if you account him a fool whom you dissent from; which may appear hence, that there are. no Warres so sharply wag'd as between Sects of the same Religion, and Factions of the same Commonweale where the Contestation is: Either concerning Doctrines, or Politique Prudence.[18]

In civil war as depicted by Butler, all perception, talk, and action are but a gloss on conspiratorial motive. We can turn yet again to Thucydides for the depiction of the schismatic character of a people at war, rivalling their own nature, protecting their own appearances.

> As the result of these revolutions, there was a general deterioration of character throughout the Greek world. The simple way of looking at things, which is so much the mark of a noble nature, was regarded as a ridiculous quality and soon ceased to exist. Society had become divided into two ideologically hostile camps, and each side viewed the other with suspicion. As for

[18] Thomas Hobbes, *Philosophic Rudiments Concerning Government and Society* (London, 1651), p. 9.

ending this state of affairs, no guarantee could be given that would be trusted, no oath sworn that people would fear to break; everyone had come to the conclusion that it was hopeless to expect a permanent settlement and so, instead of being able to feel confident in others, they devoted their energies to providing against being injured themselves. As a rule those who were least remarkable for intelligence showed the greatest powers of survival.[19]

It is precisely the deterioration of character—in a political and modal sense—that provides Butler with his narrative material in *Hudibras*. A satiric subject is a deteriorating character, an image or embodiment of faction just as it has always been from the time of Aesop's fable of the revolt of the members against the stomach or Plato's image of the deteriorating *polis* as the body and soul declaring internal warfare. For Hobbes the image of civil revolt is that of "defectuous procreation," and in *Hudibras* Butler presents his hero in open revolt against the proportion of his own character. His is the burden of factional monstrosity, the very image of the "Rump" or topsy-turvy domination.[20] As an inheritance from an epic tradition, Hudibras is a Virgilian deformity.

> His *Back*, or rather Burthen, show'd
> As if it stoop'd with its own load.
> For as *Æneas* bore his Sire
> Upon his shoulders through the fire:

[19] Thucydides, *The Peloponnesian Wars*, p. 244.

[20] Butler's description of the Rump Burning later in the poem suggests the emblematic allegiance with his titular hero.

> This shews, how perfectly, the Rump,
> And Common-wealth in Nature jump;
> For as a Fly, that goes to Bed,
> Rests with his Tail above his Head;
> So in this Mungril *State of ours*,
> The Rabble are the Supream Powers.
> (III, ii, 1607-1612)

THE INTERNECINE ROMANCE

> Our Knight did bear no less a Pack
> Of his own Buttocks on his Back.
>   (I, i, 285-291)

As Thucydides suggests, schism turns against "the mark of a noble nature." Butler's Knight, a figured parody of noble proportion, performs in a world whose image betrays its sanction. Butler writes: "No Age ever abounded more with Heroical Poetry than the present, and yet there was never any wherein fewer Heroicall Actions were performd; Nor any though the most Barbarous, ever so averse to the Practice of those examples which are dayly set before their eyes."[21] Hudibras' first important speech is a direct parody of Lucan's *Pharsalia*, an epic of Roman civil war where Lucan himself suggests how the nature of civil war turns against itself in a kind of hypocrisy: "Inminet armorum rabies, ferrique potestas / Confundet ius omne manu, scelerique nefando," ("The madness of war is upon us, when the power of the sword shall violently upset all legality, and atrocious crime shall be called heroism," Loeb trans., bk. I, ll. 666-668).

Butler begins *Hudibras* with an allusion to the Lucanic condition: "When *civil* Fury first grew high, / And men fell out they knew not why" (I, i, 1-2). The parody of the purposeless strife epos continues when Hudibras addresses the factions within his own cause, the inevitable war within the war: "What Rage, O Citizens, what fury / Doth you to these dire actions hurry?" (I, ii, 493-494). These lines compare to the opening book of the *Pharsalia* as translated by Tom May in 1627:

> What fury, Countreymen, what madnesse cou'd
> Moove you to feast your fooes with Roman Blood?

---

[21] Butler, *Characters and Passages From Note-Books*, p. 442.

And choose such warres, as could no triumphs yeeld,
Whilest yet proud Babylon unconquer'd held.

(I, 8-14)

The key line for Butler would be May's "choose such
warres, as could no triumphs yeeld." Internecine conflict is
double jeopardy, as Hudibras admits when he mimics the
Parliamentary argument that states that the attack on the
body of the King is the preservation of his office: "For as we
make War *for the King / Against himself*, the self-same thing"
(I, ii, 513-514). Hudibras, gently pricking his way upon the
plain, comes upon the bearbaiting episode at an unnamed
town in "Western Clime." The poem's initiating action is
internecine. Hudibras sees in the bearbaiting

> A deep design in't, to divide
> The well-affected that confide,
> By setting Brother against Brother,
> To claw and curry one another.
> Have we not enemies *plus satis*,
> That *Cane et angue pejus* hate us?
> And shall we turn our fangs and claws
> Upon our own selves, without cause?

(I, i, 737-744)

Supposed allies are at each other's throats.[22] Even at a
time when the War ought to be over the internecine condition prevails. Well into the Restoration the forces of civil
conflict fester.

[22] Butler first seems to have conceived the idea of the bearbaiting as a
schism within the "Cause," but he then generated something of a larger
issue out of it. Ward Miller was the first to suggest that Butler's strategy in
this episode implicated both Parliamentary and Royalist figures, giving
credence to the opening lines of the poem that men (presumably, all men)
"fell out they knew not why." See *The Allegory in Hudibras* (Ph.D. dissertation, University of Iowa, 1955) and "The Allegory in Part I of *Hudibras*,"
Huntington Library Quarterly 21 (1958): 322-343.

The *Gibellins*, for want of *Guelfs*,
Divert their rage upon themselves:
For now the War is not between
The Brethren, and the Men of sin:
But *Saint, and Saint*, to spill the Blood
Of one anothers Brotherhood.

(III, ii, 685-690)

Or worse, all action stops, all movement is exhausted, and all being suffers satiric enervation.

For Saints in Peace degenerate,
And dwindle down to Reprobate:
Their Zeal corrupts like standing Water,
In th' Intervals of war and slaughter.

(III, ii, 643-646)

In the played out satiric condition, extravagant actions cancel each other's extremes. And the "greatest extravagancies in the world are things that have ever been and ever wilbe," writes Butler. To try to reform them "is but to put them into another way, and perhaps a worse, and not to alter their Nature."[23] According to Butler there is a "universal Inclination" in mankind that "tends to the worst of our Creation."[24] And the divisive or schismatic satiric scene is, by design, the measure of heroic worsening: "All great Actions derive one half of their Greatness from the meaness of other mens Performances. For when all particulars meet upon even terms, there is seldom any great Difference in the success."[25] *Hudibras* is grounded on just such a premise, and the actions Butler represents can only be subdued and levelled, they can never be resolved. Just as the temporal scheme of the poem dwindles "down

[23] Butler, *Characters and Passages From Note-Books*, p. 345.
[24] Butler, "Satire upon the Weakness and Misery of Man," in *Satires and Miscellaneous Poetry and Prose*, ed. René Lamar (Cambridge, 1928), p. 34, ll. 35-36.
[25] Butler, *Characters and Passages From Note-Books*, p. 292.

to Reprobate," so too does Butler's hero who, by embody-
ing the status of degenerative heroism, takes the mode of
the poem down with him. His chivalric and martial humili-
ation is of epic disproportion.

> I WHO was once as great as *Caesar*,
> Am now reduc'd to *Nebuchadnezar*.
> And from as fam'd a Conquerour,
> As ever took degree in War,
> Or did his *Exercise*, in battle,
> By you turn'd out to *Grass with Cattle*.
>
> ("To his Lady," 1-6)

At poem's end Hudibras is in virtually no different a position than he was at poem's beginning. Butler begins with a
formulaic construction *in medias res*: when-then. But the
course of the narrative is a joke at the expense of such easy
causality: "men fell out they knew not why." For many of
Butler's commentators, the most pressing issue in the
poem is exactly how its actions allegorically convey the
phases of the Civil Wars and Interregnum. But a more
troubling point is how the satiric strategy of the poem ob-
literates the import of specific historical details in the total
collapse of value. Allegory counts on a doctrine of superior
meanings; satire, like faction, is a record of collapsed
meaning. The focus on the revolutionary period seems sustained, yet the poem's chronology is jumbled and its sequential moorings are not altogether clear. There are hints
that the first part of *Hudibras* centers on the earlier
episodes of the Civil War when the Presbyterians, with their
Scottish connection, were on the border, so to speak, of
protecting the King and opposing the extreme measures
of their regicide-planning Independent allies.[26] But the

[26] See Hardin Craig, "*Hudibras*, Part I and the Politics of 1647," in *The
Manly Anniversary Studies in Language and Literature* (Chicago, 1923), pp.
144-155. Craig offers a different allegorical reading of the sequence than
the one cited above by Ward Miller.

larger fable (the marriage suit) seems a conflation of three decades of rebellious history (even into the Restoration). Butler the allegorist manipulates events in which Hudibras and Ralpho serve the "Cause" as Presbyterian and Independent "Saint," while the Widow is of the more sound Royalist breed of the "Wicked." But for Butler the satirist, neither the Saints nor the Wicked, the rebels nor the Royalists differ much in nature. The admixtures of satire contaminate each other.

> And yet the Actions be contrary,
> Just as the *Saints* and *Wicked* vary.
> For as on land there is no *Beast*,
> But in some *Fish* at Sea's exprest,
> So in the *Wicked* there's no *Vice*,
> Of which the *Saints* have not a spice.
> (II, ii, 239-244)

A sustained allegorical reading of *Hudibras* runs into more difficult problems. Allegory argues for an awareness by the readers of the events represented in an allegorical sequence. But the potentially allegorical scenes of *Hudibras* are perceived by characters *in* the narrative as a digression from the struggle that they know they are in. For example, if the bearbaiting sequence is the allegorical representation of the Presbyterian-Independent rift over the disposition of the King, then it seems odd that Hudibras himself would perceive the bearbaiting as diversionary.

> What Towns, what Garrison's might you
> With hazard of this bloud subdue,
> Which now y' are bent to throw away
> In vain, untriumphable fray?
> (I, ii, 499-502)

As a factionalist Hudibras is inside the action against the Independent "dogs" and in support of the monarchical bear. But as a commentator he does not see the allegorical potential—he mocks the event as a literal "happening," a minor riot in a small town, less *of* history than *against* history: "Shall *Saints* in Civil bloudshed wallow / Of *Saints*, and let the *Cause* lie fallow?" (I, ii, 503-504). In his speech to the rabble, Hudibras wishes to displace the action represented in the canto and replace it with the political sentiment he supports. (Of course his call for union is itself hypocritical.) Whether or not he wants it both ways, Hudibras seems to have it both ways: he is in the action and he talks around the action; he is an allegorical being and he denies allegorical connection. Once again he is representative of the condition of the poem both as historical allegory and satiric commentary on allegorically conceived action. But the constant satirical palaver around the central allegorical episodes diminishes the conviction with which the allegorical import is registered for the reader. Allegory, which is a kind of commentary, is satirically buried in commentary. Interpretation itself is schismatic, and the allegory of *Hudibras* is made part of the cohesive irony of the narrative where the madness of the times is mirrored in the madness of the mind's record.

Hudibras is filled with allegorical details, but Butler rarely rests content until he has reconditioned even the smallest item into its satiric antitype. Hudibras' famous beard is a case in point. The beard has always intrigued commentators as a possible clue to the real identity of the allegorical Hudibras.[27] Butler compares his knight to the "valiant *Mamaluke*" for "Person, Parts, Address, and Beard" (I, i,

[27] Butler's *Oxenden Letter*, first revealed by Ricardo Quintana, suggests the personal basis of the knight's conception. See "The Butler-Oxenden Correspondence," *MLN* 48 (1933): 1-11. Hudibras is modelled on a "West Countrey Knt"; guesses center on Sir Samuel Luke and Sir Henry Rosewell of Forde Abbey in Devonshire. Discoursing generally on beards, Mr. Spectator mentions that of Hudibras: "During the Civil Wars there appeared one, which makes too great a Figure in Story to be passed over in Silence; I mean that of the redoubted *Hudibras*, an Account of which *Butler* has transmitted to Posterity." See *Spectator*, no. 331 (20 March 1712), in *The Spectator*, ed. Donald F. Bond (Oxford, 1955), 3: 222.

895; 898). The obvious candidate is Sir Samuel Luke, an energetic, if deformed, Presbyterian colonel in the Parliamentary forces. But we learn very little about Luke in the poem, and the historical record presents only one portrait (in Sir Luke's *Letter Books for 1644-45*) in which the colonel sports no beard at all. We are far safer concluding that for Butler the beard is, like Hudibras' hump, a symbol of degenerative government.

> His tawny *Beard* was th' equall grace
> Both of his wisdome and his face;
> In Cut and Dry so like a tile,
> A sudden view it would beguile:
> The upper part thereof was Whey,
> The nether Orange mixt with Gray.
> This hairy Meteor did denounce
> The fall of Scepters and of Crowns;
> With grizly type did represent
> Declining Age of Government.
>
> (I, i, 239-248)

Butler goes on to allude to the practice of numerous Puritan votaries during the wars who had vowed never to cut their beards until the final defeat of the monarchy, but even more local color is involved. Hudibras' beard, like Bottom's in his portrayal of the ill-fated Pyramus, is orange-tawny. Military historians tell us that orange-tawny is a particularly contentious color. During the Wars it was often impossible to distinguish between the leaders of the rival armies because officers dressed "much as they pleased."[28] One distinction, however, was fairly reliable. Officers on both sides wore scarves as battle insignia. Peter Young writes: "There was little to distinguish the officers of

[28] Peter Young, *Marston Moor 1644, The Campaign and the Battle* (Kineton, Eng., 1970), p. 22.

the two Armies but the crimson silk scarves habitually worn by the Royalists and the orange-tawny ones of their opponents.[29] Butler knows of the practice because, by way of a passing allusion to the Smectymnus controversy of the early 1640s, he alludes to the "Canonical *Crabat* of *Smeck*" (I, iii, 1166) worn as insignia by the Parliamentary factions "When Church and State they set on flame" (I, iii, 1168). The *"Crabat"* or *"hand-kercher* about the neck" (I, iii, 1165) was worn "by them as badges then / Of *Spiritual Warfaring* men" (I, iii, 1169-1170).

Hudibras' beard colors his cause—it is but another emblem of his allegorical self. When confronted by the Widow after his defeat in battle, he complains that his Lady is forced to view him in the stocks "with *Beard* and *Face*, / By you, in such a homely case" (II, i, 163-164). The Widow jokingly responds: "A torn *Beard's* like a tattered Ensign, / That's bravest which there are most rents in" (II, i, 173-174). Once again, the action of the poem provides additional commentary on the status of allegorical representation. Butler tells us what he thinks of the internecine "Cause" when in the Skimmington episode of Part II Sir Hudibras runs full face into a well-aimed egg, which "running down his Cheek, besmear'd / With Orenge-Tawny-slime, his *Beard*" (II, ii, 817-818). For Butler, the tiny allegorical detail is the occasion of a much larger burlesque spectacle wherein Hudibras is humiliated and what he "represents" is bespattered. That events and details have actual analogues in the history of the times is finally of less importance to the author than the patterns that accrue in a general state of civil war where all faction is riot and all commentary is a kind of verbal anarchy. His deeper subject is not the external circumstances of rebellion but the violation of measured reason, the apostolic succession where no

[29] Young, *Marston Moor*, p. 22.

force in the land escapes the "perturbations that possess / The Mind" (I, iii, 1019-1020).

✧

Perhaps the best way to perceive the satiric structure of *Hudibras* is to return to the narrative models upon which the poem is based. Near the beginning of the poem Butler claims that his fable relates the story of Hudibras, "Chief of Domestic Knights and Errant" (I, i, 21). As in *Don Quixote*, domesticity is both native and localized. When the domestic is allowed to wander, the hero, in effect, is turned out of house and home. But the anterior domestic model for Sir Hudibras is not Quixote. Rather, Butler kidnaps an obscure figure who appears in a small episode of an earlier epic of errantry, *The Faerie Queene*. Commentators have long known the Spenserian source for Sir Hudibras, but they have paid scant attention to the episode from which he is drawn, an episode that is itself a miniature of the larger internecine romance.[30]

Spenser's Sir Huddibras[31] appears in the midst of a family at war, a house internally divided and barely surviving. Three sisters share their inheritance—their father's castle. As in the folk motif, sharing is disguised discord, a theme Jonathan Swift adapts for the allegorical fable in *A Tale of A Tub*. The castle of the three sisters is the domain of faction, and all domestic relations are "but continuall jarre" (*Faerie Queene*, II, ii, xxvi). Spenser's sisters are of a "sundry sort,"

---

[30] Zachary Grey's notes cite the relevant Spenserian sources and so do those of Butler's modern editor, John Wilders. Among critics, Ian Jack mentions Butler's debt to the appropriate canto of the *Faerie Queene*, but he fails to probe much further (*Augustan Satire*, p. 15).

[31] James Nohrnberg, *The Analogy of the Faerie Queene* (Princeton, 1976), derives Huddibras' name as follows: "Erasmus draws a contrast between the recalcitrance of Agamemnon ('no high deed or show of spirit is recorded of him except that he flew into a rage over the removal of Chryseis') and the 'undisciplined impulses' of Achilles. Achilles and Agamemnon are the *bradeōs* and *speude* components of the proverb, Erasmus suggests. The same contrast is at work in Spenser's Huddibras—whose name sounds like the Greek phrase in reverse" (p. 306).

daughters of one father but of three different mothers. The eldest and youngest are perpetually in strife. As her name indicates, Dame Elissa gives too little, while the younger sister, given to excess, is named Perissa or "too much." Medina marks the name and position of the middle sister. Spenser's figure of temperance or moderation, Guyon, is naturally allied to Medina. Perissa is wooed by Sans-loy, a reckless holdover from the first book of the *Faerie Queene*. Dame Elissa is courted by the blustering Sir Huddibras.

> He that made love unto the eldest Dame,
>> Was hight Sir *Huddibras*, an hardy man;
>> Yet not so good of deedes, as great of name,
>> Which he by many rash adventures wan,
>> Since errant armes to sew he first began;
>> More huge in strength, then wise in workes he was,
>> And reason with foole-hardize over ran;
>> Sterne melancholy did his courage pas,
> And was for terrour more, all armd in shyning bras.
>
> (II, ii, xvii)

Dame Elissa neither gives nor receives much from Sir Huddibras. Her nature is hard, like that of the Widow in Butler's poem.

> *Elissa* (so the eldest hight) did deeme
>> Such entertainment base, ne ought would eat,
>> Ne ought would speake, but evermore did seeme
>> As discontent for want of merth or meat;
>> No solace could her Paramour intreat
>> Her once to show, ne court, nor dalliance,
>> But with bent lowring browes, as she would threat,
>> She scould, and frownd with froward countenaunce,
> Unworthy of faire Ladies comely governaunce.
>
> (II, ii, xxxv)

Spenser's allegory is set in balance, lack and excess flanking moderation. When Guyon arrives, Sans-loy and Huddibras unite to oppose "temperance," but they end up, like all extremes, in a kind of perverse embrace: they take each other in and are taken in when "themselves at discord fell, / And cruell combat joynd in middle space; / With horrible assault, and furie fell" (II, ii, xx). Middle space, when taken over by extremes, is space without Medina. Contested space is undifferentiated—no one possesses it, no one owns it, no one controls it. Guyon and Medina sue for peace, as befits them, but initially they are implicated by faction in a "tripple war" in which "a house was raysd, and all that in did dwell" (II, ii, xx). Spenser resolves the episode by allowing moderation to win over excess and restraint (as he does throughout Book II).

The image of concord that ensues is drawn from mythological reserves. If the *Faerie Queene*'s twelve-book prospectus announces for each book an ideal virtue in the formulation of the complete heroic courtier, the allegorical hero can in the course of his adventure meet anything that can be brought into imaginative being. And when the poem's title figure, the Faerie Queene, or its salvation figure, King Arthur, arrive on the scene, they are free from the contingent historical world of internecine ambition, religious schism, and dynastic hegemony. That is, they are released in and protected by heroic space.[32] Civil war seems to fade away in pageantry of native rule when the Faerie Queene herself occupies the episode's contested ground: "That with her soveraigne powre, and scepter shene / All Faery lond does peaceably sustene" (II, ii, xl).

Such a vision is noticeably absent in Butler's *Hudibras*, and it is fitting that an inconsequential figure drawn from a poem with a Glorianist title (*Faerie Queene*) should take over

[32] In the later, more bitterly political of Spenser's books, the saving mythology weakens in the presence of the blatant beast. Finally, the conservation of heroic type in fully conserved spaces is threatened by a naturally powerful and inclusive sense of contingency in the temporal and spatial world of *Mutabilitie*. Nohrnberg's *Analogy of the Faerie Queene* is superb on the final fragments of the poem (pp. 737-757).

the role of titular hero in a poem about a land whose king has had his head cut off. Butler elects Hudibras for the purpose of arousing contention among the elect. Spenser's contentious parasites become Butler's satiric hosts. In the Spenserian allegory he seeks a model for discord but not a model for resolution. The temporary "horrible assault, and furie fell" of Spenser's episode is transformed into perpetual "civil Fury" (I, i, 1) in *Hudibras*. Without moderation all that remains for Butler is what he calls "odde perverse antipathies." Extremes simply alternate, and all action is appropriating. Ralpho points out to Hudibras that by conquering the Royalists, the Puritans in effect hold title to their natures as well as to their properties.

> The property is in the *Saint*,
> From whom th' injuriously detain't;
> Of him they hold their Luxuries,
> Their Dogs, their Horses, Whores and Dice,
> Their Riots, Revels, Masks, Delights,
> Pimps, Buffoons, Fidlers, Parasites:
> All which the *Saints* have *title* to,
> And ought t'enjoy, if th' had their due.
> (I, ii, 1011-1018)

In an allegory of chivalric conflict, Spenser's rival knights, Sans-loy and Huddibras, fight for ladies who represent the impulses of political and religious extremes. Ready to "observe *Romantique* Method" (II, i, 1) in representing war and love, Butler sets his factionalists loose to "fight, like mad or drunk, / For Dame *Religion* as for Punk" (I, i, 5-6). Spenser's knights are "all for their ladies froward love to gaine," but before moderation arrives they gain only a love "which gotten was but hate" (II, ii, xxv). Butler seizes this bit of romance machinery by having the Widow confuse the courting Hudibras with the paradoxical notion that "She could love none but onely such / As scorn'd and hated her as much" (I, iii, 335-336). In the *Faerie Queene* the factious ladies hate the contentious knights; in *Hudibras* the duplicitous knight has to learn to hate the conniving Lady. The logic of both situations fulfills the pattern of factional extremes.

Hudibras, who "never bent his stubborn knee / To any thing but Chivalry" (I, i, 17-18), accedes to the Widow's antithetical demands. He argues the opposite of what he would express, but he speaks the truth about his motives. In perpetrating one kind of hypocrisy, Hudibras penetrates another. He speaks with a double tongue and damns himself with the truth. In satire, hypocrisy will sooner or later be laid bare.

> I do confess, with *goods* and *land*,
> I'd have a wife, at second hand;
> And such you are: Nor is't your person,
> My stomach's set so *sharp*, and *fierce* on,
> But 'tis (your better part) your *Riches*,
> That my enamour'd heart bewitches.
>
> (II, i, 471-476)

The only other occasion in the poem when Hudibras will admit his unembellished motives is when Ralpho, disguised as a kind of seventeenth-century Wizard of Oz, frightens the wits out of his colonel and forces him to "fess-up" to what for Butler was the ur-motive of the wars embodied in the material quest: "*What makes all Doctrines Plain and Clear?* / About two Hundred Pounds a Year" (III, i, 1277-1278). But his admission to the Lady earlier on is something of a double embellishment—he hopes it will be taken as a lie serving chivalric truth rather than as truth underlying a chivalric lie. The Lady's first reaction to Hudibras, however, is to laugh at his person, which appears to her as an ill-proportioned hulk masquerading in the lineaments of knighthood. The Lady "laugh'd out, until her back / As well as sides, was like to crack" (II, i, 84-85).

Spenser's model episode with its knights of suspect motive and extreme relations courting mates of tempera-

mental suitability had set the dubious chivalric potential for
Hudibras. Butler makes the episode into a chivalric epic and
changes the rituals of romance into the propertied settle-
ments of war. His Lady is aware of the expanded allegorical range: "I find (quoth she) my *Goods and Chattles* / Are
like to prove, but meer *drawn Battles*" (III, i, 533-534), and
she opens up the narrative action to its mid-century revision by closing off the mode of heroic romance: "Such
hideous Sots, were *those obedient* / *Old Vassals*, to their *Ladies
Regent*" (III, i, 609-610). In a curious sense, the Lady serves
as the reader's guide to inverted ideals of civil conflict, and
the logic of inversion perhaps explains the power that
women seem to exert in the world of *Hudibras*.[33] The defla-
tion of the heroic is a masculine apostasy, and the antithetical inspiration of feminine power produces what Northrop
Frye would call the *omphale* archetype, the woman-domi-

---

[33] The role of women during the Wars and Interregnum was a matter
that received considerable contemporary attention. The Royalist peri-
odical, *Mercurius Aulicus*, often waxed hot against women preachers (see
issues no. 8, p. 97; no. 33, pp. 445 and 449; no. 37, p. 518). In 1647, John
Taylor considered the influence of women in state affairs and comments:
"that will be a rare World when women shall weare the breeche, & men
peticotes, this greatly tingleth in the eares of the world." See *The Diseases of
the Times or The Distempers of the Commonwealth* (1647), sig A3v. For a review
of the role of women in the period, see Keith Thomas, "Women and the
Civil War Sects," *Past and Present* 13 (April 1958): 42-62. Dan Gibson, Jr.
concludes that Butler was distrustful of the prospect of female control in
government: "Truly, even as Butler intimates, woman had power in state
affairs—a power which he clearly disapproved." See "Samuel Butler," in
Seventeenth-Century Studies, ed. Robert Shafer (Princeton, 1933), p. 286.
But the matter does not rest there. Butler had a kind of secret admiration
for women rulers.

> The Governments of women are commonly more Masculine than
> those of men. For women delight in the Conversation and Practices of
> men; and men of women. This appeares by the management of State
> Affayrs in the Reigns of Queen Elizabeth, Catherine De Medices Re-
> gent of France, and the Princes[s] of Parma in the Low Cuntrys*
> compard with the best of any other Christian Princes of those times.
> (*Characters and Passages From Note-Books*, p. 441)

* Although the pun here is a common one, I do not think Butler intended it as demeaning.

THE INTERNECINE ROMANCE

nant trope.[34] The imperious Widow, the Billingsgate warrior, Trulla, and the impersonated Skimmington Shrew are all examples. Playing out the chivalric game beyond its limits, Hudibras protests that there is something unnatural going on with women in his land, although his anarchic mind never really settles on what. The Lady's inversion of the terms and bases of chivalry turns ritual into rape, but "A *Rape*, that is the more inhumane, / For being acted by a *Woman*" (II, i, 327-328). Butler is no feminist—in fact, later in the narrative he has the Independent politician harangue his allies for implicating women in national affairs, transforming "all Wives to *Dalilahs*, / Whose Husbands were not *For the Cause*" (III, ii, 1115-1116)—and his elevation of women in the poem reveals the odd antipathies of satiric extremes.[35] If the loose allegorical action begins with men falling out "they knew not why," it is fitting that *Hudibras* should end with a couplet of inverted domestic

[34] Northrop Frye, *Anatomy of Criticism: Four Essays* (Princeton, 1957), p. 228. Butler's character of a "Henpect Husband" illustrates the trope: "He was meant to be his Wife's Head, but being set on at the wrong End she makes him serve (like the Jesuits Devil) for her Feet" (*Characters and Passages From Note-Books*, p. 47).

[35] In *The Dial of Virtue*, Ruth Nevo sets Butler's antifeminist tone as part of the general debasement of chivalric machinery. Nevo refers to Trulla as a "Billingsgate Virago" and to the Lady as "fishwifely." Earlier commentators were more generous. For the zealous, anti-Puritan Zachary Grey, anyone (man or woman) who made Hudibras look ridiculous was admirable. Grey commented on Trulla's victory over Hudibras: "What a generous and undaunted heroine is Trulla" (*Hudibras*, I, 240). In his review of Wilders' edition of *Hudibras*, Earl Miner asked: "But what should be made of the fact that in this radically antiromantic poem, the women (Trulla, the Lady) command our greatest respect and even some affection?" See *Philological Quarterly* 47 (1969): 341. In his recent *The Restoration Mode*, Miner considers Butler's women the poem's "most outrageous joke" (p. 184). He moves toward a solution consistent with the worsening processes of satire: "In all this joke I suspect of Butler a yet worse misogyny. And I believe that farther beyond that very funny use of prejudice the pessimist has permitted the sickliest of ideals to take strength in transvestism" (p. 188). A recent essay on the subject by George Wasserman, "*Hudibras* and Male Chauvinism," *Studies in English Literature* 16 (1976): 351-361, agrees with Miner's conclusion.

errantry: "Let Men usurp Th' unjust Dominion, / As if they were *the Better Women*" ("Ladies Answer," 381-382).

❖

Spenser provides Butler with an expandable strife episode, but in *Hudibras* the larger pattern of errantry derives from the semipicaresque journeys and adventures of Cervantes' Quixote and Sancho Panza. *Hudibras* is a further revision of the quixotic revision of the chivalric mission. Its Cervantick legacy is, in one sense, direct: knight and squire, knight's pathetic nag, sudden encounters of the seedy kind, bourgeois enchantments, drubbings, imprisonments, chivalric suits, learned discourses, mock-transformations. But in a more generative sense, *Don Quixote* offers Butler a subverting narrative principle, a principle allied to the satiric inheritance: the will to perform exists in inverse relation to the efficacy, legitimacy, or sanctity of the performance. Hudibras himself gives voice to his own satiric destiny, which is inevitably a burlesque, accidental descent.[36]

> For whatsoe're we perpetrate,
> We do but row, w'are stear'd by Fate,
> Which in success oft disinherits,
> For spurious causes, noblest merits.
> Great Actions are not always true sons

[36] In his notebooks, Butler has a passage on the nature of accident: "Man has an absolute Power over Fate in all things that concerne his own Distruction, but none at all in those that relate to his own Happiness, in which his greatest Care and Industry is many times defeated by an unfortunate accident" (*Characters and Passages From Note-Books*, p. 358). In one sense, Butler's parodic object in *Hudibras* is heroic destiny itself, and he turns his hero loose on that famous reader of the stars, Sidrophel, who holds the burlesque role of magus or wizard. When Sidrophel sees a boy's kite flit across the lens of his telescope he thinks the end of the world has been destined by the appearance of a doomed planet. He decides to cash in on contingent fate: "To make our best advantage of it, / And pay our losses with our profit" (II, iii, 481-482). Burlesque satire negotiates that middle distance between accident and material destiny.

Of Great and mighty Resolutions:
Nor do the bold'st attempts bring forth
Events still equal to their worth;
But sometimes fail, and in their stead
Fortune and Cowardice succeed.

                              (I, i, 873-882)

   Satiric errantry is for Butler (as it was for Cervantes) an
effect of lunatic singlemindedness. In another context he
writes of "humourists"—of those whose psychological
fancy has leapt astride their reason: "Men that are mad
upon many things, are never so extravagant, as those who
are possest with but one. For one Humor diverts another,
and never suffers the Caprich to fix. . . . So those that are
Distracted with severall Sorts of Freakes, are never so sol-
idly and Profoundly mad as those that are wholy taken up
with some one Extravagance."[37] In a literary rendering, extravagance (extra-*vagari* or wandering beyond limits) is the
very narrative impetus of both *Don Quixote* and *Hudibras*,
and in a psychological sense, both heroes wander beyond
their limits of contingent control. Butler had described the
mode of satiric narrative as a "kinde of Knight Errant that
goe's upon Adventures"[38] in a world unwilling and unpre-
pared to accommodate itself to the caprice of wit, and he is
well aware that in identifying the parodic basis of his effort
he, like Cervantes, links the satirist to the extravagancies of
the satiric subject.
   From Spenser Butler borrowed a fable of moderation
and then strategically proceeded to eliminate the moderat-
ing principle from the narrative action. From Cervantes he
borrowed a fable of monomania, but he adjusted that fable
in different ways. Although *Don Quixote* submits its hero to
an extravagant chivalric prototype revised by a satirically
contingent fable, Cervantes' purpose is to educate (or "lead

---

[37] Butler, *Characters and Passages From Note-Books*, p. 327.
[38] Butler, *Characters and Passages From Note-Books*, p. 469.

out") Quixote from the damaging madness of his errantry. Quixote is imaginatively educable throughout because he learns those things that are finally necessary to him. He refuses, for example, to retest his knightly helmet after it has previously proven more fragile than his imagination would have wished. The crucial resolution of Quixote's case comes at the end of the narrative when the hero confines his converting fancy and "returns" to sanity. That conversion is equivalent to a kind of narrative homecoming, and it allows for a final comic, even pathetic, chord in a satirically dispersed action. Butler allows nothing of the sort. At the end of the narrative, Hudibras is as deluded in his quest as he was at the beginning. There is no principle of thematic and narrative conversion—extravagance reigns to the end.

In *Don Quixote* Cervantes includes three separate journeys so that the world of the novel becomes too wide for Quixote's transforming imagination to encompass it. The three-voyage structure is very deliberate in leading the knight errant back to sanity. But in Butler's three-part structure he makes sure that his hero learns nothing and that his plot only shows signs of hysterical advance. In *Hudibras* the first day's sally is local and fairly restricted. Like Quixote, Hudibras ventures out and meets only what finds *him*. He seeks to correct a rural abuse (bearbaiting), gets drubbed for his efforts, and is committed to the stocks. In the second adventure—not a journey in the quixotic sense but another *journeé* or day—the scope of the poem widens. And, as in the second section of *Don Quixote*, the second part of *Hudibras* implicates a set of more "romantic" participants. The Widow and Sidrophel arrive on the scene and the chivalric plot thickens or, if one prefers, becomes more dense. Like Quixote, Hudibras confuses love and mortification—their chivalric suits entail whippings that both would escape if they could. Quixote's third journey takes him to Barcelona on the Mediterranean coast of Spain. The third part of *Hudibras* opens the Interregnum

adventures to the dawn of the Restoration, and it changes
the scene to London. For a good part of Quixote's third
journey he literally drops out of the action—the Duke and
the Duchess take over for him. Something of the same occurs in *Hudibras* when, after his gulling by Ralpho, the
Widow, and Sidrophel, Butler's knight leaves the poem in
fright. Butler fills the narrative gap with the "Rump" canto,
a long debate between an Independent and a Presbyterian
politician set in the 1660s.

Quixote's monomania is visionary: he creates his adventures because the transforming necessities of his imagination tell him to see what he believes. When Hudibras sets
his own errant plot in motion he does so by guile. Thus for
Butler belief is anything but visionary. Hudibras' lunacy is
not the quester's self-sanction but the deluding energy of
the hypocritical spirit. What makes him ridiculous is not
that he believes in himself but that he could think anyone
else would. Hypocrisy is blind, and in the satiric spectacle
of *Hudibras* the blind lead the blind. Whereas Cervantes
works with the complication of vision, Butler works with
the cynicism of belief. Satiric ground is littered with characters who live by deception, and if they manage to become
totally deceptive, they have, in effect, foisted themselves
upon the world.

Cervantes generates sympathy for Quixote because he is
a being capable of conversion—Quixote learns to believe
what is best for him. In *Hudibras* only fear, force, and
power can change behavior; nothing can change belief because almost nothing is believed in. One of the only touching moments in the poem occurs when the Widow, charged
with coldness by a meretricious Hudibras, stares her knight
down and says almost wistfully, "For if I thought you could
be *true*, / I could *love* twice as much as you" (II, i, 551-552).
Nowhere in the narrative do we see a whit of love—the
Widow's or any one else's—and the strong implication is
that we do not see a whit of truth either. What we do see

are greed and material deserts: men of unbelief live in the realm of the senses. Whereas Quixote feeds on the generative spirit, Hudibras at best fears a future *separatio a mensa et thoro*. This is a subject upon which both narratives consciously touch. Quixote explains to Sancho.

> "How little you understand!" . . . "You must know, Sancho, that it is the pride of knights-errant to remain for a whole month without eating, and when they do, they eat only what is ready at hand. You would know this if you had read as many books as I have. In all the books I have delved into I have never found that knights-errant ate, unless by mere chance or at some costly banquets prepared in their honor." (P. 115)

If we read Cervantes' book with any imaginative sympathy, we find that Quixote is right. Like Christ or Achilles, he is starved for something beyond food. On the other hand, Butler's Hudibras is an eater of great repute and a consumer of reputation. To eat is to express material motive. "Put food on thy table," says Butler, who adjusts his contestants' theory of politics to the availability of marrow-puddings and plum-cakes. The underbelly of rebellious action is nurtured by nonconformist delicacies. Knights are cared for by their Ladies who

> Pamper'd and edifi'd their *Zeal*,
> With *Marrow-puddings*, many a meal;
> Enabled them, with store of meat,
> On controverted *Points* to eat.
> And cram'd 'em till their Guts did ake
> With *Cawdle*, *Custard*, and *Plum-cake*.
> (II, ii, 793-798)

Hudibras goes into battle with his hose "lin'd with many a piece / Of Ammunition-Bread and Cheese" (I, i, 311-312), and Butler has him cross palates with Don Quixote himself.

And though Knights Errant, as some think,
Of old did neither eat nor drink,
Because when thorough Deserts vast
And Regions desolate they past,
Where Belly-timber above ground
Or under was not to be found,
Unless they graz'd, there's not one word
Of their Provision on Record:
Which made some confidently write,
They had no stomachs, but to fight,
'Tis false: For *Arthur* wore in Hall
Round-Table like a Farthingal,
On which, with shirt pull'd out behind,
And eke before, his good Knights din'd.
Though 'twas no Table, some suppose,
But a huge pair of round Trunk-hose;
In which he carry'd as much meat
As he and all his Knights could eat,
When laying by their swords and truncheons,
They took their Breakfasts or their Nuncheons.

(I, i, 325-344)

King Arthur is the model knight and the king of the *Faerie Queene*. For Butler to reconstruct Arthur's Round Table as a chivalric support-store so that he might refute Quixote's theory of knightly abstinence is a witty union of narrative sources. Both the norms of moderation imaged in the picture of knighthood and the strength of vision enacted by the gentleman farmer of La Mancha are subverted by material intake and suspicious outgrowths. In *Hudibras*, lack is the prime mover and surfeit is the final cause. Coincidentally, these are the demonstrable extremes in civil war as well as the materialist extremes of the internecine legacy.

Chapter Five

A HOUSE DIVIDED: MARVELL'S *LAST INSTRUCTIONS* AND DRYDEN'S *ABSALOM AND ACHITOPHEL*

At one point in his panegyric *To Sir Godfrey Kneller*, John Dryden asks pardon for inserting what appears to be an insulting reference to the origin of Kneller's art, painting. Dryden traces the artist's craft to Eve "making-up" in the garden. He doesn't really mean it, after all, "But Satire will have room, were e're I write" (l. 94). The growth of the satiric spirit—what Swift called the "Satyrical Itch"—is in a way endemic for the seventeenth century. Dryden was the first practitioner and theorist to understand the full transforming potential of satiric action. He recognized the ranging power of satire in appropriating the strategies of other modes and genres while changing the perspective from which those modes and genres reflect material. In his *Discourse Concerning the Original and Progress of Satire*, Dryden writes of satire as variously manifest, from the negative reflections (*médisance*) of invective to the sublimities of heroic mockery.[1] In essence, "Why shou'd we offer to confine free

---

[1] George Lord's explanation of the title of his recent book, *Heroic Mockery: Variations on Epic Themes from Homer to Joyce* (Newark, Del., 1977), is worth citing because, following Dryden, he lends stature to the mock-heroic: "My title, *Heroic Mockery*, is an attempt to avoid the bias inherent in the more familiar term *mock heroic*. Where *mock heroic* usually designates a kind of literature in which the heroic past is used to satirize the contemptible present, this book is principally concerned with literature that criticizes and modifies the heroic tradition or appeals from it to other standards, standards that, while often appearing to be unheroic, attain in the long run a greater validity than those they replace" (p. 13).

Spirits to one Form, when we cannot so much as confine our Bodies to one Fashion of Apparel?"[2]

In one of the many attacks on Dryden at the time of the Exclusion Crisis, his arch enemy, Elkannah Settle, wrote in frustration of what Dryden had refined as a satiric strategy: "you have got a damnable trick of turning the Perspective upon occasion, and magnifying or diminishing at pleasure."[3] Settle is onto the counterfeit. At least in theory, Dryden knows that literary genre is a matter of separable parts. But in practice the satirist is mercurial. In his *Parallel of Poetry and Painting* Dryden writes: "In the character of an hero, as well as an inferior figure, there is a better or worse likeness to be taken: the better is panegyric, if it be not false, and the worse is libel."[4] The idea is not new. Aristotle has a witty passage in the *Rhetoric* where he speaks of contraries and metaphoric values: "And if we wish to ornament our subject, we must derive our metaphor from the better species under the same genus; if to depreciate it, from the worse. Thus, to say (for you have two opposites belonging to the same genus) that the man who begs prays, or that the man who prays begs (for both are forms of asking) is an instance of doing this" (Loeb trans., 1405a). But what is new, or at least dominant, for Dryden's period is the urge to expand the paradigm from metaphor to mode—to scratch, as Swift put it, wherever satire itched.

What lies behind a good deal of Dryden's thinking on the cross-generic and cross-modal "room" for satire is expressed by Neander in the *Essay of Dramatick Poesie*. According to Neander, literary change accommodates the genius of an age. Thus modernity is the battle against

[2] John Dryden, *Discourse Concerning the Original and Progress of Satire*, in *The Works of John Dryden*, ed. A. B. Chambers, William Frost, and Vinton Dearing (Berkeley and Los Angeles, 1974), 4:78.

[3] Elkannah Settle, Preface to *Absalom Senior: or Achitophel Transpros'd* (London, 1682).

[4] John Dryden, *A Parallel of Poetry and Painting*, in *Essays of John Dryden*, ed. W. P. Ker (New York, 1961), 2:146.

anachronism, and modes, genres, and styles (what Claudio Guillén calls "literary systems") actually change their character as a matter of course. In the literature of his own age Dryden sees an essential flexibility in representation: modal and stylistic range counter generic rigidity.[5] In the *Discourse Concerning Satire*, he even goes so far as to challenge conventional Horatian wisdom on satiric "lowness":

> But how come Lowness of Style and the Familiarity of Words to be so much the Propriety of Satire, that without them, a Poet can be no more a Satirist, than without Risibility he can be a Man? . . . If *Horace* refus'd the pains of Numbers, and the loftiness of Figures, are they bound to follow so ill a Precedent? Let him walk a Foot, with his Pad in his Hand, for his own pleasure; but let not them be accounted no Poets, who choose to mount, and shew their Horsmanship.[6]

Later in the *Discourse*, Dryden makes his famous observation on Boileau's *Le Lutrin*, pointing out that, when well-executed, heroic counterfeits are but a species of the higher forms of heroic poetry.[7] Although he is the most elegant theorist of satire in the century, some of Dryden's better ideas had been anticipated and put into practice by others. In 1666 Dryden wrote *Annus Mirabilis*, an heroic-historical poem on the great fire of London and a victory at sea over the Dutch. A year later, when the English lost a famous sea battle, Andrew Marvell turned Dryden's perspective. In his *Last Instructions to A Painter*, he forged a re-

---

[5] In his essay, "The Augustan Mode in English Poetry," *Eighteenth-Century Studies* 1 (1967): 3-32, Ralph Cohen describes (among several features of Augustan poetry) the "organizational strategy of the inherited mixed form, with its varied tones or varied speakers, varied poetic features, varied political and social attitudes, implying a social and natural world in exhilarating, anxious, or dangerous change." Cohen sees the mixed form as a negotiating strategy in the two major generic systems of the period, the Georgic-descriptive poem and the satiric poem.

[6] Dryden, *Discourse*, 4:78.   [7] Dryden, *Discourse*, 4:85.

placement not only for Dryden's *Annus Mirabilis* but for the historical subgenre or "instructions to a painter" poems intended as Stuart panegyric. Marvell's *Last Instructions* are *last* in two senses: latest, hence the most recent accommodation of contingent event to historical narrative; and last, hence final, as befits a satirically revealed scene of fraud and folly. Satire is the last word in heroic fashion.

In his *Last Instructions* Marvell included a panel from a semiserious poem, *The Loyall Scot*, in which he portrayed the heroism of Lord Douglas in defending his ship against the 1667 incursion up the Thames by the Dutch Admiral De Ruyter. Marvell notices the double response to contingent events and the implied modal crossover in recording them. He writes of "Worth Heroick or Heroick Crimes" (l. 241). The chiasmus is strategic—in all Marvell's major political poems, both heroism and heroic enormity are matters of timing. Worth can sometimes sanction criminality, but the untimely abrogation of heroic power is as bad as its excessive tyrannic abuse. Heroism is circumstance. Isolated from appropriate expression, it can look absurd. And it is a subtle satiric mind that sees a kind of criminal barbarity in heroic absurdity. In *The Growth of Popery and Arbitrary Government*, Marvell writes of the misappropriation of power: "For by how much a thing is more false and unreasonable, it requires more cruelty to establish it: and to introduce that which is absurd, there must be somewhat that is barbarous."[8]

Marvell's *Last Instructions* reviews a state conspiracy in crimes of greed, collective guilt, paranoia, lust, improperly allocated monies and taxes, poor defense planning, and shameful bureaucratic scapegoating.[9] The important

[8] Andrew Marvell, *The Growth of Popery and Arbitrary Government*, in *The Works of Andrew Marvell*, ed. Alexander B. Grosart (London, 1873), 4:255.

[9] For a review of the historical circumstances surrounding this trying episode in English history, see P. G. Rogers, *The Dutch in the Medway* (Oxford, 1970). Alan S. Fisher, "The Augustan Marvell: *The Last Instructions to a Painter*," *ELH* 38 (1971): 223-238, sees the literary strategy of the poem in terms of the bureaucratic fiasco and writes: "His [Marvell's] demonstra-

scenes of the poem, the Excise debates in Parliament and the naval invasion up the Thames, are separated by months in actual historical sequence, but they conveniently overlap as satiric "instructions." Marvell reserves his mock-epic machinery for a parody of the parliamentary debates over the funding of an impossible land war on the Continent while he presents the invasion by sea as a pastoral epithalamion, the absurd marriage of violated rivers, the Thames and Medway.[10] The debates have the trappings of battle; the battle has the trappings of parody. The chicanery of Parliament is glorified by the heroic; the necessarily heroic resembles a regatta on the Thames. Admiral De Ruyter meets little resistance, so he participates in the only action available to him: he sports with water nymphs. The violator ceremoniously takes his pleasure.

> *Ruyter* the while, that had our Ocean curb'd,
> Sail'd now among our Rivers undisturb'd:
> Survey'd their Crystal Streams, and Banks so green,
> And Beauties e're this never naked seen.
> Through the vain sedge the bashful *Nymphs* he ey'd
> Bosomes, and all which from themselves they hide.
> The Sun much brighter, and the Skies more clear,
> He finds the Air, and all things, sweeter here.
> The sudden change, and such a tempting sight,
> Swells his old Veins with fresh Blood, fresh Delight.
> Like am'rous Victors he begins to shave,
> And his new Face looks in the *English* Wave.
> His sporting Navy all about him swim,
> And witness their complaisance in their trim.
>
> (Ll. 523-534)

tion comes from the way heroic *convention* acts upon things that do not exactly belong in a heroic context" (p. 232).

[10] Marvell recalls the Spenserian marriage of the rivers Thames and Medway in the *Faerie Queene*, IV, xi. For a discussion of the allusion in the full context of the *Last Instructions*, see Michael Holahan's dissertation, "The Poet and the Civic Crown: The Theme of Political Participation in the Poetry of Andrew Marvell" (Yale University, 1967).

De Ruyter's ravishment of England's spaces defines not so much the intent of the perpetrator as the willingness of the perpetrated. The absence of one force defines the presence of another. The first sound of Dutch gunfire sends the English viewers from the shore, running back to the safety of the court and town, running out on the heroic action. That De Ruyter ravishes the land is not so important as the fact that he can do whatever he pleases. And he can do so because England is heroically (and financially) spent, her body (land, water, defenses, commercial lifelines) raped, her inheritance as a naval power diminished.

Marvell leads up to the generic condition of the poem by beginning with a series of court portraits. His strategy is to represent the decaying body of heroic lineaments, and he opens with the King's ambassador to France, Henry Jermyn, Earl of St. Albans. The Earl has inherited a title from Francis Bacon, but he has debased Bacon's interests: "Well he the Title of St. *Albans* bore, / For never *Bacon* study'd Nature more" (ll. 35-36). A more telling portrait is reserved for Anne Hyde, the King's sister-in-law and the daughter of his recently dismissed first minister. Anne is of Diana's ilk, a perverse pastoral nymph who "after Childbirth" can "renew a Maid" (l. 54). Like England, she "hides" her condition. What's in a name? In the portrait of Lady Castlemaine, Charles's aging mistress, the sexually profligate network continues and touches yet closer to the King. Like one of Pope's veteran "Sex of Queens," Lady Castlemaine finds herself sexually used up, passed from Charles to Jermyn to her footman. When Charles finally appears later in the poem, we are primed for his behavior. The virgin and naked image of *"England* or the *Peace"* comes to him (and he to it) in a Pharsalian vision, and in the most absurd gesture of all Charles exercises his libido as a function of state (or a function of *his* state). If De Ruyter rapes a spent victim and enemy, Charles attempts to possess his own body ("the Country is the *King"*), thus adding a kind of incest to lust.

There, as in the calm horrour all alone,
He wakes and Muses of th' uneasie Throne:
Raise up a sudden Shape with Virgins Face,
Though ill agree her Posture, Hour, or Place:
Naked as born, and her round Arms behind,
With her own Tresses interwove and twin'd:
Her mouth lockt up, a blind before her Eyes,
Yet from beneath the Veil her blushes rise;
And silent tears her secret anguish speak,
Her heart throbs, and with very shame would break.
The Object strange in him no Terrour mov'd:
He wonder'd first, then pity'd, then he lov'd:
And with kind hand he does the coy Vision press,
Whose Beauty greater seem'd by her distress;
But soon shrunk back, chill'd with her touch so cold,
And th'airy Picture vanisht from his hold.
In his deep thoughts the wonder did increase,
And he Divin'd 'twas *England* or the *Peace*.

(Ll. 889-906)

In the *Last Instructions*, the satiric perspective implies so
lost an order of things that even the elegiac is subject to
parody. Only one stylized figure remains as a kind of ves-
tige from a previous world. He is a lone and somewhat hapless Scotsman, Lord Douglas. And in the separate poem,
The Loyall Scot (part of which Marvell inserted in the *Last
Instructions*), we see all too clearly the curious relation of satire to discarded systems. Marvell requests that the dead
satirist John Cleveland step forward to praise Douglas. Although Cleveland's soul has been purged of satire in the
Elysian Fields, his praise of Douglas, as mimicked by Marvell, begins with a reference to satiric impulses: "Abruptly
he began disguising art, / As of his Satyr this had been a
part" (ll. 13-14). Marvell suggests that all praise is given
over to satire. Heroic action in the Douglas poem or the
Douglas interval becomes at best part of a memorable
code—its fate is elegiac because it exists to no real effect. As

a youth, Douglas sports with nymphs and virgins who are to reappear somewhat less innocently for De Ruyter and Charles II. Marvell depicts the scene in *Last Instructions*.

> Among the Reeds, to be espy'd by him,
> The *Nymphs* would rustle; he would forward swim.
> They sigh'd and said, Fond Boy, why so untame,
> That fly'st Love Fires, reserv'd for other Flame?
>
> (Ll. 657-660)

Marvell's language is almost painfully mannered because Douglas, even as a youth, was something of a "burnt-out" case. The flame of love is the Virgilian flame of destruction, and of course in heroic death the warrior or lover either goes out like a house of fire or swoons in a sort of post battle *tristesse*.

> And, as on Angels Heads their Glories shine,
> His burning Locks adorn his Face Divine.
> But, when in his immortal Mind he felt
> His alt'ring Form, and soder'd Limbs to melt;
> Down on the Deck he laid himself, and dy'd,
> With his dear Sword reposing by his Side.
> And, on the flaming Plank, so rests his Head,
> As one that's warm'd himself and gone to Bed.
>
> (Ll. 683-690)

The very archaism of the Douglas interlude forces a re-valuation of the later seventeenth-century heroic "scene." In one sense, the Douglas sequence barely manages to skirt bathos (or modal burlesque); in another, it allows Marvell to work a legitimate hero into a poem and world that is generically insufficient for his literary image. Douglas is a dying swan, and Marvell knows that his loss, although regrettable, does not answer to what is a greater loss in the contingent world of the poem—the loss of England's commercial and military fleet. If Douglas appears ridiculous in his heroism, Marvell directs his subversive wit less at his absurdity than at his uselessness. In the later seventeenth century, satiric narrative adapts its strategies for a changing historical order, and, reflexively, the changing historical order forces the modal adaptation of the literary structures chosen to represent it. This is precisely John Dryden's tactic in *Absalom and Achitophel*.

❖

In his *Discourse Concerning the Original and Progress of Satire*, Dryden states that corruption is a source of poetic strength. For the satirist, bad times are good times almost in the same way as recessions are a boon to bankruptcy lawyers. In reference to the peaceful Augustan age and the satirist Horace, he writes: "After all, *Horace* had the disadvantage of the Times in which he liv'd; they were better for the Man, but worse for the Satirist,"[11] and he concludes that "*Juvenal* was the greater Poet, I mean in Satire. His Thoughts are sharper, his Indignation against Vice is more vehement; his Spirit has more of the Commonwealth Genius; he treats Tyranny, and all the Vices attending it, as they deserve, with utmost rigour: And consequently, a Noble Soul is better pleas'd with a Zealous Vindicator of *Roman* Liberty; than with a Temporizing Poet, a well Manner'd Court Slave, and a Man who is often afraid of Laughing in the right place: Who is ever decent, because he is naturally servile."[12]

I focus upon what amounts to Dryden's satiric field theory because in it he realizes that the mode's double perspective invites a potential for trouble. As Dryden presents him in the *Discourse*, the satirist is at his best only when he reserves the right to be illegal (even if he chooses not to exercise that right). The *Discourse* appeared late in 1692 and he is no doubt thinking of his own "post-Augustan," nontemporizing detestation of William III, but Dryden's

[11] Dryden, *Discourse*, 4:65. [12] Dryden, *Discourse*, 4:65.

"parallel" imagination was profound, and he surely remembered the career-long charge against him as a temporizing poet, whether in support of Cromwell or the Augustan Charles II. If Horace was hampered by the propriety and enforced legality of his loyalty,[13] Augustus, perhaps a bit like Charles II, "Was not altogether so Good as he was Wise."[14] And as satirist, Dryden would do well to recognize his King's philandering as well as his King's wisdom.

The subtle, ambiguous opening of *Absalom and Achitophel* suggests that Dryden wants the best of Horatian and Juvenalian satiric worlds. He wants to write in Augustan contexts but reserves the right to measure lust against leadership. In his *Life of Plutarch* he avows that all times are perhaps alike and seeing double is but one way of seeing steadily: "For Mankind being the same in all ages, agitated by the same passions, and mov'd to action by the same interests, nothing can come to pass, but some President of the like nature has already been produc'd, so that having the causes before our eyes, we cannot easily be deceiv'd in the effects, if we have Judgment enough but to draw the parallel."[15] "Judgment enough" tells us that greatness is measured by the potential for weakness, and good times by the potential for bad. It is no accident that in *Absalom and Achitophel*, the biblical David, like his kingly types Augustus and Charles II, was also not altogether so good as he was wise.

[13] Dryden writes in the *Discourse*: "But *Augustus*, who was conscious to himself, of so many Crimes which he had committed, thought in the first place to provide for his own Reputation, by making an Edict against Lampoons and Satires, and the Authors of those defamatory Writings, which my Author *Tacitus*, from the Law-Term, calls *famosos libellos*" (4:66-67).

[14] Dryden, *Discourse*, 4:68. In his ironic *Epistle to Augustus*, Pope sensed that perhaps the equivocation was even stronger, but of course Pope's model was George II rather than Charles II.

[15] Dryden, "The Life of Plutarch," from *Plutarchs Lives*, in *The Works of John Dryden*, ed. Samuel Holt Monk and A. E. Wallace Maurer (Berkeley and Los Angeles, 1971), 17:270-271.

A HOUSE DIVIDED

In the beginning of the poem Dryden takes us to the source of a paradoxical problem: the natural bounty of kingship (whenever the reign) is satirically complicating. Promiscuous impulse threatens the economy of the successive line. Legality is at odds with one kind of nature.

> In pious times, e'r Priest-craft did begin,
> Before *Polygamy* was made a sin;
> When man, on many, multiply'd his kind,
> E'r one to one was, cursedly, confind:
> When Nature prompted, and no law deny'd
> Promiscuous use of Concubine and Bride;
> Then, *Israel*'s Monarch, after Heaven's own heart,
> His vigorous warmth did, variously, impart
> To Wives and Slaves: And, wide as his Command,
> Scatter'd his Maker's Image through the Land.[16]
>
> (Ll. 1-10)

Dryden is very much aware that even if David sanctions his actions "before" law, the parallel King, Charles II, cannot—he is of latter days. But there is a more general satiric problem embedded in these brilliant opening lines, a problem that Dryden will sustain throughout the poem.[17] All history is both sacred and profane, both outside and inside of measured time. The secular (strictly legal) measure is a fall from a more natural order. Legality is time's fiction, and there is no violation until there is law. The disjunction of nature and law and their reunion (the sacred, sanctified, and restored "body" of the King's office)[18] are

---

[16] This and all subsequent citations from *Absalom and Achitophel* are from *The Works of John Dryden*, ed. H. T. Swedenberg, Jr. and Vinton A. Dearing (Berkeley and Los Angeles, 1972), 2:3-36.

[17] The poem's opening has been treated at greater length by Earl Miner, *Dryden's Poetry* (Bloomington, 1967) and by Alan Roper, *Dryden's Poetic Kingdoms* (London, 1965).

[18] For the theory of sacred-secular kingship, see Ernst Kantorowicz, *The King's Two Bodies: A Study in Mediaeval Political Theology* (Princeton, 1957), and for a sustained reading of the bipartite structure of *Absalom and*

the narrative subjects of *Absalom and Achitophel*. The poem combines historical issue and satiric progeny, a crisis of the moment with its retrospective parallel, a necessary servility with what Dryden calls laughter in the right place, a mythographic revolution (or rounding out) with a rebellious line (a *bar sinister* or illegitimate turn to political revolt).

As a succession-satire written during the bad times of the Exclusion Crisis, *Absalom and Achitophel* is a narrative deeply concerned with the form and substance of transmission. In almost every sense, its satiric strategies are focused upon a kind of legal end-game—upon those forces in England's progressive-regressive cycles that revolt, that turn the political line around. The poem's historiographic or panegyric resources image restoration as mythographic and solar, as patterned renewal. *Restore*, of course, means "restock" or "refill." And Dryden plays upon the primary and political meaning throughout: at the end of the poem, the forms of restoration are given bodily and official substance, so that what was excluded can, in a sense, be taken back in. The action of *Absalom and Achitophel* demands a metaphoric reading because the restoration of metaphoric value is one of its subjects. Metaphor invites law to partake of symbolic transfers. The final action of the poem deliberately excludes satiric violation by reconstituting a kind of natural-political balance. Whereas it first seemed that as Absalom rose in the west David set in the east, it "turns" out otherwise. The revolt or rebellion of the son (in both senses of *son-sun*) against the father is a regressive action that belongs to those "Adam-wits" or lunatic "*Jewes*" (lunatic in the sense of counterfeit or proliferate "suns"). The cyclic curved line of restoration belongs to the sustaining and successive rituals of kingship, an office that never dies, es-

---

Achitophel, see Sanford Budick, *Poetry of Civilization: Mythopoeic Displacement in the Verse of Milton, Dryden, Pope, and Johnson* (New Haven, 1974).

pecially in a land perpetually trying to kill it. Thus, the satiric phase of the poem programs a usurpation; the mythographic phase renews a dispensation. If its complex opening creates a succession-controversy by casting doubt on the integrity of line, its ending testifies to a different sort of legitimacy—one that binds sacred and secular time, one that resolves the satiric apostasy: "Once more the Godlike *David* was Restor'd, / And willing Nations knew their Lawfull Lord" (1030-1031). "Lord" is ambiguous—it refers to David and implies God, a metaphoric restoration (or carry over) in both the typological and political sense. The kingly office *is* divine.

For Dryden, England's recent history was a series of overhasty successions by a land that kept consuming itself in revolt. The forms and allied mythography of the monarchy had been forever modified by the memory of a once divested throne and beheaded king, the father of a newly ruling son who is *not* the father of any legitimate heirs. *Absalom and Achitophel* has the backward look of a narrative that sees the satiric possibility of exclusion in the language of succession. Dryden, the Restoration apologist, may have eagerly measured a series of new time with its ceremonial and majestic trappings, but Dryden, the political satirist, is sensitive to the strains of discord. He sees and elaborates the complexities of plot in the regress of constant "plotting." For many of his contemporaries, the Restoration was less the joyful end to the Interregnum winter of discontent than an accident of historical accommodation. Even well into the next century, figures such as Daniel Defoe would have preferred that the twenty-eight year Restoration had never occurred. And it is likely that Robinson Crusoe's twenty-eight year isolation on a desert island at a time almost cotemporaneous with restored Stuart rule in England is Defoe's none-too-subtle indication that for some the Restoration itself was a kind of apostasy.

In *Absalom and Achitophel* Dryden finesses the delicate

issue of Stuart tyranny by structuring the narrative so that David might lay back from precipitous action. There are two impulses at work in the narrative: one exhausts the arguments of rebel politics; the other withholds the machinery of sacred "intentions" until the time is ready. Dryden paces the narrative between hysteria and calm, *réal politique* and royal mythography, history and ceremony. If the poem's conclusion suggests that the figure and figural components of the kingly Lord resolve the cycle of the day, the body of the narrative contains an astute and flexible review of alternative schemes for contractual authority in government, schemes that existed from the early days of the Revolution and would revive again in strength for the ouster of Charles II's Catholic brother, James II. Dryden resolves the narrative action of *Absalom and Achitophel* in favor of the Stuart succession, but theories presented in the poem will, at a later date, ironically reflect the basis of Stuart exclusion: the poem has a mythic power and, to Dryden's later dismay, a proleptic intelligence. If the future rebellion of Monmouth can be extrapolated from its fable, so too can the revolution of the murmuring *Jewes*, not at the twenty-year cycle as indicated by history but at the twenty-eight year cycle, the lunatic number, in 1688.

✧

Absalom and Achitophel derives its satiric energy from the crisis of prematurity, that is, from the restlessness of a successor figure. Dryden had the subject of prematurity on his mind even before the Exclusion Crisis. In *Mac Flecknoe* (written in the late 1670s, although not published until after *Absalom and Achitophel*) another succession takes place too soon, in this instance at the request of a long-winded monarch who, like Lear, wants to hold onto the requisites of office even after he has given up the office itself. Dryden's king (Richard Flecknoe) is "blest with issue of a large increase" (l. 8), and he seeks to "settle the succession of the

State" (l. 10) on his son (Mac Flecknoe). Throughout the satire Dryden plays on the images of weight and line—that which is heavy drops, that which is sizeable displaces. In an earlier poem, *Fleckno, an English Priest at Rome*, Andrew Marvell had pictured Richard Flecknoe, a "Basso *Relievo* of a Man" (l. 63), as stuck between the railings of a staircase in Rome, and Dryden continues the joke with the enormous Mac Flecknoe (Shadwell), whose promised succession allows space for filial heaviness or "filial dullness" (l. 136).

The father-king chooses his successor not on the basis of primogeniture but according to the formulaic folk-tale pattern of inheritance—in Mac Flecknoe's case a kind of appropriate capacity. Flecknoe ponders "which of all his Sons was fit / To Reign, and wage immortal War with Wit" (ll. 11-12). No contest. King Flecknoe can be sure that all will fall into place. The controlling conceit in the poem's inheritance is that more of nothing adds up to less: "Of his Dominion may no end be known, / And greater than his Father's be his Throne" (ll. 141-142). Mac Flecknoe fulfills the promise of dulness by betraying the promise of art. His father says "Thou art my blood, where *Johnson* has no part; / What share have we in Nature or in Art?" (ll. 175-176). He gets an appropriately theatrical answer at the end of the poem when the "yet declaiming Bard" is prematurely shot through a trapdoor, thus affecting the ceremony of linear descent while literally descending. Art is the spirit of nature.

> Sinking he left his Drugget robe behind,
> Born upwards by a subterranean wind.
> The Mantle fell to the young Prophet's part,
> With double portion of his Father's Art.
>
> (Ll. 214-217)

In *Mac Flecknoe* the notion of premature succession is allied with a kind of comic or farcical satire, while in *Absalom and Achitophel* such notions are allied with a deeper sense of satiric history or even tragic irony. In the poem, Achitophel speaks a crucial line to Absalom—a line that confuses inheritable time: "But try your Title while your Father lives" (l. 462). In the normal rituals of inheritance donation is a postponed promise, although in some prearranged instances it replaces testamentary inheritance so that the son will come into his estate early, often at marriage. To fulfill the promise of inheritance while the father is still alive alleviates the strain on the son waiting to receive it or the threat of the son planning to take it. Achitophel goes a step further—he advises that the donation be assumed before given. Revolution or usurpation affronts the natural course of things, but Achitophel, tempter that he is, perverts the logic of inheritance.

> Believe me, Royal Youth, thy Fruit must be,
> Or gather'd Ripe, or rot upon the Tree.
> Heav'n, has to all allotted, soon or late,
> Some lucky Revolution of their Fate:
>
> (Ll. 250-253)

The scene recalls the temptation to partake of forbidden fruit, and Achitophel is intent on making the moment of truth more important than the consequences. He wishes to substitute political revolution for the slower revolutions of the natural order. Or to put it another way, he wants to make the premature seem naturally timed. Of David, Achitophel says:

> Had thus Old *David*, from whose Loyns you spring,
> Not dar'd, when Fortune call'd him, to be King,
> At *Gath* an Exile he might still remain,
> And heavens Anointing Oyle had been in vain.
> Let his successfull Youth your hopes engage,
> But shun th' example of Declining Age:
> Behold him setting in his Western Skies,
> The Shadows lengthning as the Vapours rise.
> He is not now, as when on *Jordan*'s Sand

The Joyfull People throng'd to see him Land,
Cov'ring the *Beach*, and blackning all the *Strand*:
But, like the Prince of Angels from his height,
Comes tumbling downward with diminish'd light.

(Ll. 262-274)

The satanic Achitophel has made a rebel angel out of
David. He sets his life and times in motion from east to
west: he represents him in decline, and he parodies the
eastern beachhead at the beginning of David's reign by its
spatial and temporal western displacement near the end of
it. Achitophel's argument seems a powerful one only because David has similar feelings himself. He, too, represents Absalom as Adamic, but he resists temptation for a
more general cyclic praise: "His motions all accompanied
with grace; / And *Paradise* was open'd in his face. / With secret Joy, indulgent *David* view'd / His Youthfull Image in
his Son renew'd" (ll. 29-32). David's nature supports the
counterfeit cycle of renewal: son in sun. After all, his
legitimate line is stymied by "A Soyl ungratefull to the Til-
ler's care" (l. 12). Absalom, "Whether, inspir'd by some di-
viner Lust, / His Father got him with a greater Gust; / Or
that his Conscious destiny made way / By manly beauty to
Imperiall sway" (ll. 19-22), seems "ready" in all senses. Furthermore, Achitophel works hard to suggest to Absalom
that he maintain his independent "being" and exchange
filial allegiance for legal power.

Urge now your Piety, your Filial Name,
A Father's Right, and fear of future Fame;
The publick Good, that Universal Call,
To which even Heav'n Submitted, answers all,
Nor let his Love Enchant your generous Mind;
'Tis Natures trick to Propogate her Kind.
Our fond Begetters, who woud never dye,
Love but themselves in their Posterity.

(Ll. 419-426)

Self-perpetuation is a vainglorious inheritance, and Achitophel makes Absalom a freak of David's ego. But the counterfeit will not work. The premature succession misses the prime, demythologizes the perfect circle of revolution to which the mythos of the poem is obedient. Of course, Achitophel tries to replicate the sacred cycle and mimic the course of the sun in arranging Absalom's magnificent (but secular) tour of the land from east to west.

> The Croud, (that still believe their Kings oppress)
> With lifted hands their young *Messiah* bless:
> Who now begins his Progress to ordain;
> With Chariots, Horsemen, and a numerous train:
> From East to West his Glories he displaies:
> And, like the Sun, the promis'd land survays.
> Fame runs before him, as the morning Star;
> And shouts of Joy salute him from afar:
> Each house receives him as a Guardian God;
> And Consecrates the Place of his aboad.
>
> (Ll. 727-736)

This is very near idolatry, and the counterfeit progress is both a political and a religious blasphemy. Earlier in the poem we learned that not only Absalom as manipulated by Achitophel but the people themselves seemed on the wrong cyclic track: "For, govern'd by the *Moon*, the giddy *Jews* / Tread the same track when she the Prime renews: / And once in twenty Years, their Scribes Record, / By natural Instinct they change their Lord" (ll. 216-219). The people, like the moon, revolve too fast on impulse, and Absalom is in danger of coming under a lunatic spell by imitating (or reflecting) the light of the sun: "Why then shoud I, Encouraging the Bad, / Turn Rebell, and run Popularly Mad?" (ll. 335-336). He realizes that "The People might assert their Liberty; / But what was Right in them, were Crime in me" (ll. 341-342).

David comes to something of the same conclusion. Although he is tortured by his queen's inability to produce an heir and thus allow for the legal renewal of succession, he comes to recognize that Absalom for all his glory is not properly "turned" out: "Had God ordain'd his fate for Empire born, / He woud have given his Soul another turn" (ll. 963-964). Absalom is not primary, and David does not intend to donate the crown prematurely. Such a gesture would undermine the inheritable line and convert succession into usurpation. David will not make Lear's mistake: "Without my Leave a future King to choose, / Infers a Right the Present to Depose" (ll. 979-980). Instead, he has already begun to set matters back on proper course. After "long revolving, in his carefull Breast" (l. 934), he inverts the order of the testaments—he is by necessity first merciful and then just. Speaking to the nation, he says: "Yet, since they will divert my Native course, / 'Tis time to shew I am not Good by Force" (ll. 949-950). It is a credit to Absalom's good nature (the same cannot be said of his biblical analogue) that he had already figured out his position before his father laid down the law. He treats his claim to the throne not as "ready" but as necessarily too ripe. His filial instincts tell him to put his rebellious impulses in arrears, and in a gesture of renunciation he disinherits himself, although with political reservations.

> I mourn, my Countrymen, your lost Estate;
> Tho far unable to prevent your fate:
> Behold a Banisht man, for your dear cause
> Expos'd a prey to Arbitrary laws!
> Yet oh! that I alone cou'd be undone,
> Cut off from Empire, and no more a Son!
> (Ll. 698-703)

Absalom is a bit of a trimmer. Politically he does not place much legal stock in divine right inheritance, which is mocked by Achitophel as "a Successive Title, Long, and Dark, / Drawn from the Mouldy Rolls of *Noah*'s Ark" (ll. 301-302). But neither would he be moved to tyrannicide (and patricide): "Were he a Tyrant who, by Lawless Might,

/ Opprest the *Jews*, and Rais'd the *Jebusite*, / Well might I Mourn; but Natures Holy Bands / Woud Curb my Spirits, and Restrain my Hands" (ll. 337-340). It could be argued that Absalom's final words in the poem ("And, tis my wish, the next Successors Reign / May make no other *Israelite* complain," ll. 721-722) are tinged with ambiguity, since the succession of James II would (and did) make the English uneasy, but there is no doubt (at least in Dryden's version of the fable) that Absalom does *not* intend to seize the day and subvert the encircling line: "No Court Informer can these Arms accuse, / These Arms may Sons against their Fathers use" (ll. 719-720). What was to happen in four years time, nephew against uncle, is literally not Dryden's problem in his depiction of son and father.

The status of David's brother is of interest in the narrative action, however, because of his collateral place in the line of succession. Absalom is resigned enough to his probable fate, but the mere existence of collateral line seems particularly galling to him.

> What more can I expect while *David* lives?
> All but his Kingly Diadem he gives;
> And that: But there he Paus'd; then Sighing, said,
> Is Justly Destin'd for a Worthier Head.
> For when my Father from his Toyls shall Rest,
> And late Augment the Number of the Blest:
> His Lawfull Issue shall the Throne ascend,
> Or the *Collateral* Line where that shall end.
>
> (Ll. 345-352)

Absalom goes on to praise David's brother (the Duke of York in the parallel), but the sentiments are more Dryden's than Absalom's. Along with Lear's Edmund, Absalom would rather stand up for bastards.

> Why am I Scanted by a Niggard Birth?
> My Soul Disclaims the Kindred of her Earth:

And made for Empire, Whispers me within;
Desire of Greatness is a Godlike Sin.
(Ll. 369-372)

Achitophel sees an opening at this point in the temptation. Perhaps Absalom can be made to adopt the "readiness
is all" argument for seizing power if that same argument
seems directed against him by his uncle: "Then the next
Heir, a Prince, Severe and Wise, / Already looks on you
with Jealous Eyes; / Sees through the thin Disguises of your
Arts, / And markes your Progress in the Peoples Hearts"
(ll. 441-444). Kill or be killed, Achitophel advises: "Your
Case no tame Expedients will afford; / Resolve on Death, or
Conquest by the Sword" (ll. 455-456). He tries to embed
the fear of uncle-nephew rivalry in Absalom's psyche, a
fear familiar in myth and literature from the legends of
Osiris, Oedipus, and Hamlet. Further, he confounds the
King's inability to produce a legitimate heir with the legacy
in store for the bastard son. His metaphoric formulation is
wonderfully duplicitous: "He to his Brother gives Supreme
Command; / To you a Legacy of Barren Land" (ll. 437-
438). These lines immediately follow Achitophel's epi-
grammatic rendering of the true nature of the satiric succession and the line of revolt: " 'Tis after God's own heart
to Cheat his Heir" (l. 436). As a satiric figure, Achitophel is
regressive—he blames the father and not the son. His appeal is to the primal moment in yet another sense—to a
primal Freudian moment of necessary rebellion where patricide is the outgrowth of generational rivalry.

The title of Dryden's narrative—like the title of another
famous narrative based on 2 Samuel, Faulkner's *Absalom,
Absalom!*—announces the struggle of fathers and sons. It is
an anguished struggle, perhaps because succession itself is
not an easy thing. Dryden centers the action of the poem
around David and Absalom, but he constructs a counter
panel or antithetical pair in Achitophel and his son.

Achitophel's son is the primordial notion of his father's spirit, "Got, while his Soul did hudled Notions try; / And born a shapeless Lump, like Anarchy" (ll. 171-172). It is the nature of Achitophel's satiric being to curse and be cursed by posterity: "A Name to all Succeeding Ages Curst" (l. 151). His name is father to bad times. Weary of body and with an overactive mind ("Restless, unfixt in Principles and Place," l. 154), Achitophel is satiric antimatter. He is so enervated ("Bankrupt of Life, yet Prodigal of Ease," l. 168) that he is used up: "A fiery Soul, which working out its way, / Fretted the Pigmy Body to decay" (ll. 156-157). He has nothing left to give his son, nothing of David's greater gusto for "that unfeather'd, two Leg'd thing, a Son" (l. 170). Achitophel's son is born lumpish—unformed and unformable, as the chaotic state before the dispensation of inheritable form.[19]

Absalom and Achitophel portrays one more father-son pair, that of the old-line Royalist family, the Butlers (figured in Barzillai, the Duke of Ormonde, and in the Duke's son, Thomas Butler, Earl of Ossory). The Butlers are victims of a fated line that should have continued by all natural rights but that was cut off in one sense by providence and in another by a kind of symbolic doom, almost as if the very age insults those whom Dryden pictures as too good for it. The Butler sequence in *Absalom and Achitophel* recalls the brief panegyric in the *Aeneid* for the snuffed-out line of Marcellus. It is always a bitter thing in a promising line for the progenitor to outlive his progeny. For Barzillai or Ormonde:

> Large was his Wealth, but larger was his Heart:
> Which, well the Noblest Objects knew to choose,
> The Fighting Warriour, and Recording Muse.

---

[19] The notes in the *Works of Dryden* state: "In Dryden's usage, *Lump* is likely to refer to the soulless body or to the primordial matter of chaos. Cf. his *Translation of the Latter Part of the Third Book of Lucretius*, l. 10: 'The lifeless Lump, uncoupled from the mind' " (II, 249).

His Bed coud once a Fruitfull Issue boast:
Now more than half a Father's Name is lost:
His Eldest Hope, with every Grace adorn'd,
By me (so Heav'n will have it) always Mourn'd,
And always honour'd, snatcht in Manhoods prime
By' unequal Fates, and Providences crime:
Yet not before the Goal of Honour won,
All parts fulfill'd of Subject and of Son;
Swift was the Race, but short the Time to run.
Oh Narrow Circle, but of Pow'r Divine,
Scanted in Space, but perfect in thy Line!

(Ll. 826-839)

Ossory's life is another premature cycle, but as Dryden draws it, it is more truly noble (and more cruelly circumspect) than Absalom's grandiose turn for the west. *Absalom and Achitophel* portrays three succession crises: David has no legitimate son; Achitophel has one who, like him, is formally deficient; and Barzillai has one who is dead. In *Plutarch's Lives*, which he dedicated to the Duke of Ormonde, Dryden writes of the Butlers as bulwarks against a satiric order:

> Tis an age indeed, which is only fit for Satyr; and the sharpest I have shall never be wanting to launce its Villanies, and its ingratitude to the Government: There are few Men in it, who are capable of supporting the weight of a just and deserv'd commendation: But amongst those few there must always stand excepted the Illustrious Names of *Ormond* and of *Ossory*: A Father and a Son, only Worthy of each other.[20]

The memory of a worthy son and a worthy father is high praise from Dryden who sees in such a pairing the integrity of the historical order. A little later in the same dedication to Ormonde, Dryden reflects on the nature of political

[20] Dryden, "Dedication to Ormond," *Plutarchs Lives*, 17:229.

crisis and on the crucial model of filial inheritance. By way
of compliment to the performance of Ormonde as lord
lieutenant in Ireland (a performance that apparently
pleased Dryden more than the Irish)[21] we hear of Irish and
English fathers and sons:

> The Crime of Rebellion was common to both Coun-
> tries; but the repentance of one Island has been steady;
> that of the other, to its shame, has suffer'd a relapse:
> Which shews the Conversions of their Rebels to have
> been real, that of ours to have been but counterfeit.
> The Sons of Guilty Fathers there have made amends
> for the disloyalty of their Families: But here the de-
> scendants of pardon'd Rebels have only waited their
> time to copy the wickedness of their Parents, and if
> possible to outdo it: They disdain to hold their Pat-
> rimonies by acts of Grace and of Indemnity: and by
> maintaining their old Treasonable principles, make it
> apparent that they are still speculative Traytors.[22]

Perhaps thinking of his own shift in loyalty from Cromwell to Charles II, Dryden sees intractability as the nation's
potential for treachery or for bastardy acting its part. In
Absalom and Achitophel he gives us a narrative of frustrated
fathers and brooding sons. And in a way that Dryden
would not have wished to predict, the elegy for Ossory
forecasts the death of another son in four years' time
(Absalom-Monmouth). To reconstitute history's disap-
pointed lines, Dryden ends the poem with an act possible

---

[21] Dryden may not have known that Charles II tried to rid himself of his
loyal supporter, Ormonde, by claiming him (and his performance as lord
lieutenant) an embarrassment. The King was reported to have said within
earshot of his courtiers: "Yonder comes Ormonde; I have done all I can to
dislodge that man, and to make him as discontented as others, but he will
not be out of humour with me, he will be loyal in spite of my teeth" (*Dictionary of National Biography*, entry on James Butler, Earl of Ormonde, p.
511).

[22] Dryden, "Dedication to Ormond," *Plutarchs Lives*, 17:231.

only in the pageantry of an undying monarchy or in the vitality of a solar myth: David, having fathered no legitimate son, renews himself in his lordly image. He inscribes the poem's conflicts, and he inscribes himself as its principle of continuity.

✧

As a parallel history, *Absalom and Achitophel* brings the source (or precursor) to the forefront. In the plan of the poem, the older biblical story is ongoing, whereas the contemporary events it parallels are recessed. For Dryden posterity is always rear-guarded. But the selection of a biblical fable for *Absalom and Achitophel* is historical in a number of ongoing senses. If seventeenth century England wavered as the land of the marvelous heroic romance, her great poets and her most vociferous factions seized onto typed patterns of sacred biblical history as a kind of prophetic repetition. In ways variously radical and conserving, the English and England were chosen people, a land in bondage, a nation seeking its proper covenant, a backsliding, murmuring host, a saving remnant, a place for prophets, martyrs, self-sacrificers, and second comers. Enfabled in types, England's providence is both the beginning and the end of the narrative-historical line, the national *telos*.

Providential design accommodates what is destined in living history: to the extent that God's plans are reenacted in time, there is no real disjunction between a providential past and an historical present. Since typology sanctions providential "readings," it offers a continuous sense of history. Unlike heroic romance, providential narratives cannot be accused of conserving atypical values.[23] Local condi-

---

[23] This is partly the position of Abraham Cowley when he argues that the ancient heroic subjects and the medieval chivalric conventions do not satisfy an ongoing heritage as powerfully as do testamentary narratives: "Why will not the actions of *Sampson* afford as plentiful matter as the

tions are easily subsumed in the greater scheme of time. In the hands of its more supple practitioners, typology becomes a sanctioned resource, a way of expanding limited options.[24] "If these be the times," Marvell writes of Cromwell, "this be the man." For poets such as Milton, Marvell, and Dryden, typology generates something equivalent to the older classical idea of *copia* or fullness by rounding out actions or, at least, *fulfilling* them in the most promising sense.

As is well known, Dryden is not the first to have seized upon the biblical story of David, Absalom, and Achitophel—his is only the culminating effort in a minitradition of contemporary typological historiography.[25] Although Dryden pillages Samuel, Kings, and Chronicles for his rogue's gallery of factionalists and his pantheon of loyalists, the more troubling and more interesting nature of the biblical fable is its evocation of the inevitable and perhaps irreconcilable sense of extended crisis. To read through the whole of 1 and 2 Samuel is to experience a narrative account that cannot be so readily concentrated, adapted, and resolved as Dryden artfully does in the parallels of *Absalom*

Labors of *Hercules*? why is not *Jephtha's Daughter* as *good a woman* as *Iphigenia*, and the friendship of *David* and *Jonathan* more worthy celebration then that of *Theseus* and *Perithous*? Does not the passage of *Moses* and the *Israelites* into the *Holy Land* yield incomparably more Poetical variety then the voyages of *Ulysses* or *Æneas*? Are the obsolete threadbare tales of *Thebes* and *Troy* half so stored with great, heroical, and supernatural actions (since *Verse* will needs *finde* or *make* such) as the wars of *Joshua*, of *David*, and divers others?" See "Preface to Poems," in *Critical Essays of the Seventeenth Century*, ed. J. E. Spingarn (Bloomington, 1957), 2:89.

[24] See, for example, Barbara Lewalski's study of Miltonic typology in *Milton's Brief Epic* (Providence, 1966) or Stephen Zwicker's study of political typology in *Dryden's Political Poetry: The Typology of King and Nation* (Providence, 1972). Both of these critics have essays in the collection, *Literary Uses of Typology from the Late Middle Ages to the Present*, ed. Earl Miner (Princeton, 1977).

[25] The other natural possibility, of course, was Charles I as Saul, Cromwell as David, and Charles II as Solomon. See the headnote and notes in the *Works of Dryden*, 2:230-233.

and Achitophel. But if Dryden hedges a few parallel bets, he
also expects his readers to do a little work on their own. His
poem is but part *of* a whole, and to read it as part *for* the
whole is to miss some of its finer ironies. While the established and coded parallels between Davidic and English Interregnum and Restoration history are striking ("Now
there was long war between the house of Saul and the
house of David but David waxed stronger and stronger,
and the house of Saul waxed weaker and weaker," 2 Sam.
3:1), Dryden's adaptation is far from slavishly exact. For
one thing, in the biblical account the level of violence and
slaughter, mostly internecine, is much greater than Dryden's poem will strategically accommodate. For another,
the biblical action provides David with a successor figure,
Solomon, who was to play a generative role in Jewish saving history. From the opening lines of *Absalom and Achitophel*, Dryden plays down the violence, exacerbates the legal
niceties of succession, and virtually ignores the matter of
Solomon.

But the memory of antecedent biblical events is nonethe-
less an important presence in Dryden's narrative. What he
omits tells an admonitory story of its own. There is barely
an event in the biblical sequence that is untinged by incest,
murder, blood vengeance, massacre, wanton disregard of
God's ordinance, self-pity, indulgence, weakness, and
greed.[26] Even Achitophel is tainted by violent melodrama.
Already damned by David's prayer that his council be
turned to foolishness, he offers advice, and when that advice is not followed, he goes home and hangs himself. This
is but a glimpse of the biblical content. Messengers get
summarily executed for the bad news they bring; scape-

[26] Faulkner's parallel in *Absalom, Absalom!*, although its cast is modern
and its reference to the biblical account mostly allusive, catches the forsaken tone of the original story. Faulkner's sweep is wider and the saga he
relays, even if updated, is more primitive and is prior to the full trappings
of monarchy.

goats and sacrificial victims fall prey to the whim of kings; betrayals are the order of the epoch. In many ways, 1 and 2 Samuel is an indictment of historical sequence. If its plot does not focus on exclusion (the prohibition of a son or a brother from a throne upon which neither yet reigns), the biblical narration sets a more sinister and personal crisis: fratricide. Perhaps Dryden sensed the satirically displaced link between exclusion and murder; throughout *Absalom and Achitophel* he certainly implies that there is a connection between constitutional challenge and regicide.

In 1 Samuel the Elders of Israel ask that Samuel "make us a king to judge us like all the nations" (8:5). As Dryden was to acknowledge in the discourse on political authority in *Absalom and Achitophel*, the source of authority and its prerogatives are not unambiguous issues. And neither are the source and nature of judgment. For the Israelites the problem turns not merely on the king judging his people but on the people's God judging their king. The reciprocity of the process is one reason that the sequence in 1 and 2 Samuel was of political significance not only to Royalists in England but to constitutionalists as well. Dryden would not wish to include the passage where Samuel warns the Israelites: "This will be the manner of the king that shall reign over you: He will take your sons, and appoint them for himself, for his chariots, and to be his horsemen; and some shall run before his chariots" (1 Sam. 8:11). With kingship comes war, tyranny, and greed. The prophet Samuel continues to warn of appropriation and bloody violence, but the people court the monarchy. Fervent Royalist interpreters remember only that the Israelites wish for a king. They tend to forget what Dryden has only briefly suppressed: that the crisis of authority is an all too reenactable one in Western history.

As much as Dryden feared crises of authority, he recognized the principles of their origin, principles brought to bear on his more general reading of the events in 1 and 2

Samuel and on the specific events represented in *Absalom and Achitophel*. Briefly formulated: authority is in a state of crisis when nature and law recoil in the face of each other. From his early heroic plays to his later *Fables*, Dryden returns again and again to the confrontation or confusion of nature and law. The opening of *Absalom and Achitophel* is set back in natural time ("When Nature prompted, and no law deny'd," l. 5), somewhat like Dryden's translated version of the Virgilian Golden Age when the only laws were those "Impos'd by Nature, and by Nature's Cause" (*Georgics*, I, 92). To force legality upon nature is to introduce some form of authority or limiting power, as when Cortez arrives amidst the Aztecs' *"pleasant* Indian *Country"* to "unteach what Nature taught" (*The Indian Emperour*, I, i, 14). The sword is a great instructor. Law as authority is a belated phenomenon, but paradoxically there is an even more barbaric potential in it: violence. Such was Samuel's god-given insight in the Old Testament.

To say that Dryden wishes to "two-time" the action in his narrative by beginning before law and revealing the natural David before the authoritative David ("So willing to forgive th' Offending Age, / So much the Father did the King asswage," ll. 941-942) is to misrepresent the matter slightly. In one sense, the poem begins in sacred time so that David can return and redeem those times, yet the only law David predates is monogamy. In contrast, the biblical account begins with a strong statement of another interdicted law. Although it is not material that Dryden wishes to dwell upon, the Absalom story in Samuel begins with the rape of his sister Tamar, who sets the tone for the sequence to follow by reminding her attacker, Amnon, that such violations bear blighted fruit. Sexual license is treated very differently in Samuel than by Dryden. Tamar lays down the law: "And she answered him, Nay, my brother, do not force me; for no such thing ought to be done in Israel: do not thou this folly" (2 Sam. 13:12). For Dryden, on the other hand, David's sexual folly is a lesser violation, partly because in the teasing time scheme of the poem's opening David's license is a kind of second nature. Nature without law is always indulgent, and law does not know about such things as the gusto of conception. But neither does nature know the measure of such things as strict legal succession. Dryden's first several couplets tease time in yet another way. Even if David can legally turn to nature for love, Charles II cannot. Charles has a real succession crisis on his hands, a crisis only fabricated by Dryden for David—certainly it is never mentioned as a pressing legal matter in 2 Samuel. The ensuing plot of the poem evolves from the confusing necessity at the beginning: succession forces nature to act legally, that is, authoritatively. Tellingly, it is Absalom who sees the confusion of David's nature—the tenderness to an "illegal" son perverts the structure of authority, and David's second nature is antagonistic to his legal self: "And all his pow'r against himself employs" (l. 712).

That Dryden creates a temporal dialectic for the poem (timeless nature; temporal law) is conveyed by a shifting series of mythographic and historical parallels. The Davidic analogy is not enough. In scattering his maker's image throughout the land, David is typed as Adam. Adam conveniently lived in two times, paradisiacal and post-lapsarian, and Dryden wants to suggest that, in a way, this is David's problem too. Further, David nostalgically refers to Absalom as himself renewed and thus as another Adamic man: "And *Paradise* was open'd in his face" (l. 30). The metaphoric logic makes David, as Absalom's progenitor, a kind of godhead, removing him from time entirely. As Dryden will later realize when he traces the problem of authority back to Eden ("How then coud *Adam* bind his future Race? /. How coud his forfeit on mankind take place?" ll. 771-772), a recession into mythic time can define the origins of law as well as nature. And in this sense (to repeat an observation of Louis Bredvold's about Dryden), law "must save human nature from itself."[27]

If Dryden turns Hobbist, natural man turns perpetual rebel. Absalom's followers fall back into a time unblessed by law but damned because in need of it. Dryden calls the rebel factions in the narrative "Adam-wits"; they do not recede into sacred time but rather into the caves of Hobbes's state of nature where license is regress: "They led their wild desires to Wood and Caves, / And thought that all but Savages were Slaves" (ll. 55-56). In the poem's longer discourse on politics, Dryden makes the same point about the people's license: "If they may Give and Take when e'er they please, / Not Kings alone, (the Godheads Images,) / But Government it self at length must fall / To Natures state; where all have Right to all" (ll. 791-794). Thus, if the myth of Eden (Paradise opened in Absalom's face) has been replaced by the myth of violent nature, any kind of restoration is going to have to recreate a version of sacred time. Of course, this is precisely what happens in the scheme of the poem when at the end David proclaims "a Series of new time" (l. 1028), perhaps a final satiric joke at the expense of his own historical era, infamous for revolutions and for new models *in* time.

In addition to the typological scheme of nature and law in *Absalom and Achitophel*, Dryden suggests that historical necessity requires movement from natural rest to legal action. As father, David idles away his image as king; as king, he wills events—his office takes over where his son fails him. The idle king at the beginning is counterfeited into an "idol" king by the murmuring Jews—idol in both the sense of empty and falsely worshipped.

> Those very *Jewes*, who, at their very best,
> Their Humour more than Loyalty exprest,

[27] Louis I. Bredvold, *The Intellectual Milieu of John Dryden* (Ann Arbor, 1934), p. 145.

Now, wondred why, so long, they had obey'd
An Idoll Monarch which their hands had made:
Thought they might ruine him they could create;
Or melt him to that Golden Calf, a State.
(Ll. 61-66)

Dryden's subtle suggestion at the beginning of the poem is that David has set himself up. His own idleness is nature run rampant, not unlike his own people, "God's pamper'd people whom, debauch'd with ease, / No King could govern, nor no God could please" (ll. 47-48). In Dryden's flexible mythology, the timeless "idyll" of nature's state is close to license. By not acting David has become an idol. The empty space of his authoritative being is temporarily filled by another idle fabrication, a plot.

The Good old Cause reviv'd, a Plot requires.
Plots, true or false, are necessary things,
To raise up Commonwealths, and ruin Kings.
(Ll. 82-84)

The Popish Plot, a scheme born of Catholic dispossession and nurtured by parliamentary ambition, does what all good plots ought to do: it conspires against action. The embellishments of plot lead only to ruin. Implying more than it could ever explain, the plot in *Absalom and Achitophel* is an event that awaits reaction from an institutionally careful King.[28] David moves into position only at the end of the narrative. As a man, his impulses are paternal (father assuages king); as a monarch, his impulses are monumental

---

[28] Charles II could afford to bide his time for reasons that Dryden did not know. On 22 May 1670 Charles and Louis XIV of France negotiated the Treaty of Dover that stipulated, among other provisions, that should Charles declare himself Catholic, at an appropriate time he would be funded and supported by French troops. Charles's reluctance to act quickly against the Popish Plot was understandable, but the Exclusion Bill was another matter entirely. On that issue it was in his immediate interests to act forcefully, which he did. See the note on the Triple Alliance in the *Works of Dryden*, 2:249.

("Kings are the publick Pillars of the State," l. 953). No longer idle or an idol, he balances his natural and legal constituencies, ends his "revenge delay'd" (l. 940), and acts by diverting what he calls his native course into its regal channel: "But 'tis to Rule, for that's a Monarch's End" (l. 946). Although Samuel Johnson complained that *Absalom and Achitophel* suffered from an incomplete plot, its action is perfect in some ways. Succession, which is the narrative's putative subject and occasion, demands the balancing of nature and law. The mythos of the poem allows for renewal in kingship or inclines "the Ballance to the better side" (l. 76). When the King indulges his body and ignores his office, the action is subject to a sort of vertigo, an unresisted and unstable course, the course of the plotters: "But wilde Ambition loves to slide, not stand; / And Fortunes Ice prefers to Vertues Land" (ll. 198-199). But when the King stands firm, he is (almost by biblical definition) nonidolatrous. He is the *one* action; his antagonists, like Dryden's Zimri, are "every thing by starts, and nothing long" (l. 548).[29]

As Dryden implies, the idol invites toppling; the state resists toppling as testimony to its balanced nature. Dryden's state is both a structure and a body.[30]

> If ancient Fabricks nod, and threat to fall,
> To Patch the Flaws, and Buttress up the Wall,
> Thus far 'tis Duty; but here fix the Mark:
> For all beyond it is to touch our Ark.
> To change Foundations, cast the Frame anew,
> Is work for Rebels who base Ends pursue:

---

[29] Zimri (or Buckingham) is Dryden's favorite bit of satiric work in *Absalom and Achitophel*. The perfectly satiric character is always disinherited in one fashion or another: "Beggar'd by Fools, whom still he found too late: / He had his Jest, and they had his Estate" (ll. 561-562).

[30] For an extended discussion of the architectural metaphor in *Absalom and Achitophel*, see the treatment of the poem in Alan Roper's *Dryden's Poetic Kingdoms*.

> At once Divine and Humane Laws controul;
> And mend the Parts by ruine of the Whole.
> The Tampering World is subject to this Curse,
> To Physick their Disease into a worse.
>
> Ll. 801-810)

To plot against the state is to follow the satanic line of bias or ruin, to wind the springs of material authority so taut against monarchy that "they Crack'd the Government" (l. 500). The line of bias, of course, threatens not only the "architecture" of kingship but the natural succession of the office. The poem asks (with a deep concern for the crisis at hand), when is a king's son not a son? And it answers (with a full sense of what the answer means), when he is a bastard. Bastardy is the biased line of nature: restless, unstable, and illegitimate (lawless). Near the end of the poem, in the lines spoken by David about his son, Absalom, Dryden draws together some of the issues present throughout:

> If my Young *Samson* will pretend a Call
> To shake the Column, let him share the Fall:
> But oh that yet he woud repent and live!
> How easie 'tis for Parents to forgive!
>
> (Ll. 955-958)

In the Bible, of course, the column does not belong to the Israelites but to the Philistines, and this may be another instance in which Dryden's defense of the secular order is tinged with some ambiguity. But of greater moment is the recombination of justice and mercy, law and nature. To shake the column and share the fall is in one sense political ruin, but in another sense it suggests the more general Adamic condition of all fathers and sons. To forgive is the parent's right, and the forgiving impulse projects the greater redemptive inheritance at the end of time. *Absalom and Achitophel* is balanced between ruin and redemption, between the biased line of satirical history and the mythic curve of natural authority.

Chapter Six

FATHERS AND SONS: SWIFT'S
A TALE OF A TUB

"Know," says King Lear, "that we have divided / In three our kingdom; and 'tis our fast intent / To shake all cares and business from our age, / Conferring them on younger strengths, while we / Unburthen'd crawl toward death" (I, i, 36-40). Of the partible estate, Cordelia has nothing to say. "Nothing?" asks Lear, "Nothing will come of nothing" (I, i, 89). *A Tale of A Tub* accommodates Lear's paradox—it follows the partible estate through to its natural end. Nothing comes in complicated ways. The allegory of the *Tale* is a fable of misinheritance; the legacy conveyed by the allegory reveals the diminished mental integrity of the allegorist. In all respects, the *Tale* is about satirically weakened lines of descent: fathers to sons, ancients to moderns. The *Tale* is dedicated to a Prince of Posterity who never escapes a kind of infantile status because his minions die hard upon their births. The inheritors of the modern spirit in the *Tale* "spend their judgment as they do their estate, before it comes into their hands," and it is tempting to suspect a last satiric joke here, an onanistic ritual at the expense of wasted spirit.

The putative subject of the *Tale* is the inability to transmit donated value across historical and generational boundaries. And as is usually the case in satire, the satirist's thematic subject is objectified—even overcompensated—in the satire's form. To complete or satisfy the narrative is to enervate its subject.[1] At the end of the *Tale*, its exhausted

[1] For a full-length study of the *Tale* from this perspective, see John R. Clark's *Form and Frenzy in Swift's A Tale of A Tub* (Ithaca, 1970). My discussion is also greatly indebted to Frank Palmeri's work in progress on short satiric narratives (a Columbia University dissertation).

author, having forgotten what he is doing and not possessing the memory to remember just what he has done, contemplates writing on nothing, recognizing insofar as his powers allow him exactly what is left him, that is, what he has inherited and what he still controls.

The narrative strategy of *A Tale of A Tub* is subversive. To comment authoritatively upon Swift's meaning or, more suggestively, upon his "positioning" within the *Tale* risks a kind of aimless vertical bobbing against the line of the narrative horizon—like a tub itself in satirically fickle waters. The personated, benighted, once-and-future Bedlamite of Swift's concoction makes a special point of complaining that he can hardly bear the mode that accommodates him—his overstrained sensibilities resist "the Satyrical Itch" that so irritates "this part of our Island" (pp. 48-49).[2] The "Apology" affixed to the 1710 edition of the *Tale* admits the parodic and satiric thread of irony running through the piece, but the represented author has "neither a Talent nor an Inclination for Satyr" (p. 53). Rather, he is in a hurry to judge the world all too well; but partly for intellectual and partly for domestic reasons (perhaps recommitment to Bedlam), he judges it not at all.

> On the other side, I am so entirely satisfied with the whole present Procedure of human Things, that I have been for some Years preparing Materials towards *A Panegyrick upon the World*; to which I intended to add

[2] All citations from the *Tale* and from the *Mechanical Operation of the Spirit* will be from *A Tale of A Tub, To which is added The Battle of the Books and the Mechanical Operation of the Spirit*, ed. A. C. Guthkelch and D. Nichol Smith (Oxford, 1958). Swift borrows the phrase, satirical "itch," from Sir William Temple's "Of Ancient and Modern Learning," in *The Works of Sir William Temple* (London, 1814), 3:486: "I wish the vein of ridiculing all that is serious and good, all honour and virtue, as well as learning and piety, may have no worse effects on any other State: it is the itch of our age and climate, and has over-run both the Court and the Stage; enters a house of Lords and Commons as boldly as a coffee-house, debates of Council as well as private conversation."

a Second Part, entituled, *A Modest Defence of the Proceedings of the Rabble in all Ages.* Both these I had Thoughts to publish by way of Appendix to the following Treatise; but finding my Common-Place-Book fill much slower than I had reason to expect, I have chosen to defer them to another Occassion. Besides, I have been unhappily prevented in that Design, by a certain Domestick Misfortune, in the Particulars whereof, tho' it would be very seasonable, and much in the *Modern* way, to inform the *gentle Reader*, and would also be of great Assistance towards extending this Preface into the Size now in Vogue, which by Rule ought to be *large* in proportion as the subsequent Volume is *small*; Yet I shall now dismiss our impatient Reader from any farther Attendance at the *Porch*; and having duly prepared his Mind by a preliminary Discourse, shall gladly introduce him to the sublime Mysteries that ensue. (Pp. 53-54)

In rejecting satire for panegyric, Swift's author performs neither but is victimized by both. The process is complicated by the author's dismissal of satire as a peculiarly modern pursuit—a mode that followed the Stuarts out of Scotland to England ("first brought among us from beyond the *Tweed*," p. 49). Even though a nominal modern, he rests uncomfortably with those modern arts that could (and probably were) turned against him and his like. He goes on to observe that the Stuarts replaced the Tudor rose with the Scottish thistle, a progress from sweetness to blight.[3] It may be that the thistle replacing the rose wittily

[3] In *The Formation of English Neo-Classical Thought* (Princeton, 1967), James William Johnson points out that the parallel of English and Roman history that occasioned the name the "Augustan Age" could well identify the height of English civilization, not in the time of the Restoration but in the Elizabethan "Golden Age." Johnson ponders the implications: "But if the classicist accepted the idea of the Elizabethan Age as the culmination of English history, and if he also believed that a nation followed a 'life'

confuses satire's cause with its effect,[4] but whatever the emblematic joke, the author blames his times for the itch he refuses to scratch. Swift, of course, insists we recognize that the author *is* the itch that the ironist who conceived of the *Tale* feels compelled to scratch.

Recent critics have become increasingly wary of trying to pin Swift down as the man behind the voices in the *Tale*, a man standing firm as a principle of reason like Mr. Ramsay in Virginia Woolf's *To the Lighthouse* who "as a stake driven into the bed of a channel upon which the gulls perch and the waves beat inspires in merry boat-loads a feeling of gratitude for the duty it is taking upon itself of marking the channel out there in the floods alone." John Traugott, for example, has put aside what to earlier commentators was the most important question of all: How far does Swift

---

cycle like that of Rome, he was forced to some disturbing conclusions. From the 'high instances of power and sovereignty,' the 'happy times,' and the *imperium et libertas* of the Age of Elizabeth, said Clarendon in his *History of the Rebellion*, there was no way for England to go but downward into strife and corruption" (p. 60).

[4] Pope sees satire rising at about the same period, but for different reasons. At the end of Elizabeth's reign Archbishop Whitgift decreed a censorship proclamation (1599) because of what the government deemed an unwholesome spate of scurrilous satiric productions in the older satiric invective vein. Satirists such as Marston, Guilpin, and Marlowe were interdicted. Pope argues that the 1599 edict forced the tone of satire to change and encouraged a more sophisticated, indirect satiric strategy. He writes in his ironic *Epistle to Augustus*.

> But Times corrupt, and Nature, ill-inclin'd,
> Produc'd the point that left a sting behind;
> Till friend with friend, and families at strife,
> Triumphant Malice rag'd thro' private life.
> Who felt the wrong, or fear'd it, took th' alarm,
> Appeal'd to Law, and Justice lent her arm.
> At length, by wholesom dread of statutes bound,
> The Poets learn'd to please, and not to wound:
> Most warp'd to Flatt'ry's side; but some, more nice,
> Preserv'd the freedom, and forbore the vice.
> Hence Satire rose, that just the medium hit,
> And heals with Morals what it hurts with Wit.
>
> (Ll. 251-262)

stand apart from the represented author, the Hack, in the comprehensive pattern of "authorship" that controls the *Tale*? Rather, Traugott assumes that anyone who would produce such a "thing" is himself deeply recessed in its structure, and the paramount question to ask is, what could so plague and unsettle a young man to make him write it?[5]

Traugott's partial answer is that Swift was strikingly unsure about the nature of his relationship to his pseudo or surrogate father, Sir William Temple, and to the values in whose "ancient" cause Swift undertook to defend Temple. Another critic, Gardner Stout, argues that satire is unsure and protean by the dictates of its modal nature and that Swift's position in the *Tale* is inevitably inconsistent.[6] *A Tale of A Tub* may well be the product of Swift's psychic and generic dilemma. To represent anything seems to subvert it in some shape or form. It may be that the mind behind such a satiric extravagance knows as little security as the mind represented in it, but there is at least one notion we can entertain about the *Tale* and that, characteristically, is a notion eschewed in it. From its staggered beginning(s) to its exhausted ending, the *Tale* disinherits itself. Its author claims he has no truck with satirists, that "large eminent Sect of our *British* Writers" (p. 49), but the very mode of the

[5] See John Traugott, "*A Tale of A Tub*," in *Focus: Swift*, ed. C. J. Rawson (London, 1971). Rawson himself has touched on these matters in an essay, "Order and Cruelty: A Reading of Swift (with some Comments on Pope and Johnson)," *Essays in Criticism* 20 (1970): 24-56, as has Gardner Stout, Jr. in two important essays, "Speaker and Satiric Vision in Swift's *Tale of a Tub*," *Eighteenth-Century Studies* 2 (1969): 175-199 and "Satire and Self-expression in Swift's 'A Tale of A Tub,' " in *Studies in the Eighteenth Century*, ed. R. F. Brissenden (Canberra, Australia, 1973), pp. 323-339.

[6] In "Speaker and Satiric Vision," Stout writes: "[Swift's] vivid personations express essential aspects of his own personality—they embody his radical, antagonistic kinship with his satiric butts and his complicity in their extravagance, aggressive pride, and subversiveness" (p. 184). Stout, Rawson, and Traugott recognize Swift's stated Anglican rationalism and moderation in all this, but they choose to concentrate on some of the potentially deeper implications of psychological strategies in Swift's satiric works.

work is given over to the thing its author (in one of his avatars) protests it is not. Swift will return to this satiric problem later in his career with Gulliver, a born-again satirist who wishes he were the thing he can never be, a horse.

That Swift should speak of the satiric art as practiced by a "sect" calls to mind the sectarian spirit of the times and its radical and "enthusiast" manifestations. Besides the satiric sect, the only significant sect mentioned in the *Tale* are the Aeolists, the winded-spirit (or exhaust) of factional lunacy. Because it is characteristic of satiric fiction to take on the nature of what it represents, the Aeolist beliefs become a version of satiric strategy. The impulse to radical inversion is common to both of Swift's "sects." The Aeolists are not alone in believing

> that, as the most unciviliz'd Parts of Mankind, have some way or other, climbed up into the Conception of a *God*, or Supream Power, so they have seldom forgot to provide their Fears with certain ghastly Notions, which instead of better, have served them pretty tolerably for a *Devil*. And this Proceeding seems to be natural enough; For it is with Men, whose Imaginations are lifted up very high, after the same Rate, as with those, whose Bodies are so; that, as they are delighted with the Advantage of a nearer Contemplation upwards, so they are equally terrified with the dismal Prospect of the Precipice below.[7] (P. 158)

There is a kind of universality in the revelation of an extravagant state of mind, and in the *Tale* Swift's procedure as satirist relies on the "Aeolist" imagination, which is akin

[7] In his *Language as Symbolic Action: Essays on Life, Literature, and Method* (Berkeley, 1966), Kenneth Burke offers a few remarks on appropriate literary modes that bear indirectly on the content of Swift's analysis of the general Aeolian mind: "Insofar as language is intrinsically hortatory (a medium by which men can obtain the cooperation of one another), God perfectly embodies the petition. Similarly, insofar as vituperation is a 'natural' resource of speech, the Devil provides a perfect butt for invective" (p. 20).

to that presented in the *Mechanical Operation of the Spirit*: *"the Corruption of the Senses is the Generation of the Spirit"* (p. 269). Such a connection or satiric crossover is obvious to Swift's critics, but what is perhaps less obvious is the full implication of what his scheme means for satire. It would appear that only the satiric subject is elevated by corruption, thus inverting normative hierarchies of order and worth. But the real question is how can anyone escape from the descendent intellection produced by ascendant bodily pressures?[8] Two hundred years after Swift, Nietzsche posed the same question: "Tell me, my brothers: what do we consider bad and worst of all? Is it not *degeneration?* . . . Upward goes our way, from genus to overgenus. But we shudder at the degenerate sense which says, 'Everything for me.' Upward flies our sense: thus it is a parable of our body, a parable of elevation. Parables of such elevations are the names of the virtues."[9] For Nietzsche and perhaps for Swift, elevation of the human spirit into that which breathes virtue is a saving fiction. The truth is closer to the satiric spirit—the fear that remains when the promise of regeneration becomes a natural and opposing fiction, when the contemplation upwards determines the plunge below. For Swift, the mind and body in perpetual vertical motion is madness, and in the *Tale*'s elaborate "Digression on Madness" we see pathology in action.

As "modern" commentators are insistent in pointing out, when Swift presents or parodies the processes of modern thought and apprehension he does not absolve himself as victim of these processes. Curiously, neither does Sir William Temple, who supposedly stands behind the *Tale*'s indictment of modern values. In his writings, Temple con-

[8] This is the subject of Norman O. Brown's discussion of Swift and the excremental vision in *Life Against Death: The Psychoanalytic Meaning of History* (Middletown, Conn., 1959). See also, Michael V. Deporte's fascinating book, *Nightmares and Hobbyhorses: Swift, Sterne, and Augustan Ideas of Madness* (San Marino, Calif., 1974).

[9] Nietzsche, *Thus Spoke Zarathustra*, in *The Portable Nietzsche*, trans. Walter Kaufmann (New York, 1976), p. 187.

firms a universal insecurity of human character. What follows could well serve as a strategic program for Swift's author—a sympathetic, if extreme, representative of the generic human mind. Temple writes that there is

> a certain restlessness of mind and thought, which seems universally and inseparably annexed to our very natures and constitutions, unsatisfied with what we are, or what we at present possess and enjoy, still raving after something past or to come, and by griefs, regrets, desires, or fears, ever troubling and corrupting the pleasures of our senses and of our imaginations, the enjoyments of our fortunes, or the best production of our reasons, and thereby the content and happiness of our lives.[10]

Thus an "ancient" voice in the modern controversy. And if Temple is privileged to say what he says, Swift ought to be privileged to represent in the condition of authorship not merely the elevated values of the reasoning writer but the descendent insecurities of a complex and often troubled satiric impersonator. In the *Tale*, Swift plays off both ancients and moderns as Laurence Sterne will later do in *Tristram Shandy*. In addressing his readers, Tristram seems to remember Swift's author.

> Thus,——thus my fellow labourers and associates in this great harvest of our learning, now ripening before

[10] Sir William Temple, "Of Popular Discontents," *Works*, 3:32. Temple goes on to write of the natural instability of the entire body politique:

> This is the true, natural, and common source of such personal dissatisfactions, such domestic complaints, and such popular discontents, as afflict not only our private lives, conditions, and fortunes, but even our civil states and governments, and thereby consummate the particular and general infelicty of mankind: which is enough complained of by all that consider it in the common actions and passions of life, but much more in the factions, seditions, convulsions, and fatal revolutions that have so frequently, and in all ages, attended all or most of the governments in the world. (P. 32)

Temple's remarks read like a version of Swift's "Digression on Madness."

our eyes; thus it is, by slow steps of casual increase, that our knowledge physical, metaphysical, physiological, polemical, nautical, mathematical, ænigmatical, technical, biographical, romantical, chemical, and obstetrical, with fifty other branches of it, (most of 'em ending, as these do, in *ical*) have, for these two last centuries and more, gradually been creeping upwards towards that Ακμὴ of their perfections, from which, if we may form a conjecture from the advances of these last seven years, we cannot possibly be far off.

When that happens, it is to be hoped, it will put an end to all kind of writings whatsoever;——the want of all kind of writing will put an end to all kind of reading;——and that in time, *As war begets poverty, poverty peace*,——must, in course, put an end to all kind of knowledge,——and then——we shall have all to begin over again; or, in other words, be exactly where we started. (Vol. I, ch. 21)

✧

In his commentary on the caves of the nymphs in the *Odyssey*, Porphyry has occasion to allude to a Platonic metaphor from the *Gorgias* (493) where Socrates describes the desiring soul as a vessel or a jar because it can be so easily swayed. Porphyry explains: "Souls, however, are tubs, because they contain in themselves energies and habits, as in a vessel."[11] In similar fashion, Swift's *Tale of A Tub* contains the energies and habits of its teller. The teller is the "tale"—the allegory (the narrative of the tailored coats) is but a thread in the larger fabric of the satiric whole. Like Socrates' vessel, the teller *as* tub is allegorical in a comprehensive sense. He is the *one* who represents the variable *other*.

[11] "On the Cave of the Nymphs," 13, trans. Thomas Taylor, in *Select Works of Porphyry* (London, 1823), pp. 194f. I am indebted to James Nohrnberg's study, *The Analogy of the Faerie Queene* (Princeton, 1976), p. 16, for this reference.

FATHERS AND SONS

Although the whole of *A Tale of A Tub* is a representation of the momentary mind and the time it takes to express its phenomenal profusions, the allegorical line, *sub specie aeternitatis*, is reconstructable. The tale within the tale has folk roots in the partible succession. Inheritance is tripartite and usually competitive. In many of the examples collected by the Grimms of the inheriting brothers (or sisters) tale, each child possesses a special talent and employs that talent in competing for paternal favor or wealth (most often land).[12] In comic forms of the structure, talents may be negative and the person with the least claim of worthiness inherits. One of Grimms' *Tales* depicts three sluggard brothers in a laziness contest. Life's "loser" is declared the winner by proving, when provided with a sword, that he lacks the energy to sever the rope that will hang him. In another Grimms story, the brother who has learned his occupation as fencing master so well that he can slice raindrops as they fall inherits over two brothers, one who can shave the whiskers off a hare running at full speed and the other who can shoe a horse in full gallop.

In the folk tale the ritual of transference may or may not have anything to do with laws of inheritance or with relevant qualifications for succession. A contest seems an arbitrary way to avoid rivalry or to concentrate rivalry in the hopes of settling it at once. Of course, the tragic dimensions of such a scheme are present in a play such as *King Lear*, where the old man demands more than equally divided loyalties for a share he tells his youngest daughter is "more opulent" than those he has already doled out in a self-flattering competition. The folk motif appears with

[12] For a review of the structure of many of these inheritance tales, see Vladimir Propp, *Morphology of the Folk Tale*, trans. Lawrence Scott; revised Louis A. Wagner; introduction Alan Dundes (Austin, 1975). Propp speaks of departure and marriage as the flanking structures of the folk tale, but in between he marks various stages of familial competition, lack, or desire. The three-brother and three-sister variety partakes of all structural stages, depending upon the narrative sequences unfolded in the specific tale.

even more sinister motives in Shakespeare's *The Merchant of Venice*, when the three-siblings story is replaced by a tale in which there is a choice of three objects. In his analysis of the three-casket tale, Freud discovers an inversion of the three-children inheritance myth or perhaps a revulsion toward what the inheritance motif represents. The choice is no longer one that allows the line to continue whole; rather, it becomes a suppressed wish for extinction. Tired of life's rivalries, the blind choice is a choice for death.

Although it is not so dark, the allegoric fable of the three brothers in *A Tale of A Tub* has its mysterious devolutions. Possibly recognizing the unstable, frenetic quality of all transmitted things, Swift understands that the father's will (literally a "will" to inertia) stands scant chance of having its stipulations fulfilled. The brothers are obligated to do nothing (a task more appropriate to the *Tale's* author). Their inheritance comes to them unadorned—it is their legal and organic portion.

> ONCE upon a Time, there was a Man who had Three Sons by one Wife, and all at a Birth, neither could the Mid-Wife tell certainly which was the Eldest. Their Father died while they were young, and upon his Death-Bed, calling the Lads to him, spoke thus,
>
> SONS, *because I have purchased no Estate, nor was born to any, I have long considered some good Legacies to bequeath You; And at last, with much Care as well as Expence, have provided each of you* (here they are) *a new Coat. Now, you are to understand, that these Coats have two Virtues contained in them: One is, that with good wearing, they will last you fresh and sound as long as you live: The other is, that they will grow in the same proportion with your Bodies, lengthning and widening of themselves, so as to be always fit.* (P. 73)

We learn from the *Tale* that the accomplishment of nothing is an elaborate procedure. Inevitably, the brothers overcompensate—they adorn their inherited coats. The outline of the fable as representative of the history of

Christianity assumes the nonpartible nature of truth: "Their Father having left them equal Heirs, and strictly commanded, that whatever they got, should lye in common among them all" (p. 121). The Romish Peter, however, reinstitutes rivalry by arguing for primogeniture: "HE told his Brothers, he would have them to know, that he was their Elder, and consequently his Father's sole Heir" (p. 105). The argument is not only for ascendancy but for "title" and authority: "Nay, a while after, he would not allow them to call Him, *Brother*, but Mr. *PETER*; and then he must be styl'd, *Father PETER*; and sometimes, *My Lord PETER*" (p. 105). Later he signs pardons, which do no good, as "Emperor Peter" (p. 113). Our "generous Author" follows the progress; he "finds his Hero on the Dunghil, from thence by gradual Steps, raises Him to a Throne, and then immediately withdraws, expecting not so much as Thanks for his Pains: in imitation of which Example, I have placed *Lord Peter* in a Noble House, given Him a Title to wear, and Money to spend" (p. 133).

Lord Peter is too big for his britches and too good for his allegorical coat. Not only does he usurp the entire inheritance but he further inflates his image by beginning to call himself "*God Almighty*, and sometimes *Monarch of the Universe*" (p. 115). The act of usurpation is given its emblematic image with Peter's three-tiered hat, a parody of papal bearing and an alternative to the three coats. It is as if Peter has taken all the family onto his head. He locks up the original will of the father, and he allows doctrines to be pronounced "*ex Cathedra*" with "*Points* [that] were absolutely *Jure Paterno*" (p. 90). He absorbs even secular space, robbing a Lord of his estates by "the way of contriving a *Deed of Conveyance* of that House to Himself and his Heirs" (p. 91).[13]

[13] Wotton's note on this passage explains the historical significance of the allegory: "Thus the Pope, upon the decease of the duke of Ferrara without lawful issue, seized the dutchy, as falling to the holy see, *jure divino*" (p. 91).

Inheritance becomes usurpation. Peter begins dividing a house against itself, and nothing divided against itself (even Satan, as Christ points out in the *Gospels*) can stand. Martin remembers what everyone else seems to forget: *"the Testament of their good Father was very exact in what related to the wearing of their* Coats; *yet was it no less penal and strict in prescribing Agreement, and Friendship, and Affection between them. And therefore, if straining a Point were at all dispensable, it would certainly be so, rather to the Advance of Unity, than Increase of Contradiction"* (p. 139). But we see very little of Martin in the *Tale*: he represents unity and satire treats of contradiction. Rather, we see too much of Peter and Jack, both alike in their extremity. Trying to abrogate the terms of their father's will by avoiding each other, they meet— like the extremes of the imagination—by coming full circle: "Yet after all this, it was their perpetual Fortune to meet. The Reason of which, is easy enough to apprehend: For, the Phrenzy and the Spleen of both, having the same Foundation, we may look upon them as two Pair of Compasses, equally extended, and the fixed Foot of each, remaining in the same Center; which, tho' moving contrary Ways at first, will be sure to encounter somewhere or other in the Circumference" (pp. 198-199). The allegory is similar to the *Tale*'s general theory of momentous expression. Swift's compass extends far and wide, and it would be risky to assume that anyone's energies and habits are fully or even partially exempted from patterned extravagancies.

AND, whereas the mind of Man, when he gives the Spur and Bridle to his Thoughts, doth never stop, but naturally sallies out into both extreams of High and Low, of Good and Evil; His first Flight of Fancy, commonly transports Him to Idea's of what is most Perfect, finished, and exalted; till having soared out of his own Reach and Sight, not well perceiving how near the Frontiers of Height and Depth, border upon each other; With the same Course and Wing, he falls down plum into the lowest Bottom of Things; like one who travels the *East* into the *West*; or like a strait Line drawn by its own Length into a Circle.[14] (Pp. 157-158)

The mind is allegorically quixotic, and for every upward venture there is a bottoming out. When the Father dies early his sons are set in contradictory motion; when the authorizing mind gives vent it turns round upon itself. In the *Tale* Swift sets out not merely to catalogue abuses in religion and learning (thus joining the allegorical narrative with the digressive one) but to reveal the underlying structure of satiric succession. Fathers, no matter what they "will," generate multiplicity. In this sense, the testamentary father of the allegory stands in the same relation to the corruption of his will as a figure such as Sir William Temple stands in relation to Swift's personated digressiveness in the *Tale*. After all, the controversy that the *Tale* inherits and carries on—a local skirmish in the perpetual crusade of ancients against moderns—has essentially the same structure as the allegory of the one coat and the many.

Inheritance is dwindled substance. Writing "In Praise of

---

[14] Freud has some intriguing things to say on the process of reversal in dreams that bears on this famous passage from the *Tale*.

Incidentally, reversal, or turning a thing into its opposite, is one of the means of representation most favoured by the dream-work and one which is capable of employment in the most diverse directions. It serves in the first place to give expression to the fulfilment of a wish in reference to some particular element of the dream-thoughts. 'If only it had been the other way round!' This is often the best way of expressing the ego's reaction to a disagreeable fragment of memory. Again, reversal is of quite special use as a help to the censorship, for it produces a mass of distortion in the material which is to be represented, and this has a positively paralysing effect, to begin with, on any attempt at understanding the dream. For that reason, if a dream obstinately declines to reveal its meaning, it is always worth while to see the effect of reversing some particular elements in its manifest content, after which the whole situation often becomes immediately clear.

See *The Interpretation of Dreams*, trans. James Strachey (London, 1953), 4:327.

Digressions," the *Tale*'s author takes stock of the modern estate: "For this great Blessing we are wholly indebted to *Systems* and *Abstracts*, in which the *Modern* Fathers of Learning, like prudent Usurers, spent their Sweat for the Ease of Us their Children. For *Labor* is the Seed of *Idleness*, and it is the peculiar Happiness of our Noble Age to gather the *Fruit*" (pp. 145-146). Fruit-gathering suggests a patrimonial inheritance that may not exist. In fact, as in Pope's *Dunciad*, the modern inheritance is maternal and reversionary, especially for the *Tale*'s "*dark* Authors" who have "found out this excellent Expedient of *Dying*" (p. 186). Modern progeny are the seeds of chaos.

> For, *Night* being the universal Mother of Things, wise Philosophers hold all Writings to be *fruitful* in the Proportion they are *dark*; And therefore, the *true illuminated* (that is to say, the *Darkest* of all) have met with such numberless Commentators, whose *Scholiastick* Midwifry hath deliver'd them of Meanings, that the Authors themselves, perhaps, never conceived, and yet may very justly be allowed the Lawful Parents of them: The Words of such Writers being like Seed, which, however scattered at random, when they light upon a fruitful Ground, will multiply far beyond either the Hopes or Imagination of the Sower. (P. 186)

Some books are freaks of nature. Modern fathers have already defrauded nature by turning the process of transmission around and trying to produce unity from multiplicity: "And indeed, it seems not unreasonable, that Books, the Children of the Brain, should have the Honor to be Christned with variety of Names, as well as other Infants of Quality. Our famous *Dryden* has ventured to proceed a Point farther, endeavouring to introduce also a Multiplicity of *Godfathers*; which is an Improvement of much more Advantage, upon a very obvious Account" (pp. 71-72). With Dryden as a model, the modern author (father of his *Tale*) divides his progeny only to find himself entirely disinherited: "having employ'd a World of Thoughts and Pains, to split my Treatise into forty Sections, and having entreated forty Lords of my Acquaintance, that they would do me the Honor to stand, they all made it a Matter of Conscience, and sent me their Excuses" (p. 72). The author's progeny is satirically cut out of an inheritance because modern progenitors spread their seed too thin. As in the violation of the allegorical will of the father, contradiction (or division) weakens unity.

Sons and "moderns" in the *Tale*, therefore, take on analogous roles. And where, one wonders, does the author of the whole enterprise fit in? One answer is that as an "extreme" mind he circulates as both progenitor and progeny, ancient and modern, father and son. His commission to write the *Tale* makes him modernity's putative enemy, and in the *Apology* we learn that the author writes in support of the Ancient's cause and waves the paternal banner of one *Sir W.T.*, "*a certain great Man then alive, and universally reverenced for every good Quality that could possibly enter into the Composition of the most accomplish'd Person*" (p. 11). Furthermore, the volume is dedicated to Lord Somers, who as a father has title to the first place if only because the modern brood keep naming him second: "For, I have somewhere heard, it is a Maxim, that those, to whom every Body allows the second Place, have an undoubted Title to the First" (p. 24).

But "*there generally runs an Irony through the Thread of the whole Book*" (p. 8), and father-Swift engenders a son-author who is liege slave to modernism. "I have profess'd to be a most devoted Servant of all *Modern* Forms" (p. 45), he writes, and a bit later he refers with reverence to one of the works at the source of arguments "bandied about both in *France* and *England*, for a just Defence of the *Modern* Learning and Wit, against the Presumption, the Pride, and the Ignorance of the *Antients*" (p. 69). The work is titled

THE *Wise Men* of Gotham, and it parodies Wotton's attack on Temple by perverting one fable (the approach of three kings to one holy source) while echoing another (the three-brothers tale of the allegory of the coats). It is not surprising that the *Tale*'s author should represent inconsistent positions. Such is precisely his impulse. He counts himself a deep writer but advises that surfaces are preferable to depths (that is, if one wishes to remain sane, and the author may not wish to do so). Writing seems deepest for the author when, like a well, it contains no contents (that is, when it aims at shallowness by design).

The author's only inspiration is likely to come from a deficient muse. The son seeks the status of father and in so doing betrays the integrity of line. For example, the author follows "the Examples of our illustrious *Moderns*" (p. 92) in discovering from "*Antient Books and Pamphlets*" (p. 92) "the proper Employment of a *True Antient and Genuine Critick*" (p. 95). To do so, he reveals the counterfeit inheritance.

> THE Third, and Noblest Sort, is that of the *TRUE CRITICK*, whose Original is the most Antient of all. Every *True Critick* is a Hero born, descending in a direct Line from a Celestial Stem, by *Momus* and *Hybris* who begat *Zoilus*, who begat *Tigellius*, who begat *Etcæt-era* the Elder, who begat *B—tly*, and *Rym—r*, and *W—tton*, and *Perrault*, and *Dennis*, who begat *Etcætera* the Younger. (Pp. 93-94)

The generational status of the true critic is parodically testamentary: "their Admirers placed their Origine in Heaven, among those of *Hercules, Theseus*, and *Perseus*, and other great Deservers of Mankind" (p. 94). Such a descent is counterheroic and proliferate at the same time, connecting the deeper structure of the allegory (a descent by threes from a heavenly original) and the parodic state of modernity, an overelaborated contribution of one or another "Etcætera." When the true (modern) critic, "*a Dis-*

coverer and Collector of Writers Faults" (p. 95), accommodates his descent, he does what the brothers do to their inherited coats: he corrupts tradition. The author of the *Tale* feels an obligation to take up his pen against a true literary source, the Homeric father: "IT was to supply such momentous Defects, that I have been prevailed on after long Sollicitation, to take Pen in Hand" (p. 129) against Homer.[15]

No fathers in the *Tale*—from the father of poetry, to the allegorical father of three brothers, to Sir William Temple—shall escape whipping from some of their sons. Even the epigraph parodies the father as source: "Basima eacabasa eanaa irraurista, diarba da caeotaba sobor camelanthi." Wotton identifies this seeming gibberish (for which Swift heaps some added abuse at his feet) as a transcription from the original Syriac of an initiation form used by the heretic gnostic sect, the Marcosians: *"I call upon this, which is above all the Power of the Father, which is called Light, and Spirit, and Life, because thou hast reigned in the Body"* (p. 323).[16] The epigraph is from Irenaeus, a Church Father, who stands in relation to the self-sufficient content of the citation in the same manner as the *Tale*'s father to the sons' coats or as Temple to the parodic impersonations of his modern "son" Swift.

[15] Sir William Temple, of course, sees Homer as "the most universal genius that has been known in the world." See "Of Poetry," in *Works*, 3:415. He continues: "there cannot be a greater testimony given, than what has been by some observed, that not only the greatest masters have found in his works the best and truest principles of all their sciences or arts, but that the noblest nations have derived from them the original of their several races, though it be hardly yet agreed, whether his story be true or a fiction" (p. 416).

[16] Wotton's notes to the epigraph appear on p. 187 and p. 323 of the Guthkelch and Smith edition of the *Tale*. The editors also reprint the response to Wotton included in *A Complete Key to the Tale of a Tub* (1710) where an appendage to a note records: *"Irenæus corrected by Mr. Wotton: O! the depth of Modern Learning"* (p. 348). For a discussion of gnosticism in *A Tale of A Tub*, see Ronald Paulson's chapter, "The Gnostic View of Man," in *Theme and Structure in Swift's A Tale of A Tub* (New Haven, 1960), pp. 87-144.

As its epigraph says, the *Tale* is sufficient unto itself, but perhaps for different reasons. A mind that is "en-tubbed" drifts or bobs on its own—it has no connections with a past and can barely anticipate the future. Modernity knows only its own moment, and moderns tend to forget memorable transmission because their entire being is momentous. It is as Paul de Man says in describing Nietzsche's position on modernity: "Modernity invests its thrust in the power of the present moment as origin, but discovers that, in severing itself from the past, it has at the same time severed itself from the present."[17] Memory is an ancient enemy to modern being, or as the author of the *Tale* puts it: "*Memory* being an Employment of the Mind upon things past, is a Faculty, for which the Learned, in our Illustrious Age, have no manner of Occasion, who deal entirely with *Invention*, and strike all Things out of themselves, or at least, by Collision, from each other" (p. 135). Always complaining of an "unhappy shortness of my Memory" (p. 92), the author dips into his well and comes up dry: "Thrice have I forced my Imagination to make the *Tour* of my Invention, and thrice it has returned empty; the latter having been wholly drained by the following Treatise" (p. 42). This is another of many instances in which the author fulfills his plans to write upon nothing before having announced that such is precisely his plan: "I am now trying an Experiment very frequent among Modern Authors; which is, to *write upon Nothing*" (p. 208). With no memory, the subject is well chosen. Nothing is held, therefore nothing is produced. Laurence Sterne sums up the modern dilemma when in *Tristram Shandy* he writes about the failure of Lockean human memory: "Dull organs, dear Sir, in the first place. Secondly, slight and transient impressions made by objects when the said organs are not dull. And, thirdly, a memory

[17] Paul de Man, "Literary History and Literary Modernity," in *Blindness and Insight: Essays in the Rhetoric of Contemporary Criticism* (New York, 1971), p. 149.

like unto a sieve, not able to retain what it has received" (vol. II, ch. 2).

Like the gnosticism of the epigraph, modernity is almost pathological. Our author is a mad scribbler—some of his visits to Bedlam are homecomings. And in the "Digression of Madness" we learn the symptoms of self-conceived and self-extinguished imaginings. A madman, knowing little of things outside himself, "did ever conceive it in his Power, to reduce the Notions of all Mankind, exactly to the same Length, and Breadth, and Height of his own" (p. 166). Swift's scheme for madness is a kind of bodily sabotage: madmen finally consume their own excrement, eat their words, and whisper nothing. We learn to admire the manifestations of nothing because, in effect, we will learn nothing else. In the midst of the most crucial explanation in the *Tale*—the "knotty Point" of why forms of madness proliferate and vary—there is a hiatus in the text. The author has again written upon nothing, and "this I take to be a clear Solution of the Matter" (p. 170). To explain madness is to explain modernity, and such an explanation is too much to expect from a book with gaps for a memory.

The appropriate figure for modernity in the *Tale* is, naturally enough, the infant. Infants are brand new—they have nothing to remember. At the same time, to be an infant is to have just entered the scene, to be last: "But I here think fit to lay hold on that great and honourable Privilege of being the *Last Writer*; I claim an absolute Authority in Right, as the *freshest Modern*, which gives me a Despotick Power over all Authors before me" (p. 130). The author claims his inheritance or his birthright without waiting for either his talent or his estate to mature. In coming last, moderns come too fast—they spend themselves. Later in the *Tale* we learn that delusions of authority, "any Thought of subduing Multitudes to his own *Power*" (p. 171), are a symptom of madness. To be born a modern is to be born mad.

In terms of the structure of the *Tale*, picturing modernity as an infant has the advantage of connecting the fable of allegorical inheritance with the greater theme of cultural inheritance. In both cases past time is forgotten. The author dedicates his *Tale* to Prince Posterity, partly because his memory may fail him at any moment and partly because the future needs all the help it can get. Posterity's children—the works of his authors—rarely last until the next revolution of the sun: "Unhappy Infants, many of them barbarously destroyed, before they have so much as learnt their *Mother-Tongue* to beg for Pity" (p. 33). These infants, tainted by time's breath, "die of a languishing Consumption" (p. 33). The labors of Grub-Street are reminiscent of the perpetual labor of Sin in *Paradise Lost*: "These yelling Monsters that with ceaseless cry / Surround me, as thou saw'st, hourly conceiv'd / And hourly born, with sorrow infinite / To me . . ." (II, 795-798). The *Tale*'s momentary productions are unluckier—they are not only hourly born but they hourly die. Swift may have remembered Sir William Temple's essay "Of Ancient and Modern Learning": "For the scribblers are infinite, that, like mushrooms or flies, are born and die in small circles of time; whereas books, like proverbs, receive their chief value from the stamp and esteem of ages through which they have passed."[18]

In the dedication to Prince Posterity Swift continues to ponder the problem of infant mortality by having the author put in a plea for "our Corporation of *Poets*," whose "*never-dying* Works" time has committed to "unavoidable Death" (p. 33). Such a corporation is the organic body of poetry that cannot hold to form. Its proliferated "beings" escape "our Memory, and delude our Sight" (p. 34) like Hamlet's protean clouds.

[18] Sir William Temple, "Of Ancient and Modern Learning," *Works*, 3:446.

If I should venture in a windy Day, to affirm to *Your Highness*, that there is a large Cloud near the *Horizon* in the Form of a *Bear*, another in the *Zenith* with the Head of an *Ass*, a third to the Westward with Claws like a *Dragon*; and *Your Highness* should in a few Minutes think fit to examine the Truth, 'tis certain, they would all be changed in Figure and Position, new ones would arise, and all we could agree upon would be, that Clouds there were, but that I was grossly mistaken in the *Zoography* and *Topography* of them. (P. 35)

In a sense, books are free form; their modern authors inherit no models and thus produce nothing but monstrosities. A monster is *sui generis*—its only property or possession is itself. What is come is done: "Books, like Men their Authors, have no more than one Way of coming into the World, but there are ten Thousand to go out of it, and return no more" (p. 36). In the "Digression on Madness," the conceit of the quick birth and perpetual death is picked up in the Lockean discourse on imaginary birth versus memorial death, fiction versus truth.

If we consider that the Debate meerly lies between *Things past*, and *Things conceived*; and so the Question is only this; Whether Things that have Place in the *Imagination*, may not as properly be said to *Exist*, as those that are seated in the *Memory*; which may be justly held in the Affirmative, and very much to the Advantage of the former, since This is acknowledged to be the *Womb* of Things, and the other allowed to be no more than the *Grave*. (P. 172)

Since the works of the modern imagination are conceived and extinguished in virtually the same short breath, the womb *is* the grave. The author of the *Tale* has "a strong Inclination, before I leave the World, to taste a Blessing, which we *mysterious* Writers can seldom reach, till we have got into our Graves" (p. 185). There fame's "Trumpet sounds best and farthest, when she stands on a *Tomb*, by the Advantage of a rising Ground, and the Echo of a hollow Vault" (p. 186). Once again the author comes up empty. In this case monuments are not exactly memories. Since memory is not an issue of the modern imagination, it is not *even* the record of the imagination laid to rest. If we return to the dedication to Prince Posterity, we learn that the infants of the pen are buried in thin air; they come so fast from the womb that they earn no fixed grave: "the *Memorial of them was lost among Men, their Place was no more to be found*" (pp. 34-35).

✧

Part of the design of *A Tale of A Tub* proclaims that a kind of zero-narrative time takes over from a more primitive concept of narrative advance. The very title of the work is digressive or diversionary, and the author announces that his commission is to decoy the modern destroyer, Hobbes's *Leviathan*, from imperiling the state. The author writes in a conservative cause as the defender of "Religion and Government" (p. 39). Of course, he is the perfect choice because his *Tale* is the perfect tub: "That Sea-men have a Custom when they meet a *Whale*, to fling him out an empty *Tub*, by way of Amusement, to divert him from laying violent Hands upon the Ship. This Parable was immediately mythologiz'd: The *Whale* was interpreted to be *Hobs's Leviathan*, which tosses and plays with all other Schemes of Religion and Government, whereof a great many are hollow, and dry, and empty, and noisy, and wooden, and given to Rotation" (p. 40).[19]

[19] The suggestion of rotation recalls the schemes for government around the time of the *Leviathan* and the English Civil Wars and Interregnum, specifically James Harrington's Republican Rota Club. Like Butler and Dryden, Swift seems to set the satiric principle of diversionary necessity in literature back to the internecine romance. From revolution (or rotation) comes the need for ironic countersubversion, a need that produced elaborate satiric structures. In this sense, it is interesting that

FATHERS AND SONS

The whale and the tub are versions of each other and, just as in the allegory of the coats, moderation is not part of this satiric spectacle. We see nothing of sound government and little of sound religion (with the exception of Martin) in the *Tale*'s allegory and digressions because satiric mimicry is itself extreme. What we do see are extremes coming "around." Section VIII is nominally distinguished as part of the allegory, but in actuality the discourse on the Aeolists *becomes* a digression. For the allegorical relation, time ought to be diachronic; for the digressions, time is inevitably synchronic. But Swift collapses allegorical time, first into the history of one family, then into local episodes, then into the synchronic state of religious faction—the perpetual Aeolian moment. The *Tale* reaches a point of narrative stasis when its author confuses progress and regress, when the diversion (or tub) takes over the tale. This happens quite literally in the Aeolist section when the allusionary tub materializes as a wind-container whose original was Odyssean.

It was an Invention ascribed to *Æolus* himself, from whom this Sect is denominated, and who in Honour of their Founder's Memory, have to this Day preserved great Numbers of those *Barrels*, whereof they fix one in each of their Temples, first beating out the Top; into this *Barrel*, upon Solemn Days, the Priest enters; where, having before duly prepared himself by the methods already described, a secret Funnel is also convey'd from his Posteriors, to the Bottom of the Barrel, which admits new Supplies of Inspiration from a *Northern* Chink or Crany. Whereupon, you behold

---

another tale of a tub crops up in the context of wartime in Rabelais when we hear of Diogenes' diversionary attempt to avoid enlistment in Philip of Macedon's campaign against the Corinthians. Rabelais writes of Diogenes: "he was giving his tub a thrashing in order not to seem the one lazy idler among a people so feverishly busy" *Gargantua and Pantagruel*, trans. J. M. Cohen (Harmondsworth, 1955), p. 283.

him swell immediately to the Shape and Size of his *Vessel*. (Pp. 155-156)

The tub is a mechanism for the compression and forcing of air, an operation that, when it occurs naturally, produces insanity (as we learn later from the "Digression on Madness"). But more important for the design of the *Tale*, the tub becomes an aid to organic self-sufficiency. With such a "digression" surrounding one's being, there are no sequences outside of one's self. The very idea of narrative sequence, then, is subsumed by digressive usurpation: "*Digressions* in a Book, are like *Forein Troops* in a *State*, which argue the Nation to want a *Heart* and *Hands* of its own, and often, either *subdue* the *Natives*, or drive them into the most *unfruitful Corners*" (p. 144). Earlier, in his "Digression in the Modern Kind," the author had distinguished between his tale and its digressions (later indistinguishable) on the basis of the Horatian formula of instruction and diversion.

That the Publick Good of Mankind is performed by two Ways, *Instruction*, and *Diversion*. And I have farther proved in my said several Readings, (which, perhaps, the World may one day see, if I can prevail on any Friend to steal a Copy, or on certain Gentlemen of my Admirers, to be very Importunate) that, as Mankind is now disposed, he receives much greater Advantage by being *Diverted* than *Instructed*; His Epidemical Diseases being *Fastidiosity*, *Amorphy*, and *Oscitation*; whereas in the present universal Empire of Wit and Learning, there seems but little Matter left for *Instruction*. (P. 124)

Like moderation and stability, instruction is not particularly fertile ground for the extremes of modernity or satire, and the author accurately describes the plan of the *Tale* in presenting "throughout this Divine Treatise" a "*Layer* of *Utile* and a *Layer of Dulce*" (p. 124). If usefulness is the measure of instruction and diversion the measure of sweetness, one concludes that the *Tale*'s digressions are pretty well useless. But as satiric mimicry they are delightful. They are such effective parodies of a world not in love with the productions of time that they have done exactly what Swift's perverse imitative genius represented them as not being able to do: they have lasted. This is satire's parodoxical testament. The "transitory State of all sublunary Things" (p. 66)—things on earth and under the moon (thus lunatic)—are given a permanent space in time by the power of satiric representation. Because the represented author is not capable of grasping time, the *Tale*'s digressive time becomes most memorable in the genius of a real author able to transcend it. Swift's author is similar to the increasingly schizoid lunatic in Dostoevsky's *Notes from Underground*, whose best sense of time is digressive but whose mental fabrications hold a more secure literary place than the sequential goings-on above ground from which he isolates himself. We are told in the *Tale* that "there is no inventing Terms of Art beyond our Idea's; and when Idea's are exhausted, Terms of Art must be so too" (p. 50). The writer *in* the *Tale* is a figure of exhaustion: he was sick when he wrote it; he cannot finish it; he can barely remember it. But the parody and energy of the effort is inexhaustible. Swift was amazed at his own genius when he "writ it," and in terms of its art the *Tale* creates and lives in its own satiric culture.

✧

Much of the anxiety created by the subject of *A Tale of A Tub*, by Swift's place in it and by the reader's reading it, has to do with the temporal and spatial insecurities of its satiric vision. To represent a world of compressed time where it seems there is not enough time to get anything done is to distort the rhythms of life. In the *Tale*, Swift's spatial sense is constructed on the same axis as his temporal sense. All goes up and down in the same place; nothing seems to extend very far backward or forward. Metaphor is what fits in a tight place—a kind of materialized psychology of vapors, spirits, bulges, and barrels. From the great movements in history to the freaks of individual and sect behavior, accountability derives from the crowding of objects, temperaments, and ideas. Satire is that proliferate number from which it is impossible to "get quit." The incontinent, the mad, the shapeless, and the shiftless cram into every available space. We are given only the option of the vertical line, and comprehension itself becomes an imitation of descendent moments in time.

> However, being extreamly sollicitous, that every accomplished Person who has got into the Taste of Wit, calculated for this present Month of *August*, 1697, should descend to the very *bottom* of all the *Sublime* throughout this Treatise; I hold fit to lay down this general Maxim. Whatever Reader desires to have a thorow Comprehension of an Author's Thoughts, cannot take a better Method, than by putting himself into Circumstances and Postures of Life, that the Writer was in, upon every important Passage as it flow'd from his Pen; For this will introduce a Parity and strict Correspondence of Idea's between the Reader and the Author. (P. 44)

In the "Digression on Madness" we are warned to shy away from depths, but here we are asked to mimic profundity. And when we descend to the bottom of the sublime, we become vertically ambiguous. The sublime—the *sub limit* or the "tops"—ought to have nothing to do with the bottom. Of course, the spatial scheme is a scatological metaphor, and it is precisely the bottom's influence on the top (head; mind) that drives men mad. The "Digression on Madness" is the same spatial nightmare that appeared earlier in the section on Aeolists, but the directions are reversed. In the Aeolist discourse all things bottom out ("the imagination of what is Highest and Best, becomes over-shot, and spent, and weary, and suddenly falls like a dead Bird of Paradise, to the Ground," p. 158); in the "Digression on Madness" a *"Phœnomenon* of *Vapours*, ascending from the lower Faculties to over-shadow the Brain" distills "into Conceptions, for which the Narrowness of our Mother-Tongue has not yet assigned any other Name, besides that of *Madness* or *Phrenzy*" (p. 167). Down or up, sexual or scatological, bodily inclinations are compressed anxieties.

The vertical line in the *Tale* is the line of satire, the line of digression, the line of compression. Elevation and debasement do not allow advance or transmission, merely mechanical operation. The directional scheme insures against the extension of the individual's properties in a beneficial line. In his *Mechanical Operation of the Spirit*, Swift borrows the Hobbist conceit of the artificial man at the beginning of the *Leviathan* and makes him into the natural man of satire: "Besides, there is many an Operation, which in its Original, was purely an Artifice, but through a long Succession of Ages, hath grown to be a natural" (pp. 267-268). Here the satiric inheritance is the result of material compressibility. Bound and squeezed heads of infant Scythians produced a sugar-loaf protrusion above the compressed area, a protrusion later passed on naturally as a deformation. A similar artificial production of natural monsters occurred during England's Civil War period. History's forms are materially shaped:

> For, in the Age of our Fathers, there arose a Generation of Men in this Island call'd *Round-heads*, whose Race is now spread over three Kingdoms, yet in its Beginning, was meerly an Operation of Art, produced by a pair of Cizars, a Squeeze of the Face, and a black Cap. These Heads, thus formed into a perfect Sphere in all Assemblies, were most exposed to the view of the

Female Sort, which did influence their Conceptions so effectually, that Nature, at last, took the Hint, and did it of her self; so that a *Round-head* has been ever since as familiar a Sight among Us, as a *Long-head* among the *Scythians*.[20] (Pp. 268-269).

Bodily pressures (up and down) in Swift's material satire produce the distortions that make life a history of natural opinions. A man like Jack in *A Tale of A Tub*, tongue up nose, braying like an ass, ears erect, dog-mad at the sound of music is subject to carnal forces that cannot help but produce monstrous human expressions of behavior and opinion. Whomever the satirist would destroy he first drives mad. Naturally, the scheme of the *Tale*'s material line appears most naturally in the "Digression on Madness."

For, if we take a Survey of the greatest Actions that have been performed in the World under the Influence of Single Men; which are, *The Establishment of New Empires by Conquest: The Advance and Progress of New Schemes in Philosophy; and the contriving, as well as the propagating of New Religions:* We shall find the Authors of them all, to have been Persons, whose natural Reason hath admitted great Revolutions from their Dyet, their Education, the Prevalency of some certain Temper, together with the particular Influence of Air and Climate. Besides, there is something Individual in human Minds, that easily kindles at the accidental Ap-

[20] In the *Tale*, Swift makes a similar point about deformed Puritan ears: "And how can it be otherwise, when in these latter Centuries, the very Species is not only diminished to a very lamentable Degree, but the poor Remainder is also degenerated so far, as to mock our skillfullest *Tenure?* For, if the only slitting of one *Ear* in a Stag, hath been found sufficient to propogate the Defect thro' a whole Forest; Why should we wonder at the greatest Consequences, from so many Loppings and Mutilations, to which the *Ears* of our Fathers and our own, have been of late so much exposed" (p. 201).

proach and Collision of certain Circumstances, which
tho' of paltry and mean Appearance, do often flame
out into the greatest Emergencies of Life. (P. 162)

All that is "individual" is potentially mad. And the
greatest of individuals in the *Tale* represents the greatest
expression of modernity. Modernity sustains madness, the
pretense that ascendancy, however insecure, is permanent.
And all engines of the satirically spirited mechanical system
are geared for the purpose of sustaining the higher or
superior fiction. The author speaks of three necessary
"Oratorial Machines" at the beginning of the *Tale*: "These
are, the *Pulpit*, the *Ladder*, and the *Stage-Itinerant*" (p. 56).
He rejects the Bar, for "tho' it be compounded of the same
Matter, and designed for the same Use, it cannot however
be well allowed the Honor of a fourth, by reason of its level
or inferior Situation, exposing it to perpetual Interruption
from Collaterals" (p. 56).[21] Engines of public performance
are as principles of psychological elevation—they move toward sublime manifestations: "FROM this accurate Deduction it is manifest, that for obtaining Attention in Publick,
there is of necessity required a *superiour Position of Place*" (p.
60).

Power is also a question of superior dimension. In the
preface to the *Tale* Swift's author had spoken of a mountebank addressing a crowd in Leicester Fields. Here domi-
nance becomes a metaphorical need to take in and control
compressed space.

---

[21] The rejection of the fourth engine is commensurate with everything
else in the *Tale* that seems to go by threes. Three is a parody of the mystical number, but it is also an exclusion of the middle by the extremes. The
brothers of the *Tale* and the engines are not the only threesomes: "Now
among all the rest, the profound Number *THREE* is that which hath most
employ'd my sublimest Speculations, nor ever without wonderful Delight"
(p. 57). Three is the subject of a planned panegyrical essay: there are
three parts to the *Tale* (prefatory material, allegory, digressions), three
critics, three winds, three London societies, three madmen, three types of
readers. Three is both the odd number and the extreme thought.

FATHERS AND SONS

A Mountebank in Leicester-Fields, *had drawn a huge Assembly about him. Among the rest, a fat unweildy Fellow, half stifled in the Press, would be every fit crying out, Lord! what a filthy Crowd is here; Pray, good People, give way a little, Bless me! what a Devil has rak'd this Rabble together: Z————ds, what squeezing is this! Honest Friend, remove your Elbow. At last, a* Weaver *that stood next him could hold no longer: A Plague confound you* (said he) *for an overgrown Sloven; and who (in the Devil's Name) I wonder, helps to make up the Crowd half so much as your self? Don't you consider (with a Pox) that you take up more room with that Carkass than any five here? Is not the Place as free for us as for you? Bring your own Guts to a reasonable Compass (and be d————n'd) and then I'll engage we shall have room enough for all.* (P. 46)

The desire to subdue multitudes is a characteristic of madness, and physical displacement is the quest for power—what Hobbes has called a "general inclination of all mankind, a perpetual and restless desire of power after power, that ceaseth only in death" (*Leviathan*, pt. 1, ch. 11). Swift presents the Engines of his tale as power machines and then converts the press of the crowd into the satirically vertical line.

AND I am the readier to favour this Conjecture, from a common Observation; that in the several Assemblies of these Orators, Nature it self hath instructed the Hearers, to stand with their Mouths open, and erected parallel to the Horizon, so as they may be intersected by a perpendicular Line from the Zenith to the Center of the Earth. In which Position, if the Audience be well compact, every one carries home a Share, and little or nothing is lost. (Pp. 60-61)

Head back, mouth open, comprehension vertical: the share carried home by such an audience is little or nothing indeed, but the image is memorable. The "Physico-logical

Scheme of Oratorial Receptacles or Machines" (p. 61) in action is both the subject and the strategy of *A Tale of A Tub*. And in satire the scheme for transmission is violated by the substance transmitted: in religion the audience carries home an embellished suit of clothes and a bag of wind; in poetry its reward is an earful of impropriety and a confusion of property ("a confounding of *Meum* and *Tuum*," p. 63); in learning its recompense is a mirror of brass "without any Assistance of *Mercury* from behind" (p. 103). The *Tale* ends with its author's finger on his own and his world's pulse. It is difficult to determine whether he plans to renew his efforts when the pulse beats again or when it stops beating forever.

Chapter Seven

STRANGE DISPOSITIONS: SWIFT'S *GULLIVER'S TRAVELS*

In the third book of *Gulliver's Travels*, a person of Luggnuggian quality asks Gulliver if he has seen any of "their *Struldbrugs* or *Immortals*" (p. 207).[1] A progressivist by nature, having "been a Sort of Projector in my younger Days" (p. 178), Gulliver is in raptures at the prospect of the immortal Struldbrugs—he is "struck with inexpressible Delight upon hearing this Account" (p. 207). Why? Because the Struldbrugs "being born exempt from that universal Calamity of human Nature, have their Minds free and disingaged, without the Weight and Depression of Spirits caused by the continual Apprehension of Death" (p. 208). Although Gulliver's reflection here does not seem particularly outrageous, it is just such a notion of bodily integrity in time that the satiric design of the *Travels* subverts. Gulliver is goaded by the Luggnuggian gentleman into the next unfortunate error: he is asked to imagine himself a Struldbrug and to speculate on his immortal rewards. An older and wilier heroic wanderer, Odysseus, had a similar opportunity to test immortality on Calypso's island, but he was forced into it almost against his will. The promise of immortality delayed homecoming, and Odysseus, the all too human traveller, desired nothing so much as a return to the temporally measured life. But not so Gulliver.

Gulliver knows little restraint in pursuing the wrong course. He "projects" the life of an immortal into an expansive and ameliorative view of human "being" and assumes that he and his fellow Struldbrugs "would probably

[1] Jonathan Swift, *Gulliver's Travels*, ed. Herbert Davis (Oxford, 1965). All subsequent citations will be to this edition.

prevent that continual Degeneracy of human Nature, so justly complained of in all Ages" (p. 210). What he soon sees, however, proves otherwise. In suspending the temporal limitation of life, the Struldbrugs incorporate the ravages of time into their nature. The best of their lot are the prematurely senile. At fourscore "they are looked on as dead in Law; their Heirs immediately succeed to their Estates, only a small Pittance is reserved for their Support" (p. 212). At this point, Gulliver ought to realize that continuity and biological life are at imperfectible odds, but he will make the same mistake in Houyhnhnmland when he wishes himself a more perfectible being than his body allows. "In its Etymology," we are told, Houyhnhnm means *"the Perfection of Nature"* (p. 235). It may be that an abstract or artificial notion of the body of man, like that presented in the opening of Hobbes's *Leviathan*, can hold to perfect form,[2] but the natural human body cannot. The Luggnuggians make the Struldbrugs into satiric fictions. As beings, the Struldbrugs's condition is desperate and degenerate.

At Ninety they lose their Teeth and Hair; they have at that Age no Distinction of Taste, but eat and drink whatever they can get, without Relish or Appetite. The Diseases they were subject to, still continue without encreasing or diminishing. In talking they forget the common Appellation of Things, and the Names of Persons, even of those who are their nearest Friends

[2] Hobbes's giant form in the beginning of the *Leviathan* is the kind of mechanical being that Gulliver might have seemed to the Lilliputians, a *homo mechanicus*.

For what is the *Heart*, but a *Spring*; and the *Nerves*, but so many *Strings*; and the *Joynts*, but so many *Wheeles*, giving motion to the whole Body, such as was intended by the Artificer? *Art* goes yet further, imitating that Rationall and most excellent worke of Nature, *Man*. For by Art is created that great LEVIATHAN called a Common-Wealth, or State, (in latine Civitas) which is but an Artificall Man; though of greater stature and strength than the Naturall, for whose protection and defence it was intended. (*Leviathan*, Introduction)

and Relations. For the same Reason they never can amuse themselves with reading, because their Memory will not serve to carry them from the Beginning of a Sentence to the End; and by this Defect they are deprived of the only Entertainment wereof they might otherwise be capable. (P. 213)

The Struldbrugs are condemned to decay—they lose their memories and are thus "ancients" made all too "modern." For the suddenly educated Gulliver the Struldbrugs "were the most mortifying Sight I ever beheld; and the Women more horrible than the Men. Besides the usual Deformities in extreme old Age, they acquired an additional Ghastliness in Proportion to their Number of Years, which is not to be described" (p. 214). What is worse, they are exiles at home; they cannot communicate in any but a dead language, "and thus they lye under the Disadvantage of living like Foreigners in their own Country" (p. 213). Although Gulliver had no way of knowing it at the time, the condition of the Struldbrugs would finally reflect his own—that of a permanent exile in his own land. By believing in the perfectibility of the species (any species), Gulliver drives himself crazy. At the end of his *Travels*, if not "despised and hated by all Sorts of People" (p. 213) as are the Struldbrugs, he himself despises and hates all sorts of Yahoos—those satirically degenerate fellow men he describes as "a Lump of Deformity, and Diseases both in Body and Mind, smitten with *Pride*" (p. 296).

The document, *Gulliver's Travels*, is written by a madman whose recollections at the time of writing are anything but tranquil. His voyagings have unsettled and dispossessed him. He begins as the middle son of a middle-class household from a middle shire of England. He ends bereft of his middling or "mediating" status. Like most of Swift's surrogate authors (or expendable selves), Gulliver *is* satiric potential—the record of his progress becomes confused with the disintegration of his recording powers. *A Tale of A*

Tub is told by an author inside his own diversionary barrel. *A Modest Proposal* is advanced by a political arithmetician obsessed by number. *Gulliver's Travels* is related as part of a narrative conspiracy to drive a fool mad. Swift begins the adventures by forcing Gulliver out of all human proportion, and Gulliver ends by wishing himself out of his own nature. Gulliver is vexed by his bodily design. Something has snapped. As a traveller who has made proximity to nature's diverse creatures a perfectible ideal, he is spoiled by his proximate status as degenerate Yahoo. In this sense, his repatriation becomes his longest voyage of all, fated to last for the rest of his life. Seeing how extensive imperfection and degeneration are in the world is discomfiting enough for Gulliver, but seeing how his own body shapes his nature as a Yahoo renders him mindless.

In *Gulliver's Travels* degeneration is literally a vision of history—ego history and human history. As has long been recognized, even the means of arrival in each strange land betray a kind of degenerate regress: shipwreck, desertion, piracy, mutiny. The 1735 edition of the *Travels* opens with Gulliver's letter to his cousin Sympson that complains among other things that Yahoo though he is Gulliver is not "so far degenerated" that he need defend his veracity to other Yahoos, especially when the "united Praise of the whole Race would be of less Consequence to me, than the neighing of those two degenerate *Houyhnhnms* I keep in my Stable; because, from these, degenerate as they are, I still improve in some Virtues, without any Mixture of Vice" (p. 8).

Gulliver may be a raving lunatic by this juncture, but even in his earlier, calmer voice he was preoccupied with degeneration. In Lilliput, ancient institutions undergo an increasingly rapid degeneration from the more noble lineaments of the past, and in relaying the laws of the land Gulliver points out that "I would only be understood to mean the original Institutions, and not the most scandalous Corruptions into which these People are fallen by the degenerate Nature of Man" (p. 60). If the Lilliputians can barely afford a further fall in stature, the Brobdingnagian giants appear enormous even as shrunken descendants of a former race. Gulliver discovers a book on the subject of Brobdingnagian morality that holds that the once mighty are now fallen. Its author writes:

> Nature was degenerated in these latter declining Ages of the World, and could now produce only small abortive Births in Comparison of those in ancient Times. He said, it was very reasonable to think, not only that the Species of Men were originally much larger, but also that there must have been Giants in former Ages; which, as it is asserted by History and Tradition, so it hath been confirmed by huge Bones and Sculls casually dug up in several Parts of the Kingdom, far exceeding the common dwindled Race of Man in our Days. He argued, that the very Laws of Nature absolutely required we should have been made in the Beginning, of a Size more large and robust, not so liable to Destruction from every little Accident of a Tile falling from an House, or a Stone cast from the Hand of a Boy, or of being drowned in a little Brook. (P. 137)

A little earlier, after listening to Gulliver's recitation of European glories, the Brobdingnagian King commented that even among "little" people the course of events seems to run from tolerable to degenerative: "I observe among you some Lines of an Institution, which in its Original might have been tolerable; but these half erased, and the rest wholly blurred and blotted by Corruptions" (p. 132). Both giants and midgets suffer from a nostalgic historiography and a degeneratively contingent inheritance.

The most sustained treatment of degeneration in the *Travels* occurs in the several lands of Book Three. The Voyage to Laputa is the whore (*la puta*) of the narrative—naturally it has many lands. On the flying doomsday island of Laputa, the local inhabitants literally experience a fear of falling. And on the magical island of Glubbdubdrib Gulliver experiences an actual descent or calling of the shades in his odyssey of strange relations. He confronts time and observes "how much the Race of human Kind was degenerate among us, within these Hundred Years past. How the Pox under all its Consequences and Denominations had altered every Lineament of an *English* Countenance; shortened the Size of Bodies, unbraced the Nerves, relaxed the Sinew and Muscles, introduced a sallow Complexion, and rendered the Flesh loose and *rancid*" (p. 201).

These are the same hundred years to which the King of Brobdingnag had reacted earlier when Gulliver performed as progressivist press agent for a land fully deserving of its bad press.

> He was perfectly astonished with the historical Account I gave him of our Affairs during the last Century; protesting it was only an Heap of Conspiracies, Rebellions, Murders, Massacres, Revolutions, Banishments; the very worst Effects that Avarice, Faction, Hypocrisy, Perfidiousness, Cruelty, Rage, Madness, Hatred, Envy, Lust, Malice, and Ambition could produce. (P. 132)

The King calls Gulliver's European civilization "the most pernicious Race of little odious Vermin that Nature ever suffered to crawl upon the Surface of the Earth" (p. 132). He does so after Gulliver had tried to defend the most noble of his people, the Lords of his native Parliament, as the "Ornament and Bulwark of the Kingdom; worthy Followers of their most renowned Ancestors, whose Honour had been the Reward of their Virtue; from which their Posterity were never once known to degenerate" (p. 128). Swift's irony and Gulliver's gullibility are manifest later when in the seance of Book Three the Roman Senate is called to stand next to Gulliver's native Parliament (Lords and Commons): "I desired that the Senate of *Rome* might appear before me in one large Chamber, and a modern Representative, in Counterview, in another. The first seemed to be an Assembly of Heroes and Demy-Gods; the other a Knot of Pedlars, Pick-pockets, Highwaymen and Bullies" (pp. 195-196). And if the political quibblers would have it that Swift means to distinguish between the noble lines in the Lords and the rabble in the Commons, Gulliver traces the decay of the highborn as an impressionable "great Admirer of old illustrious Families." He experiences a kind of perverse pleasure in the distortions of natural lines.

> And I confess it was not without some Pleasure that I found my self able to trace the particular Features, by which certain Families are distinguished up to their Originals. I could plainly discover from whence one Family derives a long Chin; why a second hath abounded with Knaves for two Generations, and Fools for two more; why a third happened to be crack-brained, and a fourth to be Sharpers.... How Cruelty, Falshood, and Cowardice grew to be Characteristicks by which certain Families are distinguished as much as by their Coat of Arms. Who first brought the Pox into a noble House, which hath lineally descended in scrophulous Tumours to their Posterity. Neither could I wonder at all this, when I saw such an Interruption of Lineages by Pages, Lacqueys, Valets, Coachmen, Gamesters, Fidlers, Players, Captains, and Pick-pockets. (Pp. 198-199)

Gulliver's vision in Book Three becomes his opinion in the maddening last voyage when he explains the decayed state of nobility's lines to his Master Houyhnhnm.

> That, *Nobility* among us was altogether a different Thing from the Idea he had of it; That, our young *Noblemen* are bred from their Childhood in Idleness

and Luxury; that, as soon as Years will permit, they
consume their Vigour, and contract odious Diseases
among lewd Females; and when their Fortunes are
almost ruined, they marry some Woman of mean
Birth, disagreeable Person, and unsound Constitution,
merely for the sake of Money, whom they hate and despise. That, the Productions of such Marriages are
generally scrophulous, rickety or deformed Children;
by which Means the Family seldom continues above
three Generations, unless the Wife take Care to provide a healthy Father among her Neighbours, or
Domesticks, in order to improve and continue the
Breed. (P. 256)

Of course it is possible to argue that when in Book Three
all history is called back to testify against its progressive
line, Swift simply follows Lucian and Rabelais in parodying
the pretense of older values. Swift is as much satiric mimic
as a defender of ancients. If in Lilliput he could have his
Cyclopean Gulliver protect his eyes, in Glubbdubdrib he
can mock the precursor poet Homer as keener of eye than
tradition itself allows. It is a Lucianic touch, indeed, that
pairs Homer and Aristotle: "*Homer* was the taller and com-
elier Person of the two, walked very erect for one of his
Age, and his Eyes were the most quick and piercing I ever
beheld" (p. 197). Satire is revisionary in every sense, and
Swift goes to such extremes to support the ancient cause
that one is compelled not only to reject the notion of modern progress but to doubt the legitimacy of past enterprise.
Perhaps Homer himself anticipated the problem. No one
appreciates the glorification of the past in the *Iliad* so much
as the old warrior Nestor, and no one is more tediously
represented than Nestor in praising the virtues of a more
perfect past order, more perfect because it is more forget-
table.

When Swift risks what is unlikely to be believed (or what
is tedious in the believing) he does so in extravagant ways.

In the last book of the *Travels* his perfectionists, his noble classicists, his reasonable traditionalists are a race of horses. They are not subject to disease; they decay gradually but only a few weeks before death, which is a kind of eternal return, a *Lhnuwnh* or a retirement to their first mother (p. 275). The Houyhnhnms' only real sense of degeneration comes from the antithetical Yahoos. But a horse is still a horse, and the inhabitants of Swift's utopia are only tentatively removed from the degenerative potential that rules the narrative.[3] If Swift's amiable quadrupeds are "placed in opposite View to human Corruptions" (p. 258), one clear and clearly satiric reason is that they are not humans by a longshot. On the other hand, Yahoos are the natural end of the satirically conceived human line. Their very beastliness conforms to the larger regressive inheritance of the *Travels*: "in most Herds there was a Sort of ruling *Yahoo*, (as among us there is generally some leading or principal Stag in a Park) who was always more *deformed* in Body, and *mischievous* in Disposition, than any of the rest" (p. 262). The Yahoos possess and are possessed by "their strange Disposition to Nastiness and Dirt" (p. 263), a disposition that no matter how much Gulliver protests otherwise also plagues him from the beginning to the end of his voyages.

Yahoos are all too human. Even the theory of their generation is degenerative. One local opinion conceived of their nature as the residual substance that once composed them: "whether produced by the Heat of the Sun upon corrupted Mud and Slime, or from the Ooze and Froth of the Sea, was never known" (p. 271). Gulliver's Master Houyhnhnm expresses a view that is more in keeping with the general structure of the *Travels*, a view ominously applicable to Gulliver: "that the two *Yahoos* said to be first

[3] These matters are explored in greater depth by John Traugott, "A Voyage to Nowhere with Thomas More and Jonathan Swift: *Utopia* and *The Voyage to the Houyhnhnms*," *Sewanee Review* 69 (1961): 534-565; and Robert C. Elliott, "Swift's Utopias," in *The Shape of Utopia: Studies in a Literary Genre* (Chicago, 1970), pp. 50-67.

seen among them, had been driven thither over the Sea; that coming to Land, and being forsaken by their Companions, they retired to the Mountains, and degenerating by Degrees, became in Process of Time, much more savage than those of their own Species in the Country from whence these two Originals came" (p. 272).

For the Houyhnhnms Gulliver is something of a time capsule of Yahoo history; he provides a look backwards. By the same argument, in the last book of the *Travels* the Yahoos are a look forward into the natural descent of man. Gulliver himself frames the issue of satiric inheritance: "And when I began to consider that by copulating with one of the *Yahoo*-Species, I had become a Parent of more; it struck me with the utmost Shame, Confusion, and Horror" (p. 289). He speaks of his own wife and children here as indistinguishable from the Yahoos of Houyhnhnmland. As the returned wanderer, Gulliver is something less than a family man.

Gulliver's experiences in the last book of his *Travels* confirm a process represented satirically throughout. When he first sets eyes on the Yahoo species, he notes that "Upon the whole, I never beheld in all my Travels so disagreeable an Animal, or one against which I naturally conceived so strong an Antipathy" (pp. 223-224). The antipathy is obviously not shared by one libidinous eleven-year-old female Yahoo who tries to mount him. Gulliver is mortified: his attacker is not even a red-head, which he might have been able to justify as an Irish-Yahoo appetite: "For now I could no longer deny, that I was a real *Yahoo*, in every Limb and Feature, since the Females had a natural Propensity to me as one of their own Species" (p. 267). When his Master sees him naked but for his shirt, he concludes that Gulliver must "be a perfect *Yahoo*" (p. 237), an observation that admits of several interpretations. The epithet "perfect" is synonymous with the name *Houyhnhnm* in Houyhnhnmnese. However *Yahoo* in the Houyhnhnm language is everything that *Houyhnhnm* is not. As perfect Yahoo, Gulliver is a living paradox. But back home and in his final madness he can make no such claim; he betrays his status as a perfect Yahoo by prancing and whinnying like a horse.

✧

Hugh Kenner has written an engaging short book called *The Counterfeiters*, which has an apt subtitle, *an Historical Comedy*. Kenner's subtitle suggests a particular vision of literary process tied to a set of preoccupations that began in the later seventeenth century and characterized "the great artists of an astonishing half-century, 1690-1740."

> We call them satirists, they called themselves (having no better word) satirists; they were, Swift and Pope, great realists, great modernists. They had responded, we are going to see, to a new definition of man, proper to the new universe of empirical fact, which definition still obtains because we are still in that universe. They transmuted, to the point of destruction, the old ritual genres, tragedy, comedy, epic, which were proper to an older universe.[4]

Counterfeit is revision with a vengeance—a sly vengeance. The "Historical Comedy" of Kenner's subtitle is itself the counterfeiting of literary history, the comic reproduction or imitation that records and debases at the same time. For the satirist the world of empirical fact works as it does for the counterfeiter: "retaining its contours, altering its nature."[5] Satirists see a double potential in all recorded action,[6] which reflects a measure of generic displacement or

[4] Hugh Kenner, *The Counterfeiters, an Historical Comedy* (Bloomington, 1968), p. 13. For a longer and more detailed study of some aspects of the notion of counterfeit and hoax in the early eighteenth century, see Joseph M. Levine, *Dr. Woodward's Shield: History, Science, and Satire in Augustan England* (Berkeley and Los Angeles, 1977).
[5] Kenner, *The Counterfeiters*, p. 158.
[6] W. Bliss Carnochan makes the same point in his study of Swift's satiric

duplicity. Gulliver is a travelling man, *homo viator*, but he is also a decentered or counterfeit hero. He shares a remembered generic destiny with sorts as variable as Odysseus and Robinson Crusoe. In parodying the idea of the nationally displaced hero, Swift addresses the epic of his time, the epic of territorial exploration and expansion in unknown continents and seas of the world. The spaces of the *Travels* are suspiciously extreme: the first and last books are set beyond *terra australis incognita* in a satirical underworld of sorts (or at least "down under"); the second adventure occurs near or about the mythical Northwest Passage (the traditional land of fallen giants); and the third adventure is set in the uncharted waters of the oriental Pacific.[7]

The conjunction of epic and travel literature can be traced back to the Greek geographer Strabo, who based a good part of his writings on the presumed accuracy of the Homeric Mediterranean adventures. Of course the counterassumption formed the ironic basis for Lucian's Homeric parody in the *True History*. Those predisposed to skepticism always treat travel literature in as antagonistic a manner as they treat heroic marvels. Thus Voltaire writes

strategies, *Lemuel Gulliver's Mirror for Man* (Berkeley and Los Angeles, 1968): "[satire] manifests ironically the hope of common assurance and the fact of common doubt" (p. 6).

[7] For a review of the geography of the *Travels*, see the second essay, "The Geography and Chronology of *Gulliver's Travels*," in Arthur E. Case's *Four Essays on Gulliver's Travels* (Gloucester, Mass., 1958). *The Memoirs of the Extraordinary Life, Works, and Discoveries of Martinus Scriblerus*, ed. Charles Kerby-Miller (New York, reissued 1966) provided Swift the more fanciful inspiration for the journeys and places of the *Travels*. Chapter Sixteen of the *Memoirs* contains a list of planned voyages for Martinus to the "Remains of the ancient *Pygmaean* Empire," to "the Land of the *Giants*," to the "Kingdom of *Philosophers*, who govern by the *Mathematicks*," to a land in which "he discovers a Vein of Melancholy proceeding almost to a Disgust of his Species" (p. 165). For the opening adventure in Lilliput, Swift may have remembered a bit of lore about another wandering hero, Hercules, who after conquering Antaeus was so exhausted by his efforts that he fell prey to a horde of attacking pigmies. The sleeping Gulliver finds himself in a similar plight.

of historical methodology in his *Philosophical Dictionary*:
"When Herodotus relates what he was told by the barba-
rians among whom he traveled, he relates nonsense; but
most of our travelers do the same."[8] And although Gulliver
is hardly one to trust, he voices a similar sentiment after his
rescue from Brobdingnag:

> I thought we were already overstocked with Books of
> Travels: That nothing could now pass which was not
> extraordinary; wherein I doubted, some Authors less
> consulted Truth than their own Vanity or Interest, or
> the Diversion of ignorant Readers. That my Story
> could contain little besides common Events, without
> those ornamental Descriptions of strange Plants,
> Trees, Birds, and other Animals; or the barbarous
> Customs and Idolatry of savage People, with which
> most Writers abound. However, I thanked him for his
> good Opinion, and promised to take the Matter into
> my Thoughts. (P. 147)

That Gulliver demurs is both a joke and a commentary
upon the state of the art. Swift's friend Frances Hutcheson
offers some observations about the status of travel literature in 1726, the same year Swift published the *Travels*.

> A Late Ingenious Author . . . has justly observ'd the
> Absurdity of the *monstrous Taste*, which has possess'd
> both the *Readers* and *Writers* of *Travels*. They scarce
> give us any Account of the *natural Affections, the Familys,
> Associations, Friendships, Clans,* of the *Indians*; and as
> rarely do they mention their Abhorrence of *Treachery*
> among themselves; their *Proneness* to mutual Aid, and
> to the Defence of their several *States*; their Contempt
> of Death in defence of their Country, or upon points
> of *Honour*. "These are but *common-Storys*—No need to

[8] Voltaire, *Philosophical Dictionary*, trans. Peter Gay (New York, 1962),
entry on "Circumcision," p. 203.

travel to the *Indies* for what we see in Europe every Day." The Entertainment therefore in these ingenious Studys consists chiefly in exciting *Horror*, and making Men *Stare*. The ordinary Employment of the Bulk of the *Indians* in support of their Wives and Offspring, or Relations, has nothing of the *Prodigious*. But a *Human Sacrifice*, a Feast upon Enemys Carcases, can raise an Horror and Admiration of the wondrous Barbarity of *Indians*, in Nations no strangers to the *Massacre at Paris*, the *Irish Rebellion*, or the Journals of the *Inquisition*. These they behold with religious Veneration; but the *Indian Sacrifices*, flowing from a like Perversion of *Humanity* by *Superstition*, raise the highest Abhorrence and Amazement. What is most suprizing in these Studys is the wondrous *Credulity* of some Gentlemen, of great Pretensions in other matters to Caution of Assent, for these *marvellous Memoirs* of Monks, Fryars, Sea-Captains, Pyrates; and for the *Historys*, *Annals*, *Chronologys*, receiv'd by Oral Tradition, or Hieroglyphicks.[9]

Hutcheson's complaint is one that had received even more eloquent expression in Montaigne's famous essay "Of Cannibals." Swift's Gulliver arrives as a satiric corrective for such complaints. But as is often the case with satire, it exacerbates before it amends. Try as he might to keep his record within the bounds of mundane description, the extravagances of the travel genre force poor Gulliver to the extraordinary. Each voyage begins with a probable destination and ends with an improbable place. Swift's strategy is primarily Lucianic, but he borrows from travels as remote as Sir Thomas More's *Utopia*, Rabelais' later Northwest Passage books, Cyrano de Bergerac's atmospheric travel histories, even Defoe's allegorical lunar journey, *The Consolidator*.[10]

[9] Frances Hutcheson, *An Enquiry concerning Moral Good and Evil* (London, 1726), pp. 203-204.

[10] Swift's pilferings from Defoe's travel works are intriguing. The ship

STRANGE DISPOSITIONS

The satiric traveller is an antithetical figure. As he "moves out," he understands less. In serious travel literature, the home order or the normative order is the basis of measured value so that in the voyage out there is both a psychological and intellectual pressure to move back in, to acclimate, familiarize, adjust, and in one way or another come home. As a narrative or strategic promise, homecoming is the final falling into place of travel literature—no voyager, imagined or actual, leaves home with the *intent* of permanent exile. Perhaps this is why the traditional utopia or *no place* is usually so alien and extreme. Utopia is home only for antithetical natures.

An essential strategy in the satiric or parodic travel narrative is the confusion of the "no place" with the "home place." Primitive forms such as the "Antipodes" satire, where the utopian realm is at geographical and cultural odds with the homeland (that is turned upside down), serve as ready examples of the process in outline, and there are antipodal elements in all of the books of *Gulliver's Travels*. But the more complex satiric parodies of travel narrative work with more subtle means of psychological and spatial unsettlement. In Swift's *Travels*, the most unsettled place is the mental territory of the traveller. Gulliver loses the will to go home because his sense of himself as a homebody deteriorates—he prefers geographical displacement. Even at home he seeks the stable rather than the house. Like Achilles, he can talk to horses, but unlike Achilles, he gains no glory from doing so.[11]

---

captain for Gulliver's third voyage is named Robinson, which could not but help recall the famous adventurer of a few years before, and the voyage's destination is Tonquin, precisely where Defoe's much earlier traveller from the *Consolidator* had journeyed to begin his lunar flight. From Tonquin Swift arrives at a flying island and parodies certain experiments of the Royal Society, a program that had also occupied Defoe in the *Consolidator*. It may be that Swift decided to repay Defoe in kind, since much of the *Consolidator* (1706) tried to capitalize on the fame and borrow the allegorical machinery of Swift's *A Tale of A Tub* (1704). The circle is made more vicious by the obvious distaste each writer had for the other.

[11] In *The Counterfeiters*, Hugh Kenner tells a different horse story about

STRANGE DISPOSITIONS

At the end of his travels Gulliver is a figure without a
ground. All of his life he has shared a characteristic feature
of the wanderer, "an insatiable Desire of seeing foreign
Countries" (p. 80), but that desire is finally subverted by an
antagonism to the place of origin. The original wanderer,
Odysseus, is sanctioned in his wanderlust partly because of
his great desire to return. Only after he reestablishes himself as a native force do the post-Homeric legends of his
further voyages begin, the most famous of which is recorded in Dante's *Inferno*. Significantly, for Dante the cen-
trifugal spirit is a kind of motion sickness, and Ulysses is
the tragic version of the perpetually exiled traveller. Hell's
exile is perhaps worse than Gulliver's home stable because
the denied home is the promised Earthly Paradise.

In the *True History*, Lucian begins his satiric subversion
of the homing epic by insisting that his narrator make the
same tragic step that Dante was later to record—the step
beyond the Pillars of Hercules into unknown waters. Lucian abandons the depth of epic values for the abnormal
range of parodic displacement. Similarly, Swift works to
undermine the measure of the home place by making Gulliver increasingly unsure of what normative measure
means. In the initial voyages, accident makes him a monster or a *lusus naturae*. Eventually he succeeds in distorting
his own lineaments by mad devise. His homing instinct is
shapeless because by the end he has no shape that he wants
to call his own. Even earlier in his *Travels*, after the Brobdingnagian adventure, he had realized that proportion was
a relative thing, but his realization made it no easier for
him to contemplate his altered physical status: "I could
never endure to look in a Glass after mine Eyes had been

---

a classical hero. For Kenner, Gulliver is a "last Odysseus" doing "his poor
best to fulfill yet another ancient scripture, one of which doubtless he has
never heard: the mysterious tradition preserved by the Pyrrhonist chronicler Sextus Empiricus, that Odysseus at the end of his life was
metamorphosed into a horse" (p. 141).

accustomed to such prodigious Objects; because the Comparison gave me so despicable a Conceit of my self" (p. 147). When at the end of the *Travels* he returns home to a place where he would rather not be and to a place that would probably prefer not to have him, he again looks in the mirror, this time with a thought to self-accommodation: "to behold my Figure often in a Glass, and thus if possible habituate my self by Time to tolerate the Sight of a human Creature" (p. 295). Satiric travel is schizophrenic, and Gulliver loses formal integrity when his spatial and proportionate insecurity befuddles his home image. After Brobdingnag all England seems Lilliputian to Gulliver (which, by satiric analogy, it was). He notes that until he can readjust, his family "concluded I had lost my Wits" (p. 149). Later, when first introduced to the estate of the Horse of Quality in Houyhnhnmland, Gulliver reaches the same conclusion about himself: "I feared my Brain was disturbed by my Sufferings and Misfortunes" (p. 229). Gulliver has been set up. His final madness is the satiric concentration of displacement in the homeless body and soul of the traveller.

In Lilliput Gulliver's stature gave him the name of mountain and allowed him the role of human arch. To the Blefuscans he was a veritable Leviathan. In Brobdingnag he is thought to be a species of weasel, toad, spider, or unnamed vermin; a piece of clockwork; perhaps even "an Embrio, or abortive Birth" (p. 104). The kitchen clerk's monkey gives him "good Reason to believe that he took me for a young one of his own Species" (p. 122), something Gulliver has occasion to remember when he is later mounted by a female Yahoo in Houyhnhnmland. At the end of his fourth voyage his wife embraces him at home, and Swift's *homo viator* faints dead away. The smell of his faithful Penelope is alien to his "perfected" nose. Earlier Gulliver's wife protested that the kind of voyaging Gulliver subjects himself to makes torture out of readjustment. She wants no more of unsettled behavior: "But my Wife protested I should never go to Sea any more; although my evil Destiny so ordered, that she had not Power to hinder me" (p. 149). For Gulliver's wife, voyaging is the equivalent of alienated affection, and it is a kind of madness constantly to test one's powers of readjustment. In a narrative sense, to send Gulliver out over and over again is to insure that he looses the capacity to return whole.

Satiric travels are something of an overextension, and at the end of his *Travels* Gulliver is like the restless author of *A Tale of A Tub*: once maddened by surfaces, his depths become lunatic. The *Tale*'s author is no more a homecomer than is Gulliver.

> For in *Writing*, it is as in *Travelling*: If a Man is in haste to be at home, (which I acknowledge to be none of my Case, having never so little Business, as when I am there) if his *Horse* be tired with long Riding, and ill Ways, or be naturally a Jade, I advise him clearly to make the straitest and the commonest Road, be it ever so dirty; But, then surely, we must own such a Man to be a scurvy Companion at best; He *spatters* himself and his Fellow-Travellers at every Step: All their Thoughts, and Wishes, and Conversation turn entirely upon the Subject of their Journey's End; and at every Splash, and Plunge, and Stumble, they heartily wish one another the Devil. (P. 188)

The author of the *Tale* views the very notion of the centripetal fiction as singleminded: he prefers the range and pace of modernity. But to be in perpetual motion is to see too much of the surface of things, to start by fits and to end by starts. When Gulliver's travels are over, he begins them again by recording them. Here, too, he feels betrayed by the home front. He protests that cuts have been made in his text after its release to an editor. As a writer, just as a traveller, he would have gone on further if he could. In another sense, his writing simply prolongs the record of his madness. Satire's wanderings do not rest upon terra firma. Gulliver begins his voyaging as a ship's surgeon whose mind is something less than surgical. At the end he is captain, and his ship is served by one Dr. Purefoy. Pure faith is satiric gullibility, and the satiric motion appears to be starting all over again. By navigating through the world, Purefoy will certainly lose the purity and the faith his name is heir to.

The displaced hero courts one or another form of madness. Insecure at home, Hamlet makes a fool of himself; sterile in his capacity as a farmer, Don Quixote travels in circles as a lunatic Hidalgo; parasitical by design, Rameau's nephew is frenetic for his supper. Homelessness is maddening. What makes *Gulliver's Travels* even more intriguing in this respect is that, as in Swift's own *Tale of A Tub* or in Dostoevsky's *Notes from Underground* or in Nabokov's *Pale Fire*, the madman is given just enough presence of mind to record the process of his own lunacy.

When Swift added the letter from Gulliver to his cousin Sympson to the 1735 edition of the *Travels*, he further complicated the problem. How can an author be trusted who rants as does Gulliver to his slightly embarrassed cousin and editor? What generates his values? The tone of the letter makes no sense until we have read the entire *Travels*. If we do read the *Travels* through (and thereby understand the prefixed letter), we are forced to conclude that even the earlier voyages are being relayed from the perspective of a madman whose sense of an audience is no more secure than his grasp on his reason. In the 1735 edition, Gulliver not only gives us an inkling of the way his condition can be held against him but of the way Swift holds a crazed Gulliver against the entire genre of travel literature: "If the Censure of *Yahoos* could any Way affect me, I should have great Reason to complain, that some of them are so bold as to think my Book of Travels a meer

Fiction out of mine Brain; and have gone so far as to drop Hints, that the *Houyhnhnms* and *Yahoos* have no more Existence than the Inhabitants of *Utopia*" (pp. 7-8).

That a madman should take so offended a tone comports with the earlier Swiftian notion from the *Tale of A Tub* that the brain's fancies have the power to leap astride reason. Of course Gulliver could point to ocular proof—the miniature cows from Lilliput or the wasp stings from Brobdingnag. But perhaps these are figments of his imagination as well. Further, he tells the professor at Lagado of his visits to the Kingdom of Tribnia (Britain) called Langden (England), and since he makes no claims to being the only European to have visited these territories, we could conclude that all his travels are but encoded versions of home as experienced by a madman. Lunacy means to be mentally far away no matter where one's body is, a state admittedly reached by Gulliver at the end of his travels.[12] The loss of powers that enables a narrator to discriminate, concentrate, and penetrate becomes part of the degenerative representation of Swift's satiric fiction. Gulliver's status as a truth teller—a man possessed by imagined truths—is a compromised status. Cousin Sympson boasts (presumably by way of relation, since he is sheepish in most regards) that Gulliver "was so distinguished for his Veracity, that it became a Sort of Proverb among his Neighbours at *Redriff* when any one affirmed a Thing, to say, it was as true as if Mr. *Gulliver* had spoke it" (p. 9). Somehow this remark by Sympson registers more loyalty than conviction.

Given free reign at home, the horse-mimicking Gulliver is likely to run away with himself. By his own testimony he worries that his manuscript has been tampered with, he offers corrections, he prepares supplementary texts detailing a more fully documented madness. Apparently the *Travels*

---

[12] In his essay, "Of Idleness," Montaigne writes: "The soul that has no fixed goal loses itself; for as they say, to be everywhere is to be nowhere." See *The Complete Essays of Montaigne*, trans. Donald M. Frame (Stanford, 1958), p. 21.

as we have them are but the ur-text of a travelling fancy. Gulliver is similar to the author of the *Tale* who has things in store for posterity. In fact, a quick glance at the proposed oeuvre of the *Tale*'s author momentarily raises the prospect that Swift's two lunatics share satiric experiences. Of the promised titles, two read: "*A Description of the Kingdom of* Absurdities" and "*A Voyage into* England, *by a Person of Quality in* Terra Australis incognita, *translated from the Original*" (p. 2). *Gulliver's Travels* fulfills a part of the *Tale*'s promise: absurdity is figured in satiric ethnocentricity, and a native of Australia might in one sense be a Hottentot but in another is a would-be Houyhnhnm.

✧

Voyages into or out of kingdoms of absurdity are by nature politically tainted. Long before Swift had begun work on the Scriblerian notion of a gullible traveller, his patron, employer, and subject in the first book of the *Travels*, Robert Harley, had participated in a scheme to cast discredit on an unfortunate traveller. In 1705 Harley, having assumed the post of Secretary of Northern Affairs, wished to fill his vacated Speaker's seat in Parliament with a candidate of his own choosing. To do so he had to block the appointment of one William Bromley. A decade before (1692), Bromley, then a young man of twenty-eight, published a personal memoir, *Remarks on the Grand Tour lately perform'd by a Person of Quality*. The remarks revealed the mind of an innocent enough but somewhat foolish admirer of Catholic Europe—a none too healthy bias at any time in England after the Stuarts. By 1705 Bromley's early exuberance had long been forgotten, except by Harley and whatever counterfeiting crew he could muster for the occasion. Harley's men arranged for the republication of Bromley's *Grand Tour*. In its own way, the hoax was ingenious and satirically economical. Its strategy damned the man through the observations of the traveller.

The *Remarks* were reprinted verbatim, but the new edition added a table at the beginning of the volume. Passages from the body of the text were excerpted or briefly described with page numbers referring to the proper context. In isolation the excerpts destroy the serious record of the *Remarks*. We learn in the table how Bromley is barely able to contain his ecstasy when offered the chance to kiss the Pope's feet, and we are informed that Bromley will discuss (as if the matter were in doubt) whether "Crosses and Crucifixes on the Roads in *France* prove it is not *England*." On page 107 of the *Remarks* as previewed, the humble "Author is Compar'd with our Savior, and wants of his Height, a Hand's breath by Measure." For Harley, the political issue is obvious. Bromley was a noted (and at that time respected) High Churchman. Harley's hoax threatens to push him over the Catholic precipice. The hoaxers undermine Bromley's allegiance to his own land by undermining his status as a traveller: rather than controlling the travels he records, he is controlled by them.

I mention this rather slight literary scheme because in a much more sophisticated manner Swift is up to the same thing in *Gulliver's Travels*. Although he has no particular wish to indict any single victim, he does wish to adjust the contours of mock travel to belittle the affairs of his nation. In this sense *Gulliver's Travels* is well-timed. Between 1699 and 1715 Swift's hero is intermittently out of his native land. There is something significant about these dates because they suggest that Swift's scheme of degeneration applies to the processes of history at large. The details of the contemporary allegory, especially in Books One and Three of the narrative, are well enough rehearsed. But the span of the four voyages sets the *Travels* during a time roughly contemporaneous with the major troubles in Europe and England beginning with the Partition Treaties of 1698 and 1699, continuing through the War of Spanish Succession (1701-1713), and concluding with the investigation of Swift's friends and patrons, Harley and Bolingbroke, in 1715.

All of Swift's important historical writings concentrate on segments near the beginning and end of the time periods encompassed by Gulliver's voyages. In his *Contests and Dissentions in Athens and Rome* (1701), he paralleled events in classical history to the Partition Treaty Trials. In his *Conduct of the Allies* (1711) and his *History of the Four Last Years of the Queen* (1713), he treated the latter conduct of the Succession Wars and the negotiations prior to the ordeal of his friends and patron ministers. The time span of *Gulliver's Travels* hints at a kind of historical apostasy—the narrative leaves England during a period of history in which Swift thought England had left her senses. Something of the same order might be argued for a narrative such as Defoe's *Robinson Crusoe*. Crusoe's twenty-eight year exile (1659-1687) roughly overlaps a period of equally charged political significance, the years of Stuart restoration in England. For a Dissenting hater of the Stuarts like Defoe, these years may just as well have been spent on Crusoe's island near the mouth of the Orinoco. Home itself, after all, was akin to political exile. Exile is a key metaphor for Gulliver as it was for Crusoe. Not only is Gulliver removed from England by navigational fate but in both the first and last books of his adventures he is barred even from the lands to which accident has consigned him. In separate legal proceedings, Gulliver leaves Lilliput because he is thought to be more scheming than he was; fifteen years later he leaves Houyhnhnmland because he was thought to be less capable than he is.

Charges of treason and sentences of exile displace greater national follies. In 1699 Gulliver starts off as an English voyager, and in 1715 he returns as an outcast from an outcast land, a misanthrope, a sick man of Europe.[13] His

---

[13] Significantly, the figure from the third book, Lord Munodi, whose name means hater of the world (although he hardly seems so), is also a political exile of sorts: "by a Cabal of Ministers [he] was discharged for Insufficiency" (p. 175). Unlike the Gulliver to be, Munodi has the discretion to keep his opinions pretty much to himself—his name is attitude enough.

giant carcass in Lilliput had made him an invading and standing army, a threat, an engulfer, a saving force and a conspiratorial force. From the first book of the *Travels* Swift announces the gigantic folly of modern politics and war and the "littleness" of all efforts for peace. Gulliver is a human Arch of Triumph as the Lilliputians march beneath him. Passing under, they look up at the holes in the mighty man's dirty breeches, a none too subtle reminder that the particular force Gulliver has to deliver comes as much from the seat of his pants as from the might of his arm. As it turns out, he is useless on land and is at best a necessary tactical force at sea.

Swift's attitude toward the land war raging in Europe was similar to that of Harley and Bolingbroke. A continued Marlborough-like commitment in Europe was madness, a madness figured in the composite of the absurd Lilliputian emperor with this Austrian lip, his fashion "between the *Asiatick* and the *European*," his gold helmet "adorned with Jewels, and a Plume on the Crest," and his symbolically drawn sword (pp. 30-31). Gulliver's efforts on behalf of this emperor's kingdom result in a conspiracy against his own powers and in a scheme to relieve the Man-Mountain of his eyes. This is either an Oedipal sentence for the land's putative savior or a strange recall of a more gigantic and barbaric Cyclopean fate.

In the second book of the *Travels*, the sweep of political degeneration is greater, even if less localized. In Brobdingnag, Gulliver, the former Lilliputian victim, becomes Gulliver, the European defender. Swift opens the satiric perspective to the hundred years of recklessness that constitutes, in his mind, the period of decline from the Renaissance to the later seventeenth century. For much of his stay in Brobdingnag, Gulliver is a figure of exhaustion, tired out by his trials. The tactician becomes a boasting domestic gladiator; the state hero betrayed by government becomes a freak of nature betrayed by a dwarf. If Gulliver reacts against political hypocrisy in Lilliput, in Brobdingnag he becomes the state hypocrite. When the King attacks England, Gulliver's "Colour came and went several Times, with Indignation to hear our noble Country, the Mistress of Arts and Arms, the Scourge of *France*, the Arbitress of *Europe*, the Seat of Virtue, Piety, Honour and Truth, the Pride and Envy of the World, so contemptuously treated" (p. 107). He follows the advice of Dionysius Halicarnassensis in his "laudable Partiality to my own Country" (p. 133), and learns after many discourses with the giant-king to "hide the Frailties and Deformities of my Political Mother, and place her Virtues and Beauties in the most advantageous Light" (p. 133). Gulliver is the child of England, unaware of most of his "mother's" deformities and hiding those he suspects: he is the child of a deformed mother that has produced, among other things, Gulliver.

Swift probably began composing the *Travels* about the time that Gulliver's voyages theoretically end, and when he continued work at his own pace through the 1720s he adjusted the allegorical scheme of the narrative to the more generally conceived issues of political and cultural degeneration in the Walpole era. In Lilliput Gulliver practices statecraft; in Brobdingnag he defends it; in Laputa he hears of its abuses; in Houyhnhnmland he attacks it. As in all of the narrative movements of the *Travels*, Gulliver's experiences grow worse and worse. And as far as the theme of political degeneration goes, history becomes something of an *end* in itself. But it remains for Pope, who in some measure acted at Swift's suggestion, to take the historical scene of the 1720s even beyond the end and back to chaos in *The Dunciad*.

Chapter Eight

THINGS UNBORN: POPE'S *THE RAPE OF THE LOCK* AND *THE DUNCIAD*

The Dunciad is a succession poem for a kingdom that ought not to be; *The Rape of the Lock* is a poem of reunion for a marriage that could not be. In the later and larger poem, Pope celebrates the law of enervation; in the earlier and miniaturized epic, he marvels at the power of denial.[1] Pope wrote *The Rape of the Lock* at the request of his friend John Caryll who had asked him to help ease tensions between two important and traditionally intermarrying Catholic families, the Petres and the Fermors. The families had quarreled over the incident depicted in the poem. Pope hoped that his jest might "laugh them together again."[2] But denial is so strong a satiric principle in the poem that intent is subverted: the very notion of rape violates the hope of renewed union. At the crucial moment, the Baron's instrument, such as it is, joins only to divide. The emblem of the poem's action, scissors upon hair, serves as the mock displacement of its proposed solution. Rape is both a violation of bodily law and a violation of marital con-

---

[1] The exclusive and shared features of the worlds of both satiric poems are treated in an essay by Murray Krieger, "The 'Frail China Jar' and the Rude Hand of Chaos," *Centennial Review of Arts and Sciences* 5 (1961): 176-194. Krieger argues that the charm of artifice in *The Rape of the Lock* was abandoned by Pope for the public ruin of *The Dunciad*. However absurd the events of *The Rape* may have seemed, Pope was, at least, writing for allies (the great Catholic families involved). *The Dunciad* was an expansive campaign against lifelong enemies.

[2] Alexander Pope, *The Rape of the Lock and Other Poems*, ed. Geoffrey Tillotson, Twickenham Edition (London and New Haven, 3rd ed., 1962), p. 81. Citations from *The Rape of the Lock* are from this edition.

sent in which to join is eventually (and legally) to divide or parturiate.

Everything about the structure of *The Rape of the Lock* diverts the issues of the day. And even the day is denied proper issue, as the sun must wait until noon to begin its mannered progress.

> *Sol* thro' white Curtains shot a tim'rous Ray,
> And op'd those Eyes that must eclipse the Day;
> Now Lapdogs give themselves the rowzing Shake,
> And sleepless Lovers, just at Twelve, awake.
>
> (I, 13-16)

Lapdogs, especially those with the curious name of Shock (another metonymic expression for hair), and lovers, announced or unannounced, reveal the epic cast and the belated epic action. *The Rape of the Lock* depicts a "shocking" or traumatic state of human affairs, and the human affairs it depicts represent the state of love without conscious lovers. Pope realized as much in the expanded five-canto version, when he added the machinery of sylphs and gnomes, the game of *Ombre*, and the descent to the Cave of Spleen (the undisplaced satiric world where denial itself is denied: "And Maids turn'd Bottles, call aloud for Corks," IV, 54). Beneath the ritualized practices of the dressing table and the codified rules of the card game (the game of man or *Ombre*), more primal activities are disguised: attraction is a kind of vanity or overcompensated desire, and sexual action is a game of displaced power.

The opening lines of *The Rape of the Lock* establish its essentially double satiric world, a world of obvious responses and misunderstood motives: "What dire Offence from am'rous Causes springs, / What mighty Contests rise from trivial Things" (I, 1-2). How small things become large is a natural subject of the mock-epic, but these first lines also hint at the hidden power of suppression.

> Say what strange Motive, Goddess! cou'd compel
> A well-bred *Lord* t'assault a gentle *Belle*?
> Oh say what stranger Cause, yet unexplor'd,
> Cou'd make a gentle *Belle* reject a *Lord*?
>
> (I, 7-10)

The answer to the first question is the overt subject of the poem; the answer to the second question is its covert subject. In satire, the covert action—that form of behavior that simultaneously disguises and betrays its purpose—provides the texture of the narrative, its ironies, its hypocrisies, its double-entendres, its obsessions, its repressions. Belinda's sexual rejection is the primary satiric subject of the poem. She is a heroine who, in a kind of game of perpetual denial, has mistaken the question of "who" for the question of "whether." Her natural instincts are determined, and she is at that crucial turn in life where the secrets of "Maids" and "Children" may no longer be valid for her. In the coded world of fashion a more mature "graceful Ease, and Sweetness void of Pride, / Might hide her Faults, if *Belles* had Faults to hide" (II, 15-16); but in the world of sexual falls and faults the imperfections of a virgin are the clue to her impulses: "Whether the Nymph shall break *Diana's* Law, / Or some frail *China* Jar receive a Flaw, / Or stain her Honour, or her new Brocade" (II, 105-107).

An amorous cause is about to spring, and as the often cited zeugmatic line implies, the abstract stain upon honor is as inevitable as the more material stain that is a sign of the same loss. In the sequence in which Diana's law seems about to be broken, the lapdog, Shock, takes a nasty little spill: "Heav'n has doom'd that *Shock* must fall" (II, 110). Such "doom" is what the virgin-inspired sylphs conceive as sexual issue: "With beating Hearts the dire Event they wait, / Anxious, and trembling for the Birth of Fate" (II, 141-142). Belinda might have guessed at all this—she was present for the omens of the mid-morning when the "tott'ring

China shook without a Wind, / Nay, *Poll* sate mute, and *Shock* was most Unkind!" (IV, 163-164). The unkindest shock of all, indeed. All along Belinda had been conscious of one *Shock* while anticipating another.

As a rhyme word, *Shock* echoes the sound of the ravished object (*Lock*) and the effect of the ravishing act (rape is traumatic). Belinda's *Shock* is a shock to her system of disguised desire. And in her grief she unconsciously tells the truth when she addresses the crime: "Oh hadst thou, Cruel! been content to seize / Hairs less in sight, or any Hairs but these!" (IV, 175-176). Perhaps inadvertently she refers to the "Shock" that sits in her lap? Earlier, when we learned what her loss meant, we were to regret the fateful action of the scissors: "The meeting Points the sacred Hair dissever / From the fair Head, for ever and for ever!" (III, 153-154). But the lost hair ought to grow back; this is one important instance where the metaphoric loss (virginity, which does not grow back) is closer to the literal description of the crucial act than to the literal act itself.

Belinda has concentrated her own energies, her libido, where only the sylphs can enjoy it—she has concentrated her libido in herself or in such seemingly neutral objects as her lapdog. In satiric narrative, coded avoidance is primed for violation. Belinda's ritual denial is both her own and others' frustration: "Oft she rejects, but never once offends" (II, 12). But denial is a kind of self-offense. The hermaphroditic sylphs—the denying militia—promote constriction. Ariel's warning, "Beware of all, but most beware of Man!" (I, 114), occludes sexual energy as effectively as the drawn curtains occlude the sun.

According to the scheme for prudery devised in the poem, nymphs exercise their sexual energies only in the air, where the sylphs take polymorphic and bisexual shapes. D. H. Lawrence would call it "sex in the head." Chastity is a natural condition only for a time; the machinery of the poem, however, would direct all instincts

forever toward incorporeal realms. At the very moment
when Ariel warns Belinda of man, Shock "Leapt up, and
wak'd his Mistress with his Tongue" (I, 116). Perhaps for
this reason, the head sylph, Ariel, posts himself as guard
not of the partitive Lock but of the sudden Shock: "Do
thou, *Crispissa*, tend her fav'rite Lock; / Ariel himself shall
be the Guard of *Shock*" (II, 115-116). Of course, at the
climactic moment, the heady brigade abandons the place of
action: Belinda's vitality invites a necessary vulnerability.

> Just in that instant, anxious *Ariel* sought
> The close Recesses of the Virgin's Thought;
> As on the Nosegay in her Breast reclin'd,
> He watch'd th' Ideas rising in her Mind,
> Sudden he view'd, in spite of all her Art,
> An Earthly Lover lurking at her Heart.
> Amaz'd, confus'd, he found his Pow'r expir'd,
> Resign'd to Fate, and with a Sigh retir'd.
> (III, 139-146)

The Baron's rape of the lock is an inarticulate mock-
tragic effort to get going. Pope does not see the Baron as a
necessary choice, but he sees choice in the abstract as a
principle of continuity. Clarissa voices this view in the fifth
canto, a view more brusquely stated by the Baron in his
own defense: "Thou by some other shalt be laid as low" (V,
98). Even if the Baron cuts himself out of the picture, his
withdrawal is still very much a part of the larger picture.
He is attracted because Belinda attracts.[3] And his impulse
"By Force to ravish, or by Fraud betray" (II, 32) sets the
metonymic action. Belinda's denial displaces response, and
the Baron exerts *his* energies on an action that is possible
not because it is publicly acceptable but because it can be
publicly done.

---

[3] The sequence of ambiguous sexual encounters in the poem is discussed in a well-known essay by Cleanth Brooks, "The Case of Miss
Arabella Fermor: A Re-examination," *Sewanee Review* (1943): 505-524.

THINGS UNBORN

Before the rape Belinda herself "Burns to encounter two adventrous Knights" (III, 26). An adventure is a thing to come which, in a sense, is what the entire poem is about, but Belinda's immediate adventure is at the game of Ombre, that is, the game of man (Spanish *hombre*). As in the later descent to the Cave of Spleen where revenge takes the form of the desire upon which it is supposed to seek retribution, the card game is of double purpose. Belinda plays at the game of "Man" with a manly and sexually confused vengeance, almost as if desire can only take its perverse form. She releases sexual energy; her King falls on the Baron's "prostrate *Ace*" (III, 98). An exhausting and sterile sexual strategy controls the poem: union of any kind is a sort of castration. Later, the Baron, too, cuts when he cannot penetrate.

Union, of course, is a comic answer to the satiric question of desire and denial posed at the beginning of the poem. If satire allows such an answer, the successor question is no less difficult: What mediating potential exists? Clarissa's speech in the fifth canto—a parody of Sarpedon's speech to Glaucus in the *Iliad* on the subject of heroic risk—provides an answer suitable for comedy but irrelevant for satire. "And she who scorns a Man will die a Maid" (V, 28), Clarissa warns, but Belinda is not attuned to the necessary compromises of a comic society. She still seeks restoration of that which is outrageously and absurdly lost. In satire the excesses of recovery are very close to the incivilities of violation. The world of the poem knows only the reaction of the hapless Belinda and the astoundingly inarticulate Sir Plume, who speaks as a satiric arbiter.

And thus broke out—"My Lord, why, what the Devil?
"Z———ds! damn the Lock! 'fore Gad, you must be civil!
"Plague on't! 'tis past a Jest—nay prithee, Pox!
"Give her the Hair"—he spoke, and rapp'd his Box.

(IV, 127-130)

The only response is the Baron's cool "It grieves me much (reply'd the Peer again) / Who speaks so well shou'd ever speak in vain" (IV, 131-132), and the only mediating spirit in the poem is the wit of its author who knows that satire is better at perceiving the irregularities of human action by imitating them than it is at making them less desperate by modifying them.

❖

In satire resolution is misproportionate by design. Rape, despite the sterility of denial, is not a mediating action. If Pope's poem hopes for reunion, the strength of its satiric resources calls for perverse coupling. In Belinda's dressing room only "The Tortoise here and Elephant unite" (I, 135)—a possibility for inlaid shell and ivory, but a trial for nature. Satire puts nature and its generic proportions on trial. Forced couplings produce a satiric birth. In *The Rape of the Lock*, the issue of Belinda's virginity is the larger birth of fate. In any Christian epic such a birth is tantamount to the loss of innocence or the fall of man. By the time of *The Dunciad* the satiric misbirth becomes a universal noncreation; the little or small-minded world bears itself as a great action. Pope's earlier mock-epic is a miniaturized *Iliad* in its design. *The Dunciad* is expansive and migrational—its model is Virgilian.

Like Milton's heavenly muse, the Queen Mother of *The Dunciad* spreads her wings to cover the production of a natural hatch: "Here pleas'd behold her mighty wings outspread / To hatch a new Saturnian age of Lead" (I, 27-28).[4] Birth is elemental, but its essence is of a suspect nature. Na-

---

[4] Alexander Pope, *The Dunciad*, ed. James Sutherland, Twickenham Edition (London and New Haven, 3rd ed., 1963). All citations from *The Dunciad* will be to this edition. Passages from the introductory material to the various editions of the poem, from the arguments of the books, and from Warburton's notes to the 1742 edition will be cited by page number in Sutherland's text.

tive sons return to mother substance.[5] In Book IV of the
1743 *Dunciad*, an antiquarian Dunce named Mummius
(identified by Warburton and others as Dr. Mead) fights
for the possession of rare coins swallowed by another crafty
collector. The account recalls the debased nature of action
in the peristaltic movements of the poem's plot. Pursued by
a band of Corsairs while travelling with his booty in the
Levant, Annius swallows the coins. Mummius remembers.

> "Down his own throat he risqu'd the Grecian gold;
> Receiv'd each Demi-God, with pious care,
> Deep in his Entrails—I rever'd them there,
> I bought them, shrouded in that living shrine,
> And, at their second birth, they issue mine."
>
> (IV, 382-385)

Mummius bargains with Annius for the base substance
within the baser field. Such Dunciadic alchemy requires a
clever obstetrician, one accustomed to strange births.

> (Reply'd soft Annius) this our paunch before
> Still bears them, faithful; and that thus I eat,
> Is to refund the Medals with the meat.
> To prove me, Goddess! clear of all design,
> Bid me with Pollio sup, as well as dine:
> There all the Learn'd shall at the labour stand,
> And Douglas lend his soft, obstetric hand."
>
> (IV, 388-394)

It was rumored around London that Douglas had delivered a woman of baby rabbits. The body of witlessness cel-

---

[5] The frontispiece of the *Dunciad Variorum of 1729* pictures an ass laden
with the works of the Dunciadic fraternity. Traditionally, on the Octave of
the Epiphany (the feast of fools) the subdeacons of the Church usher an
ass into the ceremony of the Mass. On that same day clowns appear in the
festivities and, among other ludicrous adventures, plunge and tumble in
excrement. The specific games of the second book of *The Dunciad* reflect
the baser activities of the *festa stultorum*—the general metaphoric pattern
of the poem is graced by the literal descent into waste substance.

ebrated in the poem is capable of all sorts of births, and the participants in the recorded action are usually incapable of distinguishing among them. Much of the content of *The Dunciad* is generation's dirty dance, and the Dunces' arts shine in "conglob'd" darkness. By the end of the poem, Dulness's progeny gathers around her so that—to modify an unpleasant but telling idiom—she can be said to have "gotten her shit together." Progeny seeks its source. Cibber, the natural successor figure in the poem, spends much of his time nuzzled in the lap of the Queen Mother. Insofar as he moves at all, he moves to return to a source near to that from which he came—any bodily orifice will do, but he naturally prefers reentrance at the point from which he gained egress. The celebration of Dulness is such that the end is an elaboration of the dark principles upon which the beginning was misconceived.

The Dunciad proper is a succession satire. It is set on Lord Mayor's Day, 1719, a day on which the then recently appointed poet laureate, Elkanah Settle, would have officiated as nationally sanctioned wit. Settle died in 1724, and *The Dunciad*'s most recent editor concurs in the somewhat standard speculation that Pope backdated the poem's setting (perhaps at Swift's suggestion) in order to encompass both the reign of Settle and the emptying of his office—as if the reign of a Dunce is a perpetual voiding.[6] In 1702, a very young Alexander Pope wrote a poem called "To the Author of a Poem, intitled Successio," a few lines of which reappear later in *The Dunciad*. None too coincidentally, the author in question was Elkanah Settle and the poem, Settle's *Eusebia Triumphans* (1702), honored the arrangements for the future Hanoverian succession to the English monarchy. For the young Pope, to pass on or to succeed meant the same as it had meant for Dryden in *Mac Flecknoe*: to sink down or to pass through. He writes of Set-

[6] See *The Dunciad*, p. xiv.

tle: "Wit, past thro thee, no longer is the same, / As Meat digested takes a diff'rent Name" (ll. 11-12).

In 1702 the Hanoverian succession was a political piece of paper; in 1728 the year of *The Dunciad* in three books, it resembled a political and cultural catharsis for Pope. If the spatial movement in the poem is from the entertainments of the east-end rabble to the glories of the Hanoverian court ("Till rais'd from booths, to Theatre, to Court, / Her seat imperial Dulness shall transport," III, 299-300), the satiric movement is to the jakes of idiocy.[7] Three years before the first *Dunciad*, Pope wrote to Swift: "Your Travels I hear much of; my own, I promise you, shall never more be in a strange land, but a diligent, I hope useful, investigation of my own territories. I mean no more translations, but something domestic, fit for my own country, and for my own time" (15 September 1725). Of course *The Dunciad* is very much a translation, but a translation on wasted ground. As the action moves west, the day grows darker so that the *translatio* is not simply the course of an empire that sinks to rise but the succession of day by night. When the successor figure—be it Theobald or Cibber—asks that Dulness "Secure us kindly in our native night" (I, 176), only the alliteration demands the dark estate—the cliché demands the legal inheritance or hegemony, "native right." By the end of the action Pope has provided the rightful succession—the son gets what he comes to rather than what comes to him: "My son! the promis'd land expects thy reign" (I, 292). The promised land is a place of native origin at the matrix or womb where the son had sunk his head. In essence, the son sinks as the sun sinks: "Universal Darkness buries All" (IV, 656). That the last line of Pope's satiric succession should inter the light of the race is narratively emblematic. Burial is a heavy descent, and

[7] For a full discussion of the progress of stupidity in the narrative action, see Aubrey L. Williams, *Pope's Dunciad: A Study of its Meaning* (Baton Rouge, 1955).

the final action is commensurate with satiric disinheritance. Even for Cibber's progeny, to hold one's own is to lose one's properties: "Soon to that mass of Nonsense to return, / Where things destroy'd are swept to things unborn" (I, 241-242).

The original *Dunciad* kept the translation and the succession Virgilian: "Books and the Man I sing, the first who brings / The Smithfield Muses to the Ear of Kings" (I, 1-2). When Pope revised the opening for the 1743 version, he expanded the satiric matrix: "The Mighty Mother, and her Son who brings / The Smithfield Muses to the ear of Kings" (I, 1-2). The effect of the change is multifold. It centers the action on the gestational and generational process, but at the same time it enlarges and antedates the narrative scope. Pope begins prior to time and form, thus enabling him to end with a more perfect satiric restoration of properties.

> In eldest time, e'er mortals writ or read,
> E'er Pallas issu'd from the Thund'rer's head,
> Dulness o'er all possess'd her ancient right,
> Daughter of Chaos and eternal Night:
> Fate in their dotage this fair Ideot gave,
> Gross as her sire, and as her mother grave,
> Laborious, heavy, busy, bold, and blind,
> She rul'd in native Anarchy, the mind.
> Still her old Empire to restore she tries,
> For, born a Goddess, Dulness never dies.
>
> (I, 9-18)

The properties of possession and of transmission are Dunciadic holes in narrative space. At the end of the action, Dulness swallows herself up: "More she had spoke, but yawn'd—All Nature nods: / What Mortal can resist the Yawn of Gods?" (IV, 605-606). The word *yawn* derives from the Greek *gas* or *chaos*: the gnostic eschatology is complete. Dulness yawns herself into oblivion. If the action begins with a parody of epic possession, it ends with a parody of epic *nostos*, a homecoming that is at the same time a disinheritance, a backward birth. In *The Masks of God*, Joseph Campbell writes of a gnostic or Manichean version of creation where a rival to the true God engulfs a quantity of light and ravishes it "downward" where it is entrapped in matter.[8] Pope's Dulness has like demiurges; she subsumes light and hatches it in dense deposits.

❖

Pope and his annotator for the 1743 edition of *The Dunciad*, Warburton, are cognizant of the ways in which the strategies of the action play upon structures of satiric inheritance. Of Cibber, the new successor figure, Warburton writes:

> We can easily derive our Hero's Pedigree from a Goddess of no small power and authority amongst men; and legitimate and install him after the right classical and authentic fashion: For, like as the ancient Sages found a Son of Mars in a mighty warrior; a Son of Neptune in a skilful Seaman; a Son of Phoebus in a harmonious Poet; so have we here, if need be, a Son of Fortune in an artful *Gamester*. And who is fitter than the Offspring of *Chance*, to assist in restoring the Empire of *Night* and *Chaos*? (Pp. 263-264)

Here illegitimacy, or its suggestion, becomes a kind of pedigree for the regressive estate. Further, the successor figure earns the honor by already having loaned his name to the rolls of the dead. Warburton recalls passages from Cibber's recently published *Apology*.

> "Is it (saith he) a time of day for me to leave off these fooleries, and set up a new character? I can no more

[8] Joseph Campbell, *The Masks of God: Creative Mythology* (New York, 1976), p. 156.

put off my Follies than my Skin; I have often tried, but
they stick too close to me; nor am I sure my friends are
displeased with them, for in this light I afford them
frequent matter of mirth, etc. etc." Having then so
publickly declared himself *incorrigible*, he is become
dead in law, (I mean the *law Epopœian*) and descendeth
to the Poet as his property: who may take him, and
deal with him, as if he had been dead as long as an old
Egyptian hero; that is to say, *embowel* and *embalm him
for posterity*. (Pp. 264-265)

The language of satire is so often mortifying because the
subjects of satire are so temptingly mortal. Warburton's
remarks encapsulate part of the larger satiric process—
satiric death is something of a redundancy because the
properties of posterity have already been cheated. For a
subject's being to be too closely attached to his skin is to
make him a negligible legal entity. And when such a subject
threatens to pass on only his dust, he "descendeth" quite
literally into a satiric plot. Warburton appropriates heroism for the satiric line of the poem by documenting its new
hero's nonstatus. He argues that illegitimacy is a version of
mysterious heroic origin, but Pope's readers know that
irony transforms the birth of the hero into a misconcep-
tion, a generic narrative parody in all senses. In *Richard
Aristarchus of the Hero of the Poem*, Warburton establishes the
bona fides of Colley Cibber, the substitute son of Dulness:
"And that he did not pass himself on the world for a Hero,
as well by birth as education, was his own fault: For, his
lineage he bringeth into his life as an Anecdote, and is sen-
sible he had it in his power *to be thought no body's son at all*:
And what is that but coming into the world a Hero?" (p.
263).

The notion of taking over a suspect line is not confined
to *The Dunciad*'s installation of a hero. Its very mode is
the inheritance of a dead line. Under the name of Richard

Aristarchus, Warburton claims that the little epic (or mock-epic) exists in the same relation to the greater epics as does the satyr play to the tragedies of ancient Greece. Of course, the little epics and all but one of the satyr plays are lost. Thus *The Dunciad*, to borrow the flippant reviewer's words, fills a much needed gap.

> From this delicacy of the Muse arose the *little Epic*, (more lively and choleric than her elder sister, whose bulk and complexion incline her to the flegmatic) and for this some notorious Vehicle of vice and folly was sought out, to make thereof an example. An early instance of which (nor could it escape the accurate Scriblerus) the Father of Epic poem himself affordeth us. From him the practice descended to the Greek Dramatic poets, his offspring; who in the composition of their *Tetralogy*, or set of four pieces, were wont to make the last a *Satyric Tragedy*. Happily one of these ancient *Dunciads* (as we may well term it) is come down to us amongst the Tragedies of Euripides. And what doth the reader think may be the subject? Why truly, and it is worth his observation, the unequal Contention of an *old, dull, debauched, buffoon Cyclops*, with the heaven-directed *Favourite of* Minerva; who after having quietly born all the monster's obscene and impious ribaldry, endeth the farce in punishing him with the mark of an indelible brand in his *forehead*. May we not then be excused, if for the future we consider the Epics of Homer, Virgil, and Milton, together with this our poem, as a complete *Tetralogy*, in which the last worthily holdeth the place or station of the *satyric* piece?
> (Pp. 255-256)

That Euripides' one extant satyr play treats of the incivilities of monstrosity and the brand of infamous behavior is understandable. Modally, satire is disproportionate in both its bearing and its efforts to foist itself upon its betters. Warburton provides the satiric enterprise with a place in the complex ironies of generic inheritance, a place that is itself part of the sustaining satiric joke. In this instance, not only is the worthy place of the little epic a parodic heritage but the critical advocate is the personated Aristarchus, a parodic version of the scholar, Richard Bentley, so devastated by Swift as the spider of entangling mental alliances in the *Battle of the Books*. As the interloping satiric commentator, Warburton has it both ways; he undermines the heroic descent by casting suspicion on its generic reconstruction, but he honors his poet through a kind of implied connection with Homer, Virgil, and Milton.

In the earlier mock-defense of the status of the poem for the *Variorum* edition, the heroic modern, Martin Scriblerus, wrote to justify the line of *The Dunciad*. On this occasion the supporting source was the lost Homeric small epic, the *Margites*, a perfect model if we can believe what the *Second Alcibiades* said of its comic hero: "He knew many things, and all of them badly" (Loeb trans., 1476). Scriblerus sets the appropriate lineage.

> From these authors also it shou'd seem, that the Hero or chief personage of it was no less *obscure*, and his *understanding* and *sentiments* no less quaint and strange (if indeed not more so) than any of the actors in our poem. MARGITES was the name of this personage, whom Antiquity recordeth to have been *Dunce the First*; and surely from what we hear of him, not unworthy to be the root of so spreading a tree, and so numerous a posterity. The poem therefore celebrating him, was properly and absolutely a *Dunciad*; which tho' now unhappily lost, yet is its nature sufficiently known by the infallible tokens aforesaid. And thus it doth appear, that the first Dunciad was the first Epic poem, written by *Homer* himself, and anterior even to the Iliad or Odyssey.

Now forasmuch as our Poet had translated those two famous works of *Homer* which are yet left; he did conceive it in some sort of his duty to imitate that also which was lost: And was therefore induced to bestow on it the same Form which *Homer's* is reported to have had, namely that of Epic poem, with a title also framed after the antient *Greek* manner, to wit, that of *Dunciad*. (Pp. 48-49)

Pope accommodates a generic model whose action celebrated a heroic dulness. To recreate or imitate the lost model is to honor that which fails to survive. For all purposes, then, the action of *The Dunciad* celebrates its generic inheritance elegiacally, but it leaves the tradition in the same condition in which it finds it. The paradox, of course, is that by so doing Pope provides the Dunces with a much greater fame than they might in any other way attain. The poet of deformed intellection is at the very height of his powers, and the Scriblerian commentator marks the difference between the poet and the subject of his poem: "In a word, the whole poem proveth itself to be the work of our Author when his faculties were in full vigour and perfection; at that exact time of life when years have ripened the judgment, without diminishing the imagination; which by good criticks is held to be punctually at *forty*" (p. 53).

Much of the energy of *The Dunciad* relies on the powers of its recorder; while the Dunces exhaust vitality, the poet displays it. But whereas Pope's faculties are "in full vigour and perfection," his body is not, and his sensitivity on this point may have accounted for the very material he amassed. Dunces are Dunces because they mistake the accidents of bodily form for the deformity of the spirit. The *Variorum*'s "Testimonies of Authors" cites Gildon on Pope's poor wracked body: "Certain it is, that his original is not from Adam, but the Devil; and that he wanteth nothing but horns and tail to be the exact resemblance of his infernal Father" (p. 25). And in the *Variorum*'s notes to lines,

Dennis makes disease a special case for Pope, as if he happened to it rather than it to him.

> "Natural deformity comes not by our fault, 'tis often occasioned by calamities and diseases, which a man can no more help, than a monster can his deformity. There is no one misfortune, and no one disease, but what all the rest of men are subject to.—But the deformity of this Author ⟨viz. Pope⟩ is visible, present, lasting, unalterable, and peculiar to himself: it is the mark of God and Nature upon him, to give us warning that we should hold no society with him, as a creature not of our original, nor of our species." (P. 115)

It is almost as if certain of the predestined Dunces have tried to disinherit Pope for the wrong reasons and now the poet returns in the latter day to disinherit them for what he has ordained are the right ones. At least part of the occasion of *The Dunciad* is Pope's reassertion of the line of poetic integrity in the face of charges against his bodily disintegration. In *The Dunciad* Pope's marvelling at the extent to which the literary line has admitted baser blood ("How Farce and Epic get a jumbled race," I, 70) is really a challenge to his own talents. After all, no better progeny of farce and epic exists than *The Dunciad* itself. Thus, the "thing" done better is Pope's way of getting through to those who have done the thing worse. Queen Dulness applauds herself as her own "momentary monsters" pass in review, rising and falling. Pope is but a step to the rear performing the same literary act, parodically in Dulness's honor but satirically at all her minions' expense.

Admittedly, if his intent had been only to enter the wars of monstrosity, Pope's deformed stature would have made him vulnerable. But he has other tactics in mind. Real Dulness is a kind of intellectual and creative impoverishment of the soul, a soul whose salvation, ironically, is in the very hands of a poet with the powers to make the Dunces memorable. Left to herself, Dulness is desperation made manifest—the frustration of having to pass on obscurity for a name and poverty for a legacy. In the letter to his publisher signed with the name William Cleland, Pope's defense of his enterprise becomes a defense of his own poetic store or value in contrast with an obscure and destitute host who make their presence felt rather than their lasting worth. In one passage from the letter the charges and countercharges of physical deformity take on a personal and aesthetic note:

> If Obscurity or Poverty were to exempt a man from satyr, much more should Folly or Dulness, which are still more involuntary, nay as much so as personal deformity. But even this will not help them: Deformity becomes the object of ridicule when a man sets up for being handsome: and so must Dulness when he sets up for a Wit. (P. 17)

The obscure become usurpers—they take over the goods and names of those who have something to transmit: "So shall each hostile name become our own" (II, 139). For Pope, poverty is "a neglect of one's lawful calling" (p. 15). In *Martinus Scriblerus of the Poem* the conceit is later embellished: "First, taking things from their original, he considereth the Causes creative of such authors, namely *Dulness* and *Poverty*; the one born with them, the other contracted, by neglect of their proper talent thro' self conceit of greater abilities" (p. 50). In satire, neglect and conceit are part of the same condition. What Dulness's Muses touch they debase. And what they debase they overvalue. Scriblerus speaks of *The Dunciad*'s poet recording the Dunces' poetic store: "He proceedeth to shew the *qualities* they bestow on these authors, and the *effects* they produce: Then the *materials* or *stock* with which they furnish them, and (above all) that *self-opinion* which causeth it to seem to themselves vastly greater than it is, and is the prime motive of their setting up in this sad and sorry merchandize" (p. 50).

✧

Although *The Dunciad* is about the succession to "Dull estate," we are constantly reminded that the successor figures have neither the focus nor the power to advance action, only to partake of its retardation. Warburton's note to the revised opening lines of the 1743 version remind the reader that the return of the poem is to something old and nothing new: "The Reader ought here to be cautioned, that the *Mother*, and not the *Son*, is the principal Agent of this Poem: The latter of them is only chosen as her Collegue (as was anciently the custom in Rome before some great Expedition) the main action of the Poem being by no means the Coronation of the Laureate, which is performed in the very first book, but the Restoration of the Empire of Dulness in Britain, which is not accomplished 'till the last" (p. 269). The charge of succession is therefore ambiguous. Late in the action, Dulness asks that her children go forth (presumably in time and space), but in going forth they only return to a kind of mother substance.

> Then blessing all, "Go Children of my care!
> To Practice now from Theory repair.
> All my commands are easy, short, and full:
> My Sons! be proud, be selfish, and be dull.
> Guard my Prerogative, assert my Throne:
> This Nod confirms each Privilege your own."
> (IV, 579-584)

Warburton's note to these lines recognizes the paradoxical nature of transferred power in the poem. There is no transference when the successor figures go from the source only to "Roll in her Vortex, and her pow'r confess" (IV, 84).

This speech of Dulness to her Sons at parting may
possibly fall short of the Reader's expectation; who
may imagine the Goddess might give them a Charge of
more consequence, and, from such a Theory as is
before delivered, incite them to the practice of something more extraordinary, than to personate Run-
ning-Footmen, Jockeys, Stage Coachmen, &c.

But if it be well consider'd, that whatever inclination
they might have to do mischief, her sons are generally
render'd harmless by their Inability; and that it is the
common effect of Dulness (even in her greatest efforts)
to defeat her own design; the Poet, I am persuaded,
will be justified, and it will be allow'd that these worthy
persons, in their several ranks, do as much as can be
expected from them. (P. 400)

That the line of inheritance is turned back on itself becomes clear early on in the poem. Cibber, like Theobald
before him, must rid himself of his own progeny in order
to succeed as the progeny of his mother. The sacrifice is an
easy one to make because Cibber's "monster-breeding
breast" (I, 108) produces only one-time losers.

Round him much Embryo, much Abortion lay,
Much future Ode, and abdicated Play;
Nonsense precipitate, like running Lead,
That slip'd thro' Cracks and Zig-zags of the Head;
All that on Folly Frenzy could beget,
Fruits of dull Heat, and Sooterkins of Wit.
(I, 121-126)

Cibber's productions are a kind of human version of the
slime of the Nile. A sooterkin is the vermin born for the
animal heat generated by stoves placed for warmth under
the petticoats of Dutch women. Cibber's mind is a teeming
womb, and his creations are quick to go up in the same heat
from which they came out.

THINGS UNBORN

"O born in sin, and forth in folly brought!
Works damn'd, or to be damn'd! (your father's fault)
Go, purify'd by flames ascend the sky,
My better and more christian progeny!
Unstain'd, untouch'd, and yet in maiden sheets;
While all your smutty sisters walk the streets."

(I, 225-230)

Pope alludes to Cibber's whoring daughter, but the pattern of the sacrifice suggests the ritual elimination of a forward line. Dulness's grandchildren are promiscuous, immature, and dead to life. In the last book, one travelling son is given back to the Queen Mother, who begs a blessing: "Thou gav'st that Ripeness, which so soon began, / And ceas'd so soon, he ne'er was Boy, nor Man" (IV, 287-288). In the notes Warburton explains that wit makes the boy a man and folly makes the man a fool. Since the "accomplish'd Son" was neither man nor fool, he effectively moves from birth to death; he has no maturity, therefore no integral line.

The premature return is the subject of mock-succession. Cibber returns by ridding himself of progeny (his books) and burying his head in his mother's lap. This evokes a kind of death, a descent to a visionary hell or Cimmerian gloom. When Cibber is laid "to slumber with his head on her lap; a position of marvellous virtue, which causes all the Visions of wild enthusiasts, projectors, politicians, inamoratos, castle-builders, chemists, and poets" ("Argument to Book III," p. 319), his folly brings forth past and present siblings. It is indeed a postion of marvelous virtue because Cibber lay with his head at the originally inspired *vagina stultiae*. Having sacrificed those of his own works begotten in follied frenzy, he now experiences a visionary madness or excitation of dulness: "Son; what thou seek'st is in thee! Look, and find / Each monster meets his likeness in thy mind" (III, 251-252). On this occasion, too much heat

from his mother's lap engenders the forms of dulness, all
of them *sui generis*.

Pope writes that "The King descending, views th' Elysian
Shade" (III, 14), and the compression of the language describes several actions. Cibber sees the truth of his own nature as he descends into darkness. Parodoxically, vision is
in darkness, the shade being both what is dark and the
"things" one sees (ghosts). In much the same way as Aeneas
was taught by Anchises, Cibber learns of succession from
the progenitor laureate, Elkanah Settle: "Thus the great
Father to the greater Son" (III, 42).

> "Oh born to see what none can see awake!
> Behold the wonders of th' oblivious Lake.
> Thou, yet unborn, hast touch'd this sacred shore;
> The hand of Bavius drench'd thee o'er and o'er.
> But blind to former as to future fate,
> What mortal knows his pre-existent state?
> Who knows how long thy transmigrating soul
> Might from Bœotian to Bœotian roll?"
>
> (III, 43-50)

Caught in the oblivious moment where the past is as
much a mystery as the future, the successor son is "yet unborn" because the noncreative sleep that will be the future
is at present only a preview. Aeneas, of sound line, has his
past somewhat securely behind him; Cibber, born of Dulness, must be informed of all time apart from the self. His
line is lit by dim wits. Each of Dulness's many sons confirms
the progress mapped in Proverbs 21:16: "The man that
wandereth out of the way of understanding shall remain in
the congregation of the dead." And the promise of the
third book is the fulfillment of the last—the mindless
inheritance—father to son back to mother.

> "And see, my son! the hour is on its way,
> That lifts our Goddess to imperial sway;

This fav'rite Isle, long sever'd from her reign,
Dove-like, she gathers to her wings again.
Now look thro' Fate! behold the scene she draws!
What aids, what armies to assert her cause!
See all her progeny, illustrious sight!
Behold, and count them, as they rise to light.
As Berecynthia, while her offspring vye
In homage to the Mother of the sky,
Surveys around her, in the blest abode,
An hundred sons, and ev'ry son a God:
Not with less glory mighty Dulness crown'd,
Shall take thro' Grub-street her triumphant round;
And her Parnassus glancing o'er at once,
Behold an hundred sons, and each a Dunce."

(III, 123-138)

The third book is a preview of the end in every sense: in
Book Four Cibber's head is still on the lap of the Queen
Mother ("Soft on her lap her Laureat son reclines," IV, 20)
because, having seen the end, he remains ready to drop
into it. Warburton comments: "With great judgment it is
imagined by the Poet, that such a Collegue as Dulness had
elected, should sleep on the Throne, and have very little
share in the Action of the Poem. Accordingly he hath done
little or nothing from the day of his Anointing; having past
through the second book without taking part in any thing
that was transacted about him, and thro' the third in profound Sleep" (p. 341). *The Dunciad* is always on the move,
but its action is inimical to its participants' inclination. Cibber, especially, displays an inert will. Pope parodies the
idea of action by displacing the successor son from it; yet
when action itself is a kind of enervation, no one more than
Cibber knows what to do with the estate in arrears. His
greatest vision is through and to his place of issue. And his
descent to the source, his mother's lap, readies him for
eternal inaction. Having seen his vision, Virgil's Aeneas re-

ascends to the light of time back through the gates of ivory, the prophetic teeth of Hades. Cibber watches his vision fly back through the *vagina dentata* (" 'Enough! enough!' the raptur'd Monarch cries; / And thro' the Iv'ry Gate the Vision flies," III, 339-340), but he remains behind inert. In the last book of *The Dunciad*, the inherited kingdom follows the inheriting king, and Dulness's hell-hole is covered over: "And Universal Darkness buries All" (IV, 656). The satiric action restores the prior or undifferentiated creation, *being* without generative form. It is said in law that an inheritance cannot reascend, but satire proves law illegal or irrelevant. When there is nothing to give, nothing can be perpetually taken back.

Chapter Nine

GRAVITY'S INHERITABLE LINE: STERNE'S *TRISTRAM SHANDY*

I would believe only in a god who could dance.
And when I saw my devil I found him serious,
thorough, profound, and solemn: it was the spirit
of gravity—through him all things fall.
Not by wrath does one kill but by laughter.
Come, let us kill the spirit of gravity.
—Nietzsche, *Thus Spoke Zarathustra*

"Are we not here now," asks Corporeal Trim in *Tristram Shandy*, "and are we not——(dropping his hat plumb upon the ground——and pausing, before he pronounced the word)——gone! in a moment?" The grave and funereal line in Sterne's narrative is the gravitational line: "The descent of the hat was as if a heavy lump of clay had been kneaded into the crown of it" (V, 7).[1] From clay to dust: lighter spirits always risk being beaten down—the case, alas!, of poor Yorick, literally beaten to death by all too grave and serious fellows. Comic levity submits to victimization, and Yorick is "set on by MALICE in the dark" (I, 12).

Yorick is Sterne's sacrifice to gravitational descent, and *Tristram Shandy* is the reincarnation of levity. In his Dedication to Mr. Pitt, Sterne writes: "I live in a constant endeavour to fence against the infirmities of ill health, and other evils of life, by mirth; being firmly persuaded that every time a man smiles,——but much more so, when he laughs, that it adds something to this Fragment of Life." Although the narrator's spirit remains, for the most part,

[1] I have used *Tristram Shandy*, ed. James A. Work (New York, 1940) for the passages cited. References are to volume and chapter.

light and alive, the narrative's actions suggest a counter-principle. In the Shandean household and in the physical history of its members the line of comic continuity is weighed down by satiric design and gravitational inheritance. At birth, young Tristram's head suffers the outrage of Dr. Slop's forceps. Walter Shandy laments.

> With all my precautions, how was my system turned topside turvy in the womb with my child! his head exposed to the hand of violence, and a pressure of 470 pounds averdupois weight acting so perpendicularly upon its apex——that at this hour 'tis ninety *per Cent.* insurance, that the fine network of the intellectual web be not rent and torn to a thousand tatters. (IV, 19)

Gravity is the defeat of systematic and organic continuity. Tristram's nose is pressured at birth; at the age of five another protuberance is victimized, a protuberance legally and generatively confused with noses in Shandy family history:[2] "I was five years old.——*Susannah* did not consider that nothing was well hung in our family,——so slap came the sash down like lightening upon us;——Nothing is left,——cried *Susannah*,——nothing is

---

[2] When uncle Toby tries to calm Walter by suggesting that Tristram's smashed nose is a minor price to pay for the good fortune that he had presented his head and not his hip for Dr. Slop's forceps, he ignores the living record in the Shandy household that the nose is but the upward sign of lower disgrace. Once Tristram's great grandfather confronted Tristram's great grandmother: "I THINK it a very unreasonable demand,——cried my great grandfather, twisting up the paper, and throwing it upon the table.——By this account, madam, you have but two thousand pounds fortune, and not a shilling more,——and you insist upon having three hundred pounds a year jointure for it.——'Because,' replied my great grandmother, 'you have little or no nose, Sir' " (III, 31). Walter "did not conceive how the greatest family in *England* could stand it out against an uninterrupted succession of six or seven short noses" (III, 33) and in fact felt that the family "had never recovered the blow of my great grandfather's nose" (III, 33). The narrator, of course, protests that by nose he means nothing more or less than nose, and to insure that we make no mistake he gives Tristram a double dose of family woe: a smashed nose and a damaged organ.

left——for me, but to run my country" (V, 17). Susannah's hasty amendment of her sentence at least allows for something, something ending "in a phimosis" that causes the more mature Tristram no small measure of difficulty. Each time Tristram presents something of himself, something of Tristram's is taken away. He is "a man, proud, as he ought to be, of his manhood" (VII, 29), although it is a manhood cursed by family ill luck. Tristram remembers a later encounter with his Jenny.

> 'Tis enough, said'st thou, coming close up to me, as I stood with my garters in my hand, reflecting upon what had *not* pass'd——'Tis enough, *Tristram*, and I am satisfied, said'st thou, whispering these words in my ear, **** ** **** **** ******;____**** ** ****——any other man would have sunk down to the center. (VII, 29)

Any other man, Tristram implies, would have given in to the gravity of the embarrassment because for any Shandy physical love is a trying descent ("Let love therefore be what it will,——my uncle *Toby* fell into it," VI, 37). But the Shandean narrator resists gravity even in the face of falling sashes, parabolic cannon balls, dropping hot chestnuts, and heavy impotence.[3] The narrative ends with the gravest Shandy of all, Walter Shandy, protesting that the family Bull is every inch a man—he goes about his businesss of

---

[3] In *Tristram Shandy* gravity is a controlling metaphor and joke. We learn early that "with all this sail, poor *Yorick* carried not one ounce of ballast" (I, 11), because dead or alive Yorick is the book's memorial comic principal: "For, to speak the truth, *Yorick* had an invincible dislike and opposition in his nature to gravity" (I, 11). All the misfortunes of the Shandy family are traceable to gravity—from the violated marriage article about Mrs. Shandy's one allowable lying-in trip to London ("I have ever thought it hard that the whole weight of the article should have fallen entirely, as it did, upon myself," I, 15) to uncle Toby's famous wound at the Battle of Namur ("that the great injury which it had done my uncle *Toby's* groin, was more owing to the gravity of the stone itself, than to the projectile force of it," I, 25).

faulty generation with "a grave face," but he is "as good a Bull as ever p-ss'd" (IX, 33). Thus while the comic spirit prevails to the end of Sterne's levitational cock and bull story, the satiric implication suggests that the Shandy's line has been suspect from the source. Earlier, Walter had reflected.

> The original of society, continued my father, I'm satisfied is, what *Politian* tells us, *i.e.* merely conjugal; and nothing more than the getting together of one man and one woman;——to which, (according to *Hesiod*) the philosopher adds a servant:——but supposing in the first beginning there were no men servants born——he lays the foundation of it, in a man,——a woman——and a bull. (V, 31)

Yorick points out that the Greek reads ox, not bull. Walter is wrong about the beginning of things and certainly wrong about the bull at the end—but at least through Volume IX the family seems to endure gravity's hardships.

And no one more consciously endures than Tristram, the narrator. He literally writes to escape the grave, although he is both weakened and exhausted by his efforts at continuity. At intervals he tries, in his own words, to collect himself—to gather the variable plots of his life (and opinions) together. By the help of a "vegitable diet, with a few of the cold seeds," he declares himself well enough late in the action to go on "in a tolerable straight line" (VI, 40). He then produces a series of linear squiggles as representations of where he has been, but he promises an absolutely straight progression for Volume VII.

> which is a line drawn as straight as I could draw it, by a writing-master's ruler, (borrowed for that purpose) turning neither to the right hand or to the left.
>
> This *right line*,——the path-way for Christians to walk in! say divines——

————The emblem of moral rectitude! says *Cicero*————
————The *best line!* say cabbage-planters————is the
shortest line, says *Archimedes*, which can be drawn from
one given point to another.————
    I wish you ladyships would lay this matter to heart in
your next birth-day suits!
    ————What a journey!
    Pray can you tell me,————that is, without anger, be-
fore I write my chapter upon straight lines————by what
mistake————who told them so————or how it has come
to pass, that your men of wit and genius have all along
confounded this line, with the line of GRAVITA-
TION? (VI, 40)

Tristram should not needlessly unsettle himself by pos-
ing such a question. Not only does his levitational nature
suggest that he is more likely to "send up" than "go
straight," but he has, in fact, already answered the question. Much earlier he had reflected on the course of wit and
genius from the days of the later seventeenth century. He
blamed "the graver gentry" who were opposed to the wit of
the Restoration Court for raising a hue and cry against the
"lawful owners" of a witty spirit. Even "the great *Locke*, who
was seldom outwitted by false sounds" (III, 20) and whose
associational theories generate much of the cogitation in
Tristram Shandy, "was nevertheless bubbled here." As a satire upon gravity, *Tristram Shandy* identifies the culprits or the
confounders of the line of wit as the anticourt merchant
and landed gentry class whose gravity from the Civil Wars
on "has been made the *Magna Charta* of stupidity ever
since, . . . which by the bye is one of the many and vile im-
positions which gravity and grave folks have to answer for
hereafter" (III, 20). The too grave quite naturally see the
line of advance (which for a man like Walter Shandy *is* the
inheritable line) as a matter of utmost gravity.[4] Sterne, the

---

[4] Oddly enough, Walter Shandy, the retired merchant, is a follower of
Robert Filmer, a great political enemy of John Locke. But Walter admires

comic writer, sees the line of gravity advancing straight to the grave. He cannot resist confounding his narrator in the very confusion that he tries so hard to avoid. Tristram finds it difficult to accept the notion that were he to go straight, he would succumb to gravity, but Sterne shows him succumbing willy nilly. For the satirist there is an edge to both the levitational and gravitational line, and the circumstance that controls *Tristram Shandy* is not so much the postponed advance of Tristram as the premature death of Yorick, where gravity catches up to levity.

The famous opening of the novel illustrates the convergence of comic and satiric lines. Sterne begins, all too literally, in the middle of things: "I wish either my father or my mother, or indeed both of them, as they were in duty both equally bound to it, had minded what they were about when they begot me" (I, 1). Three short chapters later Tristram follows another Horatian precedent for beginning at the beginning: "For which cause, right glad I am, that I have begun the history of myself in the way I have done; and that I am able to go on tracing every thing in it, as *Horace* says, *ab Ovo*" (I, 4). The opening sequence of *Tristram Shandy* has it both ways: conception *ab ovo* begins at the very beginning, but *coitus interruptus* begins *in medias res*. The comic narrative line attempts to establish the basis for a complete relation, but the satiric interruption threatens the health and generative strength of the narrative object. Father and mother, methodical and grave beyond the call of duty, had been delinquent. The resulting shock to the very young Tristram's system turns out to be an even greater shock to his father's inheritable system.

> Had they duly consider'd how much depended upon what they were then doing;———that not only the pro-

---

Filmer's *Patriarcha* for its "admirable pattern and prototype of this household and paternal power" (I, 18). Locke fought his political battles with Filmer when Walter was a young man; as an older man who has had such obvious difficulty with his household, Walter's allegiance to the patriarchal model is, at best, satirically amusing.

duction of a rational Being was concern'd in it, but that possibly the happy formation and temperature of his body, perhaps his genius and the very cast of his mind;——and, for aught they knew to the contrary, even the fortunes of his whole house might take their turn from the humours and dispositions which were then uppermost:——Had they duly weighed and considered all this, and proceeded accordingly,——I am verily persuaded I should have made a quite different figure in the world, from that, in which the reader is likely to see me.——Believe me, good folks, this is not so inconsiderable a thing as many of you may think it;——you have all, I dare say, heard of the animal spirits, as how they are transfused from father to son, &c. &c.——and a great deal to the purpose . . . (I, 1)

The narrative begins with its hero under organic siege. His conception has bodily and legal implicatons—all negative—and his narrative progress is threatened from its onset. His future self, a "homulculean" runner, exhausts his progress:

My little gentleman had got to his journey's end miserably spent;——his muscular strength and virility worn down to a thread;——his own animal spirits ruffled beyond description,——and that in this sad disorder'd state of nerves, he had laid down a prey to sudden starts, or a series of melancholy dreams and fancies for nine long, long months together.——I tremble to think what a foundation had been laid for a thousand weaknesses both of body and mind, which no skill of the physician or the philosopher could ever afterwards have set thoroughly to rights. (I, 2)

For different reasons, Sterne's Tristram is not unlike Swift's narrator in *A Tale of A Tub* whose disordered state makes him equally prey to sudden starts. The threat of spending too much too soon is the satiric condition of

works such as Swift's *Tale* or Pope's *Dunciad*, where at the
end the line dies out or exhausts itself. Tristram knows
such a threat from the time of his conception; his father's
gravity exacerbates it; his accident plagued life adds to it.
But even as his full inheritance mocks him, he is less satiric
than comic in returning the mockery.

The opening of the narrative hints that in the face of
time the Shandean line is weakened, if not impotent. Even
the earlier history of the family leads to such a conclusion.
Sixty years before, Tristram's great aunt Dinah was mar-
ried to and impregnated by the coachman. For Uncle
Toby, whose modesty was legendary and who did not know
the right side of a woman from the wrong, the story of
Dinah was unbearable. For Walter, the story was at the
basis of the Shandean system: it was "of as much consequence to him, as the retrogradation of the planets to
Copernicus" (I, 21). Retrograde and backsliding Aunt Dinah
is a gravitational joke, and her fate is emblematic of the
family's inheritable line: "One would have thought, that
the whole force of the misfortune should have spent and
wasted itself in the family at first,——as is generally the
case:——But nothing ever wrought with our family after
the ordinary way" (I, 21).

✧

In *Tristram Shandy* it is traditional to see Sterne's working
through of oddities in the novelistic consciousness as an attempt to render in fiction those Lockean mental trains
where private associations mature into public contracts.[5]
Narrative ought to adjust idiosyncrasy to expectation, to
reconcile a subject's thoughts with a subject's place. Sterne
suggests that the process is not so simple. He begins from
Lockean premises that he is willing to satirize because associational opinions never seem to run parallel to commun-

[5] For a discussion of the novel and philosophic rationalism, see Ian
Watt, *The Rise of the Novel* (Berkeley and Los Angeles, 1956).

ally and conventionally conceived designs for life. The narrator is "resolved never to read any book but my own, as long as I live" (VIII, 5), which is to say that he is caught up in a Lockean proposition. He tells his readers what Locke's book is: "It is a history.——A history! of who? what? where? when? Don't hurry yourself.——It is a history-book, Sir, (which may possibly recommend it to the world) of what passes in a man's own mind" (II, 2).

But it is precisely when the Lockean design is foisted upon a reading audience as a history or narration (*historia*) that the narrator faces difficulties. In order for his history not to end, he must let his mind outrace time. On the title page of *Tristram Shandy*, Epictetus's Greek motto maintains: "It is not actions, but opinions concerning actions, which disturb men." To disturb is to break lines of continuity. The title, "Life and Opinions," plays on the expectations of "Life and Adventures," but an adventure is an action to come (an advent), and Tristram's opinions are always in arrears. In terms of the narrative, he is caught between an inability to get himself properly born and a fear "that my OPINIONS will be the death of me" (IV, 13). Traditional plots and their traditional symbols are filtered through a confusing medium. Opinions convert the paths of romance into the byways of the mind: "——What a wilderness has it been! and what a mercy that we have not both of us been lost, or devoured by wild beasts in it" (VI, 1). But the narrator's mind is a kind of lost and found: "——When I can get on no further,——and find myself entangled on all sides of this mystick labyrinth,——my Opinion will then come in, in course,——and lead me out" (VI, 37).

Tristram's father, Walter Shandy, also possesses opinions that disturb and are disturbed by time. Most of them serve as the groundwork of the *Tristra-pædia*

> at which (as I said) he was three years and something
> more, indefatigably at work, and at last, had scarce

compleated, by his own reckoning, one half of his undertaking: the misfortune was, that I was all that time totally neglected and abandoned to my mother; and what was almost as bad, by the very delay, the first part of the work, upon which my father had spent the most of his pains, was rendered entirely useless,——every day a page or two became of no consequence. (V, 16)

Like his son, Walter is always getting behind himself. His opinions conflict with the natural (and predictably accidental) course of plot: "he was serious;——he was all uniformity;——he was systematical, and, like all systematick reasoners, he would move both heaven and earth, and twist and torture every thing in nature to support his hypothesis" (I, 19).

In a telling interchange between Walter and Toby Shandy, Sterne makes it clear how the principle of the narrative's organization in fact runs counter to schemes for Shandean integrity. Walter is obsessed with Aunt Dinah's marriage to the coachman, and Toby would rather close the subject.

> For God's sake, my uncle *Toby* would cry,——and for my sake, and for all our sakes, my dear brother *Shandy*,——do let this story of our aunt's and her ashes sleep in peace;——how can you,——how can you have so little feeling and compassion for the character of our family:——What is the character of a family to an hypothesis? my father would reply.——Nay, if you come to that——what is the life of a family. (I, 21)

Toby, who has problems of his own, replies that such an opinion "is downright MURDER," and Walter replies by taking the human element out of the hypothetical formulation: "for, in *Foro Scientiæ* there is no such thing as MURDER,——'tis only DEATH, brother" (I, 21). Walter's seriousness or gravity marks the satiric edge of the narrative, the final solution to all maladjusted sequences where the principles of life are countered by the blindness of opinion: "his whole life a contradiction to his knowledge!" (III, 21).

In allowing Walter Shandy to carry the brunt of an un-inheritable baggage, *Tristram Shandy* borrows from the overtly satiric narrative, Pope's *The Memoirs of the Extraordinary Life, Works, and Discoveries of Martinus Scriblerus*. Martin's father, like Tristram's, ponders the processes of inheritance and inheritable transmission while trying to insure their effect upon his son "for the generation of Children of Wit."[6] Walter Shandy, having a blockhead for a first son (the result of cranial pressure in forging the first passage out), views Tristram as a "second staff for his old age, in case *Bobby* should fail him" (I, 16). In a satiric sense, both Tristram and Martinus are overdetermined, and preparation exhausts production: "What you seest in me," writes Martinus, "is a body exhausted by the labours of the mind" (p. 92); Tristram, devitalized for other reasons, turns the matter around and delights in the inevitable by praising the Pythagoreans for *"getting out of the body, in order to think well"* (VII, 13). Perhaps more fully committed to the satiric inheritance, Martin's father wishes that his son be born with all the deformities of famous and prominent ancients—with Demosthenes' stammer, Cicero's wart, Alexander's wry neck, Marius's knots upon his legs. In a bizarre way, the fate of the body might generate the state of the mind. Walter Shandy's hopes are more normative, but the satiric results are somewhat the same.

> I see it plainly, that either for my own sins, brother *Toby*, or the sins and follies of the *Shandy*-family, heaven has thought fit to draw forth the heaviest of its artillery against me; and that the prosperity of my

[6] Alexander Pope, *The Memoirs of the Extraordinary Life, Works, and Discoveries of Martinus Scriblerus*, ed. Charles Kerby-Miller (New York, reissued 1966), p. 96. Subsequent reference is to this edition and will be cited by page number in the body of the text.

child is the point upon which the whole force of it is
directed to play——Such a thing would batter the
whole universe about our ears, brother *Shandy*, said
my uncle *Toby*,——if it was so——Unhappy *Tristram*!
child of wrath! child of decrepitude! interruption!
mistake! and discontent! What one misfortune or dis-
aster in the book of embryotic evils, that could un-
mechanize thy frame, or entangle thy filaments! which
has not fallen upon thy head, or ever thou camest into
the world——what evils in thy passage into it!—
—What evils since!——produced into being, in the decline of thy father's days——when the powers of his
imagination and of his body were waxing feeble—
—when radical heat and radical moisture, the elements which should have temper'd thine, were drying
up; and nothing left to found thy stamina in, but
negations——'tis pitiful——brother *Toby*, at the best,
and called out for all the little helps that care and attention on both sides could give it. But how were we
defeated! You know the event, brother *Toby*,——'tis
too melancholy a one to be repeated now,——when
the few animal spirits I was worth in the world, and
with which memory, fancy, and quick parts should
have been convey'd,——were all dispersed, confused,
confounded, scattered, and sent to the devil.——(IV,
19)

Comedy guarantees that the race go on; satire endures
negation. The Shandy line is intent on comedy and resigned to satire. Because of the "sinister turn, which every
thing relating to our family was apt to take," the Shandy
arms on the coach door mistakenly bore a bend sinister
across its field. Of course Walter "constantly complained of
carrying this vile mark of Illegitimacy upon the door of his
own" (IV, 25). Illegitimacy signifies the family as a mark of
error, and "it was one of the many things which the *Destinies* had set down in their books——ever to be grumbled

at (and in wiser families than ours)———but never to be mended." There is perhaps no better scene in literature where satiric mitigation works against comic abundance than the episode in which Walter Shandy, distraught over the loss of one son, rhetorically conceives another. Mrs. Shandy, who has not yet learned of the death of Bobby, eavesdrops at a slightly open door as Walter consoles himself by reciting Socrates' speech from the *Apology*:

"I have friends———I have relations,———I have three desolate children,"———says *Socrates*.———

———Then, cried my mother, opening the door,———you have one more, Mr. *Shandy*, than I know of.

By heaven! I have one less,———said my father, getting up and walking out of the room. (V, 13)

The economy, the wit, and the satiric compression of this scene are remarkable. Perhaps it is fitting to end with another extraordinary exchange, one that is descriptive of so much that is distinctly satiric. Walter Shandy, crossed at every natural turn, protests that Corporeal Trim has misappropriated his jackboots for refashioning into Uncle Toby's mortar pieces: "I have not one appointment belonging to me, which I set so much store by, as I do by these jack-boots,———they were our great-grandfather's, brother *Toby*,———they were *hereditary*" (III, 22). Toby thinks for a moment and responds: "Then I fear, quoth my uncle *Toby*, *Trim* has cut off the entail." Toby's is a comic voice articulating a satiric inheritance. What *inheres* in the satiric action is essentially what ends it.

CODICIL

I have represented narrative satire as a literary system of discontinuities or subversions. Satire's sustained actions are violations, and its generic laws subvert tradition, the *trans dare* or giving across of substance and value in form. Satire's subjects may have known a previous, perhaps higher, ancestral status, but satire's actions depict the falling-off or exhaustion of line. In a modal sense, satire is both descend*ant* and descend*ent*. It violates the bodily and mental integrity of its subjects by radicalizing rather than conserving "issue," and it confuses the moral and spatial notions of direction by divorcing descent from continuity. To be satirically conceived is to be rendered monstrous—too singular, too materially degenerate to carry on.

In satire, monstrosity becomes both an inheritable and imaginative impasse. If Giambattista Vico's first poetic men were to guarantee the preservation and continuity of inheritable forms they had to kill monsters or "destroy a subject in order to separate its primary form from the contrary form which had been imposed upon it."[1] Deprived of normative form—what Vico calls "just corporature" or that "property of human nature which not even God can take from man without destroying him"[2]—all inheritable forms are *de*formed or made abnormal. The disruption of generic and organic lines is a kind of denaturing, and the very monstrosities that natural lines of inheritance disfavor become the subjects of satire—denatured subjects that exist only as destroyed conceptions. To borrow Goya's phrase, the satirist's dreams of reason bring forth monsters.[3] The

[1] Giambattista Vico, *The New Science of Giambattista Vico*, trans. Thomas Goddard Bergin and Max Harold Fisch (Ithaca, 1970), p. 90.
[2] Vico, *New Science*, p. 81.
[3] Goya's famous observation serves as the subtitle of a book on narrative

264

CODICIL

narrative force of satire derives from the monstrous or the
unbearable occupying space for the time unbeing.

Throughout this book I have reiterated the primary
literary structures of satiric inheritance, and perhaps one
concluding example is in order. In the *Memoirs of the Extraordinary Life, Works, and Discoveries of Martinus Scriblerus*,
Alexander Pope's hero educates his readers into an accep-
tance of the satiric dispensation: "how I wonder at the
Stupidity of mankind, who can affix the opprobrious Name
of Monstrosity to what is only a Variety of Beauty, and a
Profusion of generous Nature."[4] Earlier, Pope had let Martinus's tutor, Crambe, work through a set of syllogisms on
the copulation of unlike ideas. Since there "cannot be more
in the conclusion than was in the premises; that is, children
can only inherit from their parents, [the] conclusion follows the weaker part; that is, children inherit the disease of
their parents." Crambe continues: "When the Premises or
parents are necessarily join'd (or in lawful wedlock) they
beget lawful issue; but contingently join'd, they beget bastards. . . . Therefore as an Absurdity is a *Monster*, a Falsity is
a *Bastard*."[5] Satire's dispensation is always the same: the
origin of satiric being is the absurd or suspect birth, and
the line of satiric action follows the bend sinister.

Satiric creations (births) reveal a falling-off at the very
point of origin, and satire is that phase of mimetic action
where human subjects respond to a condition described by
Pope as "active to no end": "Fix'd like a plant on his peculiar spot, / To draw nutrition, propagate, and rot" (*Essay on*

---

and narrative satire in Latin American literature that has been a great
source of ideas for me, Alfred Mac Adam's *Modern Latin American Narratives: The Dreams of Reason* (Chicago, 1977).

[4] Alexander Pope, *The Memoirs of the Extraordinary Life, Works, and Discoveries of Martinus Scriblerus*, ed. Charles Kerby-Miller (New York, reissued 1966), p. 147. Martinus happens to be referring here to a set of
female Siamese twins who share excretory and reproductive organs. One
of the twins has just been ravished by a three-foot tall black midget.

[5] Pope, *Memoirs*, p. 122.

Man II, ll. 63-64). Yet satire celebrates the very condition it has generically produced. "To decompose," as Samuel Beckett puts it, "is to live too." Satire responds to the familiar ditty presented by Joyce in *Finnegans Wake*: "Tarara boom decay." Joyce records the power, even the crazy joy, of degeneration. All things begin in Viconian thunder, and "Tarara" is the stuttering prelude to creation. "Boom" is the manifestation of forms—the big-bang theory of origin—and "decay" is the decomposition of bodies that embarrass humanity into a lifelong cover-up. "Boom decay" is also the last judgmental chord, the end of creation where, as Vico describes it, men "finally go mad and waste their substance."[6] The satiric subject is literally "wasted." As Dryden writes, satire makes a "Malefactor die sweetly,"[7] or at least it makes him thrive in such a way that his end is indistinguishable from his satiric beginnings. Subjects deprived of a progressive *hereditas* enjoy only a regressive satiric vitality.

[6] Vico, *New Science*, p. 37.
[7] John Dryden, *Discourse Concerning the Original and Progress of Satire*, in *The Works of John Dryden*, ed. A. B. Chambers, William Frost, and Vinton Dearing (Berkeley and Los Angeles, 1974), 4:71.

BIBLIOGRAPHY

The following is a selected bibliography of secondary works consulted.

Auerbach, Erich. *Mimesis: The Representation of Reality in Western Literature*. Translated by Willard R. Trask. Princeton: Princeton University Press, 1953.

Bachofen, J. J. *Myth, Religion, and Mother Right*. Translated by Ralph Manheim. Princeton: Princeton University Press, 1967.

Bakhtin, Mikhail. *Problems of Dostoevsky's Poetics*. Translated by R. W. Rotsel. Ann Arbor: Ardis, 1973.

——. *Rabelais and His World*. Translated by Helene Iswolsky. Cambridge, Mass.: M.I.T. Press, 1968.

Brown, Norman O. *Closing Time*. New York: Random House, 1973.

——. *Life Against Death: The Psychoanalytic Meaning of History*. Middletown, Conn.: Wesleyan University Press, 1959.

Budick, Sanford. *Poetry of Civilization: Mythopoeic Displacement in the Verse of Milton, Dryden, Pope, and Johnson*. New Haven: Yale University Press, 1974.

Bullitt, John M. *Jonathan Swift and the Anatomy of Satire*. Cambridge, Mass.: Harvard University Press, 1953.

Burke, Kenneth. *A Grammar of Motives*. New York: Prentice-Hall, 1945.

——. *Language as Symbolic Action: Essays on Life, Literature, and Method*. Berkeley: University of California Press, 1966.

Campbell, Joseph. *The Masks of God: Creative Mythology*. New York: Penguin Books, 1976.

Carnochan, W. Bliss. *Confinement and Flight: An Essay in English Literature of the Eighteenth Century*. Berkeley and Los Angeles: University of California Press, 1977.

Carnochan, W. Bliss. *Lemuel Gulliver's Mirror for Man*. Berkeley and Los Angeles: University of California Press, 1968.

Clark, John R. *Form and Frenzy in Swift's* A Tale of A Tub. Ithaca: Cornell University Press, 1970.

Cohen, Ralph. "The Augustan Mode in English Poetry," *Eighteenth-Century Studies* 1 (1967): 3-32.

de Man, Paul. *Blindness and Insight: Essays in the Rhetoric of Contemporary Criticism*. New York: Oxford University Press, 1971.

Deporte, Michael V. *Nightmares and Hobbyhorses: Swift, Sterne, and Augustan Ideas of Madness*. San Marino, Calif.: Huntington Library, 1974.

Douglas, Mary. *Purity and Danger: An Analysis of the Concepts of Pollution and Taboo*. London: Routledge & Kegan Paul, 1966.

Edwards, Thomas R. *Imagination and Power: A Study of Poetry on Public Themes*. New York: Oxford University Press, 1971.

———. *This Dark Estate: A Reading of Pope*. Berkeley and Los Angeles: University of California Press, 1963.

Eliade, Mircea. *Myth and Reality*. Translated by Willard R. Trask. New York: Harper Torchbooks, 1968.

———. *The Myth of the Eternal Return or, Cosmos and History*. Translated by Willard R. Trask. Princeton: Princeton University Press, 1954.

———. *The Sacred and the Profane: The Nature of Religion*. Translated by Willard R. Trask. New York: Harcourt, Brace, & World, 1959.

Elliott, Robert C. *The Power of Satire: Magic, Ritual, Art*. Princeton: Princeton University Press, 1960.

———. *The Shape of Utopia: Studies in a Literary Genre*. Chicago: University of Chicago Press, 1970.

Foucault, Michel. *Madness and Civilization: A History of Insanity in the Age of Reason*. Translated by Richard Howard. New York: Pantheon Books, 1965.

BIBLIOGRAPHY

———. *The Order of Things: An Archaeology of the Human Sciences*. Translated by Richard Howard. New York: Pantheon Books, 1971.

Frame, Donald M. *François Rabelais: A Study*. New York: Harcourt, Brace Jovanovich, 1977.

Freud, Sigmund. *Civilization and Its Discontents, The Future of an Allusion, and Other Works*. Translated by James Strachey. London: Hogarth Press, 1961.

———. *The Interpretation of Dreams*. Translated by James Strachey. London: Hogarth Press, 1953.

———. *Totem and Taboo*. Translated by James Strachey. London: Hogarth Press, 1953.

Frye, Northrop. *Anatomy of Criticism: Four Essays*. Princeton: Princeton University Press, 1957.

———. *Secular Scripture: A Study of the Structure of Romance*. Cambridge, Mass.: Harvard University Press, 1976.

Fussell, Paul. *The Rhetorical World of Augustan Humanism*. Oxford: Clarendon Press, 1965.

Girard, René. *Deceit, Desire, and the Novel: Self and Other in Literary Structure*. Translated by Yvonne Freccero. Baltimore: The Johns Hopkins University Press, 1966.

———. *Des Choses cachées depuis la fondation du monde*. Paris: Grasset, 1978.

———. "Les Malédictions contre les Pharisiens et la révélation évangélique." *Bulletin du centre protestant d'études* 27 (1975): 3-29.

———. *Violence and the Sacred*. Translated by Patrick Gregory. Baltimore: The Johns Hopkins University Press, 1977.

Greene, Thomas. *The Descent from Heaven: A Study in Epic Continuity*. New Haven: Yale University Press, 1963.

———. "The Flexibility of the Self in Renaissance Literature." In *The Disciplines of Criticism: Essays in Literary Theory, Interpretation, and History*. Edited by Peter Demetz, Thomas Greene, and Lowry Nelson, Jr. New Haven: Yale University Press, 1968.

BIBLIOGRAPHY

Greene, Thomas. *Rabelais, A Study in Comic Courage*. Englewood Cliffs: Prentice-Hall, 1970.

Guillén, Claudio. *Literature as System: Essays Toward the Theory of Literary History*. Princeton: Princeton University Press, 1971.

Heiserman, A. R. "Satire in the 'Utopia.'" *PMLA* 78 (1963): 163-174.

Highet, Gilbert. *The Anatomy of Satire*. Princeton: Princeton University Press, 1962.

Jack, Ian. *Augustan Satire, 1660-1750*. Oxford: Clarendon Press, 1952.

Jauss, Hans Robert. "Levels of Identification of Hero and Audience." *New Literary History* 5 (1974): 283-317.

Jensen, James H. and Zirker, Malvin R., eds. *The Satirist's Art*. Bloomington: Indiana University Press, 1972.

Johnson, James William. *The Formation of Neo-Classical Thought*. Princeton: Princeton University Press, 1967.

Kantorowicz, Ernst H. *The King's Two Bodies: A Study in Mediaeval Political Theology*. Princeton: Princeton University Press, 1957.

Kenner, Hugh. *The Counterfeiters, an Historical Comedy*. Bloomington: Indiana University Press, 1968.

Kermode, Frank. *The Sense of An Ending: Studies in the Theory of Fiction*. New York: Oxford University Press, 1967.

Kernan, Alvin B. "Agression and Satire: Art Considered as a Form of Biological Adaptation." In *Literary Theory and Structure: Essays in Honor of William K. Wimsatt*. Edited by Frank Brady, John Palmer, and Martin Price. New Haven: Yale University Press, 1973.

———. *The Cankered Muse: Renaissance Satire*. New Haven: Yale University Press, 1959.

———. *The Plot of Satire*. New Haven: Yale University Press, 1965.

Krieger, Murray, "The 'Frail China Jar' and the Rude Hand of Chaos." *Centennial Review of Arts and Sciences* 5 (1961): 176-194.

BIBLIOGRAPHY

Levine, Joseph M. *Dr. Woodward's Shield: History, Science, and Satire in Augustan England*. Berkeley and Los Angeles: University of California Press, 1977.

Levi-Strauss, Claude. *Totemism*. Translated by Rodney Needham. Boston: Beacon Press, 1963.

Leyburn, Ellen Douglass. *Satiric Allegory: Mirror for Man*. New Haven: Yale University Press, 1956.

Lord, George deForest. *Heroic Mockery: Variations on Epic Themes from Homer to Joyce*. Newark, Del.: University of Delaware Press, 1977.

————, general ed. *Poems on Affairs of State: Augustan Satirical Verse 1660-1714*. 7 vols. New Haven: Yale University Press, 1963-1975.

Lorenz, Konrad. *On Aggression*. Translated by Marjorie Kerr Wilson. New York: Harcourt Brace Jovanovich, 1966.

Mac Adam, Alfred J. *Modern Latin American Narratives: The Dreams of Reason*. Chicago: University of Chicago Press, 1977.

Maresca, Thomas. *From Epic to Novel*. Columbus: Ohio University Press, 1974.

Miner, Earl. *The Cavalier Mode from Jonson to Cotton*. Princeton: Princeton University Press, 1971.

————. *Dryden's Poetry*. Bloomington: Indiana University Press, 1967.

————, ed. *Literary Uses of Typology from the Late Middle Ages to the Present*. Princeton: Princeton University Press, 1977.

————. *The Restoration Mode from Milton to Dryden*. Princeton: Princeton University Press, 1974.

Nevo, Ruth. *The Dial of Virtue: A Study of Poems on Affairs of State*. Princeton: Princeton University Press, 1963.

Nietzsche, Friedrich. *Basic Writings of Nietzsche*. Translated by Walter Kaufmann. New York: Modern Library, 1968.

————. *The Portable Nietzsche*. Translated by Walter Kaufmann. New York: Penguin Books, 1976.

Nohrnberg, James. *The Analogy of the Faerie Queene*. Princeton: Princeton University Press, 1976.

Novak, Maximillian E. "Defoe's *Shortest Way with the Dissenters*: Hoax, Parody, Paradox, Fiction, Irony, and Satire." *Modern Language Quarterly* 27 (1966): 402-417.

Paulson, Ronald. *The Fictions of Satire*. Baltimore: The Johns Hopkins University Press, 1967.

———. *Satire and the Novel in Eighteenth-Century England*. New Haven: Yale University Press, 1967.

———, ed. *Satire: Modern Essays in Criticism*. Englewood Cliffs: Prentice-Hall, 1971.

Pinkus, Phillip. "The New Satire of Augustan England." *University of Toronto Quarterly* 38 (1969): 136-158.

Pollock, Sir Frederick and Maitland, Frederic William. *The History of English Law Before the Time of Edward I*. 2 vols., 1895. Cambridge: Cambridge University Press, reissued 1968.

Price, Martin. *To the Palace of Wisdom: Studies in Order and Energy from Dryden to Blake*. Garden City: Doubleday, 1964.

Propp, Vladimir. *Morphology of the Folk Tale*. Translated by Laurence Scott. Revised by Louis A. Wagner. Introduction by Alan Dundes. Austin: University of Texas Press, 1968.

Rabkin, Eric S. *The Fantastic in Literature*. Princeton: Princeton University Press, 1976.

Randolph, Mary Claire. "The Structural Design of the Formal Verse Satire." *Philological Quarterly* 21 (1942): 368-384.

Rank, Otto. *The Myth of the Birth of the Hero and Other Writings*. Edited by Philip Freund. New York: Vintage, 1964.

Ricoeur, Paul. *The Symbolism of Evil*. Translated by Emerson Buchanan. Boston: Beacon Press, 1969.

Rosenheim, Edward, Jr. *Swift and the Satirist's Art*. Chicago: University of Chicago Press, 1963.

Said, Edward W. *Beginnings: Intention and Method*. New York: Basic Books, 1975.

Scholes, Robert and Kellogg, Robert. *The Nature of Narrative*. New York: Oxford University Press, 1966.

Seidel, Michael and Mendelson, Edward, eds. *Homer to Brecht: The European Epic and Dramatic Traditions*. New Haven: Yale University Press, 1977.

Spingarn, J. E., ed. *Critical Essays of the Seventeenth Century*. Bloomington: Indiana University Press, reissued 1957.

Stout, Gardner, Jr. "Speaker and Satiric Vision in Swift's *Tale of a Tub*." *Eighteenth-Century Studies* 2 (1969): 175-199.

Sullivan, J. P., ed. *Satire: Critical Essays on Roman Literature*. Bloomington: Indiana University Press, 1963.

Sutherland, James R. *English Satire*. Cambridge: Cambridge University Press, 1956.

Todorov, Tzvetan. *The Fantastic: A Structural Approach to a Literary Genre*. Translated by Richard Howard. Cleveland: Case Western Reserve University Press, 1973.

Traugott, John. "A Voyage to Nowhere with Thomas More and Jonathan Swift: *Utopia* and *The Voyage to the Houyhnhnms*," *Sewanee Review* 69 (1961): 534-565.

Vico, Giambattista. *The New Science of Giambattista Vico*. Translated by Thomas Goddard Bergin and Marx Harold Fisch. Ithaca: Cornell University Press, revised 1961; reissued 1970.

Weinberg, Bernard. *A History of Literary Criticism in the Italian Renaissance*. 2 vols. Chicago: Chicago University Press, 1961.

Weinbrot, Howard D. *Augustus Caesar in "Augustan" England*. Princeton: Princeton University Press, 1978.

————. *The Formal Strain: Studies in Augustan Imitation and Satire*. Chicago: Chicago University Press, 1969.

Wild, John. *Plato's Theory of Man*. Cambridge, Mass.: Harvard University Press, 1948.

BIBLIOGRAPHY

Wilding, Michael. "The Last of the Epics: The Rejection of the Heroic in *Paradise Lost* and *Hudibras*." In *Restoration Literature: Critical Approaches*. Edited by Harold Love. London: Methuen, 1972.

Williams, Aubrey L. *Pope's Dunciad: A Study of Its Meaning*. Baton Rouge: Louisiana State University Press, 1955.

Zwicker, Stephen. *Dryden's Political Poetry: The Typology of King and Nation*. Providence: Brown University Press, 1972.

INDEX

Abel, 18, 20, 40-45, 46
Absalom and Achitophel, see Dryden
Achilles, 50, 64, 98, 112n, 133, 215
Adam, 27, 43, 151, 164
Aeneas, 31, 48, 113, 160n, 247, 248-249
Aeolists, 174-175, 192, 195-196
Aeolus, 192
Aesop, 113
Agamemnon, 5n, 27, 64, 122n
Alcibiades, 70
Alexander (the Great), 84, 260
allegory, 122-126; and satire, 115n, 117-121, 128, 169, 177-182, 184-185, 189, 192
Amadis (of Gaul), 89
ancient-modern controversy, 50-51, 173, 175-177, 182-191, 208
antiromance, 60, 61-62, 78-81, 86-89, 96-97, 98, 111, 125-129, 258. *See also* burlesque, narrative (revisionary), satire (action of)
Aphrodite, 48, 101
Aristophanes, 51-52, 77
Aristotle, 136, 208
Arthur (King), 64, 124, 134
Astraea, 52
Augustine, 66
Augustus (Caesar), 144
Avellaneda, Alonso Fernández de, 87, 89-93

Bacchus, 71
Bacon, Francis, 140
Bakhtin, Mikhail, 23n-24n, 65n, 66n, 69n, 70n

Baudelaire, Charles, 25
Becker, J. H., 44n
Beckett, Samuel, 15-16, 265
Benengeli, Cide Hamete, 62, 66. *See also* Cervantes
Bentley, Richard, 185, 240
Beowulf, 43
Bergin, Thomas Goddard, 5n, 26n, 63n, 263n
birth, of hero, 26-27, 36-37, 39, 100-101, 237; and satire, xi-xii, 65-69, 84-85, 156, 183-184, 188-189, 227, 233-237, 242, 244-247, 251, 255-257, 260-261, 263-264. *See also* descent, genealogy, hero
blatant beast, 55n, 124n
body, 167-168; and satire, 51-52, 55n-56n, 68-70, 69n-70n, 73-74, 77-78, 95, 113-114, 189, 196-197, 202-203, 241-242, 256
Boileau-Despréaux, Nicolas, *Le Lutrin*, 137
Bolingbroke, Henry St. John, Viscount of, 224
Böll, Heinrich, 14
Bond, Donald F., 119n
Bracton, Henry of, 47
Brady, Frank, 12n
Brailsford, H. N., 103n
Braithwaite, Richard, 101n
Bredvold, Louis I., 165
Brissenden, R. F., 173n
Bromley, William, 221-222
Brooks, Cleanth, 230
Brown, Norman O., 175n
Brutus (Marcus Junius), 64

Brutus (Trojan hero), 97n

Buckingham, George Villiers, second Duke of, 167n

Budick, Sanford, 53n, 145n-146n

Burke, Kenneth, 24n, 174n

burlesque, 48, 50, 64, 81, 83, 98-101, 121, 129-130. *See also* antiromance, descent, narrative (revisionary), satire (action of)

Butler, James, Duke of Ormonde, 156-158

Butler, Samuel, 7n, 191n; *Characters and Passages From Note-Books*, 60, 95-96, 98, 109n, 114, 116, 127n, 129n, 130; *Hudibras*, xii, 22, 97-134

Butler, Thomas, Earl of Ossory, 156-158

Cadmus, 27

Cain, 18, 20, 40-45, 46, 68

Calypso, 201

Campbell, Joseph, 237

cannibalism, 21, 59

Carnochan, W. Bliss, 211n-212n

Caryll, John, 226

Casaubon, Isaac, 7

Case, Arthur E., 212n

Cassius (Gaius), 64

Castlemaine, Barbara Villiers, Countess of, 140

Cervantes, Miguel de, 97, 98; *Don Quixote*, xii, 60-61, 66, 78-94, 95, 122, 129-134, 219

Chambers, A. B., 8n, 136n, 265n

chaos (*Chaos*), 49, 78, 237

Charles I (of England), 115, 117, 125, 147, 160n

Charles II (of England), 102, 140, 143-144, 147, 148, 155, 158, 160n, 164, 166n

Christ, 20, 23, 34, 35, 39, 48, 133, 181, 222

Chronicles (Bible), 160

Cibber, Colley, 103n, 235-238, 245-249

Cicero (Marcus Tullius), 64, 260

Circe, 36

civil war, 37, 38, 99, 103, 108, 109n, 110, 112-116, 121, 124, 127, 134; in England, 101n, 102, 103-105, 111, 115, 117, 119n, 127n, 191n, 196

Clarendon, Edward Hyde, Earl of, 172n

Clark, John R., 169n

Cleland, William, 243

Cleveland, John, 141

Cohen, J. M., 7n, 61n, 192n

Cohen, Ralph, 137n

comedy (comic), 55, 69-70, 69n, 72, 78, 80, 95, 99, 107, 231, 240, 250-251, 255, 257, 261-262

Copernicus, Nicolaus, 257

Cowley, Abraham, 96, 159n-160n

Craig, Hardin, 117n

Cromwell, Oliver, 104, 105, 144, 158, 160, 160n

Cromwell, Richard, 105

Cronos (Saturn), 33, 37

Cyclops, 224, 239

Cyrus, 39

Dante Alighieri, 91; *Divine Comedy*, 20, 55-56, 216; as pilgrim, 48

Davenant, William, 96n

David (biblical king), 144, 147-148, 150-155, 159, 160-161, 160n, 163-168

Davis, Herbert, 201n

Dearing, Vinton A., 8n, 136n, 145n, 265n

de Bergerac, Cyrano, 214

Defoe, Daniel, *Consolidator*, 214, 214n-215n; *Robinson Crusoe*, 147, 212, 223 degeneration, 52-56, 72, 175, 222; and satire, xii, 4, 11, 57-59, 64, 67-68, 70, 116-117, 140, 175, 197n, 234, 263-265. *See also* descent, dirt, satire (action of)

de Man, Paul, 187

Demosthenes, 260

Dennis, John, 108n, 185, 242

Deporte, Michael V., 175n

De Ruyter, Michael (Admiral), 138-139, 140

descent, 28, 46-52, 64n-65n, 66, 68, 100-101, 185-186, 195-196, 207-208, 263. *See also* degeneration, genealogy, hell, hero (heroic), inheritance, satire (action of)

Diderot, Denis, *Rameau's Nephew*, 219

Dido, 64

Diogenes, 192n

Diotima, 53, 77

dirt, and contamination, 12, 14-17, 66, 69, 174-175, 209, 224, 233-234, 264-265. *See also* degeneration, satire (action of), satirist (nature of)

donation, and inheritance, xi, 150, 153, 169, 178

Don Quixote, see Cervantes

Dostoevsky, Feodor, *Notes from Underground*, 194, 219

Douglas, Archibald (Lord), 138, 141-143

Douglas, Mary, 16-17

Dryden, John, 10, 50-51, 94, 97, 183, 191n; *Absalom and Achitophel*, xii, 23, 31, 53n, 56-57, 144-168; *Annus Mirabilis*, 137-138; *Discourse of Original and Progress of Satire*, 7, 8n, 135-137, 143-144, 265; *Essay of Dramatick Poesie, An*, 50n-51n, 136; *Fables*, 163; *Georgics*, 163; *Hind and the Panther, The*, 43; *Indian Emperour*, 163; *Mac Flecknoe*, 57, 148-149, 234; *Parallel of Poetry and Painting, A*, 136; *Plutarchs Lives*, 144, 157-158; *To Sir Godfrey Kneller*, 135

Dunciad, The, see Pope

Dundes, Alan, 178n

Edwards, Thomas, 97n, 102n

Eliade, Mircea, 31-32

Elliott, Robert, 5n, 13n, 23n-24n, 209n

Epictetus, 258

Erasmus, Desiderius, 78, 122n

Erebus, 49

errantry, 60-61, 82, 95, 101, 108, 122, 129-131

Esau, 40, 45-46

Euripides, 239

Exclusion Crisis, 136, 146, 148, 166n

farce, 9, 66, 89

Faulkner, William, 61n

Festa stultorum, 233n

Fielding, Henry, 7n, 8, 94

Filmer, Robert, 254n-255n

Fisch, Max Harold, 5n, 26n, 63n, 263n

Fisher, Alan S., 138n

Flecknoe, Richard, 148-149

Fletcher, John, 51n

Frame, Donald M., xin, 65n, 83n

Freud, Sigmund, 10-11, 31, 37, 155, 179, 182n

Frost, William, 8n, 136n, 265n

Fry, Paul, 38n

Frye, Northrop, 26n, 50n, 55n, 56n, 79, 127, 128n

Gargantua and Pantagruel, see Rabelais

Gay, Peter, 44n, 213n
genealogy, 27-28, 46n-47n, 61,
    68-69, 185, 237-241. *See also*
    birth (of hero), descent
George II (of England), 144n
giants, 27, 43, 55, 55n-56n, 67-69,
    205. *See also* monster
Gibson, Dan, Jr., 127n
Gildon, Charles, 241
Girard, René, xii, 17-21, 38n, 46,
    67
Glaucos, 50, 231
Goya, Francisco, 263
Greene, Thomas, 48, 69n
Grendel, 43
Grey, Zachary, 102n, 104n, 122n,
    128n
Grimm (Brothers), 178
Grimmelshausen, J.J.C. von, 6,
    99-100
Grosart, Alexander, 5n, 138n
Guillén, Claudio, 62n, 137
Guilpin, Edward, 172n
Gulliver's Travels, see Swift
Guthkelch, A. C., 50n, 109n, 170n,
    186n

Hall, Joseph, 5n
Hamlet (*Hamlet*), 155, 189, 219
Harley, Robert, 221-222, 224
Harrington, James, 191n
Hastings, James, 21n
Hector, 98
hell (Hades), 20, 31, 35, 48-49,
    55-56, 216, 246-247, 249; rivers
    of, 55
Hephaestus, 48, 101
Hera, 29, 48
Hercules, 48, 73, 84, 160n, 185
hero (heroic), conservation of,
    81-82, 159; descent of, 48-49,
    100, 237; etymology of, 29-30;

revision of, 82-84, 95-101, 116,
    127, 138-140, 159, 208, 238-239.
    See also birth (of hero), descent,
    genealogy, satire (action of)
Herodotus, 213
Hesiod, 37, 52, 55, 253
Hobbes, Thomas, 112, 113, 165;
    Leviathan, 53n-54n, 84, 95-96,
    97, 109n, 191, 196, 199, 202
Holahan, Michael, 139n
Homer, 4n, 36, 58, 62, 101, 135n,
    186, 208, 212, 216, 239-241;
    Iliad, 4, 48, 50, 208, 231, 240,
    241; *Odyssey*, 27, 36, 48, 240, 241
Hooker, Edward Niles, 108n
Horace (Horatius Quintus Flac-
    cus), 9, 64, 137, 143, 144, 255
Houyhnhnms, 63, 202, 204, 207,
    209-211, 217, 220, 221, 225. *See
    also* Swift, *Gulliver's Travels*
Hudibras, see Butler, Samuel
Hutcheson, Frances, 213-214
Hyde, Anne, 140
hypocrisy, 22-23, 25, 38, 108-109,
    111, 119, 126, 132, 228. *See also*
    satire (action of)

illegitimacy, 31, 34, 65, 146, 153-
    155, 157, 164, 237-238, 261,
    264. *See also* law (legality), satire
    (action of), succession
inheritance, and folk tales, 122,
    178-179; and narrative, xi-xii,
    26-59, 149, 263; and national
    dispensation, 110, 140, 158; or-
    ganic, 52-55, 256-257, 260-261,
    264; and sacrifice, 41; testamen-
    tary, 40-41, 179-182, 238. *See
    also* descent, donation, geneal-
    ogy, primogeniture, property,
    satire (action of)
Interregnum (English), 101n, 102,
    127, 131, 147, 191n

Iranaeus, 186
irony, 14, 24n, 41, 56n, 63, 73, 184,
    206, 228. *See also* hypocrisy,
    satire (strategies of)
Isaac, 39, 40, 45

Jack, Ian, 102n, 122n
Jacob, 45-46
James II (of England), 148, 154-
    155
Jauss, Hans Robert, 79n
Johnson, James William, 171n
Johnson, Samuel, 38, 53n, 167
Jonson, Ben, 51n, 149
Joyce, James, 111, 135n; *Finnegans
    Wake*, 26-27, 36-37, 39, 43,
    44-45, 265
Juvenal (Decimus Junius
    Juvenalis), 7, 10, 143, 144

Kantorowicz, Ernst, 145n
Kaufmann, Walter, 19n, 74n, 175n
Kenner, Hugh, 211, 215n-216n
Ker, W. P., 136n
Kerby-Miller, Charles, 212n, 260n,
    264n
Kernan, Alvin, 12-13
Kings (Bible), 160
Krailsheimer, A. J., 44n, 83n
Krieger, Murray, 226n

Lamar, René, 116n
Last Instructions to A Painter, see
    Marvell
law (legality), xi, 10-11, 18n, 21,
    23-25, 31, 34, 44, 45, 47, 109,
    111-112, 144-145, 148, 153,
    163-165, 168, 172n, 179, 180n,
    238. *See also* illegitimacy, in-
    heritance, property, succession
Lawrence, D. H., 229
Lear (*King Lear*), 148, 153, 154,
    169, 178

L'Estrange, Roger, 102n, 104n
Levine, Joseph M., 211n
Lewalski, Barbara, 160n
Lewis, Wyndham, 3, 17
Livy (Titus Livius), 18n
Locke, John, 103n, 187, 254,
    254n-255n, 257-258
Lord, George D., 135n
Louis XIV (of France), 166n
Love, Harold, 97n
Lucan (Marcus Annaeus Lucanus),
    38-39, 114
Lucian, of Samosata, 50n, 96, 208,
    214; *True History*, 4n, 61, 62, 212,
    216
Luke (gospel), 20
Luke, Sir Samuel, 119n, 120

Mac Adam, Alfred, 264n
madness (lunacy), 61, 84, 85-88,
    92-93, 130-132, 146, 152, 170,
    176n, 181, 188, 193, 196-199,
    203-204, 215, 217, 219-221. *See
    also* satire (action of)
Maitland, Frederic William, 40, 41,
    47n
Marlborough, John Churchill,
    Duke of, 224
Marlowe, Chrisopher, 172n
Mars, 48, 101, 237
Marston, John, 6-7, 172n
Marvell, Andrew, 102, 160;
    Fleckno, An English Priest at Rome,
    149; *Growth of Popery and Arbi-
    trary Government, The*, 138; *Last
    Instructions to A Painter*, xii, 137-
    143; *Loyall Scott, The*, 138, 141;
    Rehearsal Transpros'd, The, 5
Marx, Karl, 70n
Matthew (gospel), 20n
Maurer, A. E. Wallace, 51n, 144n
May, Tom, 114-115
Melville, Herman, 22n

Mendelson, Edward, 38n
Mercury (Hermes), 28, 49
Miller, Ward, 115n, 117n
Milton, John, 53n, 54, 160, 239,
    240; *Paradise Lost*, 32-35, 48, 49,
    56, 97, 189, 232
Miner, Earl, 96n, 102n, 128n,
    145n, 160n
Momus, 50, 185
Monk, Samuel Holt, 51n, 144n
Monmouth, James Scott, Duke of,
    148, 158
monster (monstrosity), 3, 5, 11,
    38-39, 43, 50, 54, 61, 74, 68-69,
    190, 242, 245, 246, 263-264. *See
    also* giants, satire (action of)
Montaigne, Michel de, xi, 83, 214,
    220
More, Sir Thomas, *Utopia*, 209n,
    214
Moses, 39, 160n

Nabokov, Vladimir, 9, 10n; *Pale
    Fire*, 219
narrative, and history, 28, 31,
    61-64, 78-80, 103-108, 119-121,
    140-143, 144-148, 154, 158-162,
    161-168, 196-198, 204-207, 211,
    222-225, 258; and inheritance,
    xi-xii, 26-59, 63; and origins,
    26-27, 31, 33, 65-69; revisionary,
    60-64, 78-84, 129; and truth,
    61-64. *See also* rivalry (in narra-
    tive), satire (action of)
Nash, Treadway Russel, 102n
Nestor, 64, 208
Nevo, Ruth, 102n, 128n
Nietzsche, Friedrich, 5, 18-19, 71,
    74n, 175, 187, 250
Noah, 37, 153
Nohrnberg, James, 55n-56n, 64n,
    122n, 124n, 177n
Numa, 64

Oedipus (*Oedipus Rex*), 36-38, 39,
    155, 224
Odysseus, 4, 5n, 27, 48, 63, 160n,
    192, 201, 212, 216, 216n
omphale archetype, 127
Osiris, 31, 155

Palmer, John, 12n
Palmeri, Frank, 169n
Panurge, 13-14, 73-77
Pascal, Blaise, 43-44, 82-83
Paulson, Ronald, 3n, 186n
Perseus, 185
Persius (Aulus Persius Flaccus), 7
Petronius (Petronius Arbiter),
    Satyricon, 8, 57-59
Pharisees, 20, 23
Plato, *Gorgias*, 177; *Laws*, 4;
    Politicus, 52-53; *Republic*, 53-55,
    113; *Second Alcibiades*, 240; *Sym-
    posium*, 51-53, 70, 77
Plautus (Titus Maccius), 18n
Pliny, the Elder, 66
Pollock, Frederick, 40, 41, 47n
Pope, Alexander, 16, 50, 51, 53n,
    97n, 140; *Dunciad, The*, xi, xii,
    19, 21, 23, 35, 49, 60, 78, 103n,
    183, 225, 226, 232-249, 257;
    Epistle to Arbuthnot, 12; *Epistle to
    Augustus*, 144n, 172n; *Essay on
    Man*, 41-42, 265; *Memoirs of Mar-
    tinus Scriblerus, The*, 212n, 260,
    264; "Preface" to *Poems* (1717),
    50n; *Rape of the Lock, The*, xii,
    226-232
Popish Plot, 166
Porphyry, 177
Poseidon (Neptune), 58, 237
Priapus, 58
Price, Martin, 12n
primogeniture, 32, 40, 41, 44. *See
    also* inheritance, succession
Proclus, 36

property (properties), xii, 26, 28, 30, 103, 125, 127. *See also* donation, inheritance

Propp, Vladimir, 178n

Proust, Marcel, 80

Ptolemy (Pharaoh), 73

Pynchon, Thomas, xi

Pythagoras, 260

Quintana, Ricardo, 119n

Rabelais, *Gargantua and Pantagruel*, xii, 7, 13-14, 60-61, 64-78, 80, 94, 192n

Rank, Otto, 26n, 36, 39

Rape of the Lock, The, see Pope

Rawson, C. J., 173n

Remus, 40, 44-45

Restoration (England), 104-105, 115, 117, 118, 132, 147, 161, 171n, 254

rivalry, in narrative, 36-41, 43-46, 67, 90, 155. *See also* primogeniture

Rogers, P. G., 138n

romanzi, 80, 89

Romulus, 40, 44-45, 64

Roper, Alan, 145n, 167n

Rosewall, Sir Henry, 119n

Rymer, Thomas, 185

sacrifice, 18, 19, 21n, 41-42

Said, Edward, 28n

St. Albans, Henry Jermyn, Earl of, 140

Sales, Sir William, 101n

Sampson, 159n, 168

Samuel (Bible), 155, 160-163, 164

Sarpedon, 50, 231

Satan, 32-35, 55-56, 181

satire, action of, xi-xii, 3-4, 14, 17, 19, 21, 23, 49-53, 56-59, 65-69, 73-74, 106, 130-132, 139-143, 148-149, 191-192, 195, 216-217, 227-228, 232, 238, 241, 248-249, 255-257, 263-264; mode of, xi, xii, 3, 10, 70-71, 113, 135-137, 263-264; strategies of, 10-14, 23, 60, 61-64, 66, 71, 91-93, 99-101, 117, 130, 135-137, 169-171, 174-175, 176, 197, 211-212, 238. *See also* body (and satire), burlesque, degeneration (and satire), descent, narrative (revisionary)

satirist, nature of, 3-6, 8, 10-12, 14, 16-17, 19-22, 88-89, 143

satura, 5-9

satyr, 5-7, 8n, 55, 70-71

Satyr Menipée, 5-6

satyr play, 239-240

Saul (biblical king), 161

Scholes, Robert, 79n-80n

Scott, Lawrence, 178n

Scriblerus (Martinus Scriblerus), 240-241, 243, 260, 264. *See also* Pope

Scythians, 18, 19, 197

Seidel, Michael, 38n

Settle, Elkannah, 136, 234, 247

Shadwell, Thomas, 149

Shafer, Robert, 127n

Shakespeare, William, 51n, 179. *See also* Hamlet, Lear

Showalter, English, Jr., 96n

Silenus, 5, 70-71

Sinon, 63

Smith, D. Nichol, 50n, 109n, 170n, 186n

Socrates, 53, 70-71, 177

Solomon (biblical king), 160n

Somers, John, 184

Sophocles, 37. *See also* Oedipus

Sorel, Charles, 94, 96n

spartoi, 37, 40, 45

Spectator, The, 119n

Spenser, Edmund, *Faerie Queene*, 54, 55n, 64, 122-130, 134
Spingarn, J. E., 97n, 160n
Spinoza, Baruch, 19
Starkie, Walter, 82n
Sterne, Laurence, 67; *Tristram Shandy*, xii, 24-25, 47, 60, 103n, 176-177, 187-188, 250-262
Stout, Gardner, Jr., 173
Strabo, 212
Strachey, James, 11n, 182n
succession, xii, 39-41, 76, 146-150, 153-155, 157, 167-168, 226, 234-235, 244, 246, 248. *See also* descent, genealogy, law, narrative (and history), primogeniture
Sutherland, James, 232n
Swedenberg, H. T., Jr., 145n
Swift, Jonathan, 57, 60, 102, 135, 136, 234; *Battle of the Books, The*, 50, 109n, 240; *Bickerstaff Papers*, 75; *Conduct of the Allies, The*, 223; *Contests and Dissentions in Athens and Rome*, 223; *Gulliver's Travels*, xii, 63, 92, 174, 201-225, 235; *Mechanical Operation of the Spirit, The*, 175, 196; *Meditation Upon a Broomstick*, 14-15; *Modest Proposal, A*, 21, 204; *Tale of A Tub, A*, xii, 8, 22, 23, 65, 122, 169-200, 203-204, 215n, 218, 220, 221, 256-257

taboo, 16-17, 23. *See also* dirt (and contamination)
Tale of A Tub, A, see Swift
Tartarus, 33
Tasso, Torquato, 82
Taylor, John, 127n
Telemachus, 27, 36
Temple, Sir William, 54, 78-80, 102n-103n, 109n, 170n, 173, 175-176, 182, 184-185, 186, 189
Thersites, 4-5

Theseus, 29, 48, 160n, 185
Thomas, Keith, 127n
Thucydides, 110-114
Tillotson, Geoffrey, 226n
tragedy, 3, 19, 56n
Trask, Willard R., 32n, 33n
Traugott, John, 172, 209n
travel literature, and satire, 58-59, 62-63, 131-132, 212-223. *See also* narrative (and history), utopia
Trimalchio, 8, 57-58
Tristram Shandy, see Sterne
typology, 159-168. *See also* allegory

ultimogeniture, 40
Uranos, 31, 33, 37
utopia, 81, 209, 214-215, 220

Vennewitz, Lelia, 14n
Vico, Giambattista, xii, 4n, 5n, 8-9, 13, 18, 26, 27, 28-29, 30, 45, 46n-47n, 47-49, 56-57, 63, 80-82, 263, 265
violation, 13, 17-21, 23-24, 31, 40-44, 90, 121, 139, 146, 164, 184, 226-227, 229-230, 263. *See also* narrative (and history), satire (action of)
Virgil (Publius Vergilius Maro), 49, 50, 142, 239, 240; *Aeneid*, 31, 63, 232, 236, 248-249; *Georgics*, 163
Voltaire (François-Marie Arouet), 44, 212-213

Wagner, Louis A., 178n
Waller, A. R., 60n, 98n
Warburton, William, 237-238, 244, 246, 248
Warner, Rex, 110n
Wasserman, George, 102n, 128n
Watt, Ian, 257n
Weinber, Bernard, 89n
Whitgift, Archbishop, 172n
Wild, John, 53n

INDEX

Wilders, John, 97n, 102n, 105n, 122n, 128n

Wilding, Michael, 57n, 97n

William III (of England), 143

Williams, Aubrey L., 235n

Wimsatt, William K., 12n

Woolf, Virginia, 172

Work, James A., 250n

Wotton, William, 50, 180n, 185, 186

Xerxes, 64

Yahoos, 203-204, 209-211, 217, 219-220. *See also*, Swift, *Gulliver's Travels*

Young, Peter, 120, 121n

Zeus (Jove, Jupiter), 33, 39, 48, 52, 99, 100

Zwicker, Stephen, 160n

LIBRARY OF CONGRESS CATALOGING IN PUBLICATION DATA

Seidel, Michael, 1943-
  Satiric inheritance.
  Bibliography: p.
  Includes index.
    1. Satire—History and criticism   2. Inheritance and
succession in literature.   I. Title
PN6149.S2S44   809.7   79-84016
ISBN 0-691-06408-3